Cruising Ireland

Cruising
Ireland

A Companion to the Irish Cruising Club Sailing Directions

Mike Balmforth
and
Norman Kean

Irish Cruising Club Publications

First published 2012 by Irish Cruising Club Publications Ltd
Burren, Kilbrittain, County Cork
email: books@irishcruisingclub.com
www.irishcruisingclub.com

© Mike Balmforth and Norman Kean

ISBN 978 0 955 81993 3

Designed and typeset by Irish Cruising Club Publications Ltd.
Printed by W & G Baird Ltd, Greystone Press, Antrim, Northern Ireland BT41 2RS

Cover: *Saint Macdara's Island, Connemara*

Frontispiece: *Inishlackan, Co.Galway*

Title pages: *Mullaghmore, Co.Sligo*

Opposite: *The Howth 17* Leila*, built in 1898, rounds the Fastnet Rock*

0 10 20 30 40 50
nautical miles

ATLANTIC OCEAN

SEA of MOYLE

Tory I
Malin Head
Rathlin I
Fair Head
Bloody Foreland
Coleraine
Arranmore
Derry/
Londonderry
Larne

NORTH CHANNEL

Rathlin O'Birne
Donegal
Belfast
ULSTER
Strangford L
Inishmurray

Erris Head
Sligo
Carlingford L
St John's Point
Belmullet

CONNACHT

IRISH SEA

Achill I
Westport
Drogheda

Inishbofin

IRELAND

Clifden
Dublin
Howth
Slyne Head
Galway
Dun Laoghaire
LEINSTER
Wicklow
Aran Is
Wicklow
Head

Limerick
Arklow

Loop Head
MUNSTER
Wexford

Tralee
Waterford
Carnsore
Point
Dingle
Kenmare
Youghal
Hook Head
ST GEORGE'S CHANNEL

Blasket Is
Cork
Kinsale
Skelligs
Bantry
Old Head of Kinsale
Mizen Head
Fastnet Rock

CELTIC SEA

Contents

As a Companion to the *Sailing Directions*, this volume is laid out in similar fashion to them. The **South and West Coasts** are described clockwise from Carnsore Point to Bloody Foreland, followed by the **East and North Coasts** anti-clockwise between the same two points.

Foreword

Local knowledge is a time-honoured term in publications giving advice to the mariner. Usually it is deployed in pilot books in such warnings as "this channel is not to be attempted without local knowledge". However, the phrase can equally be applied to being in the know when enjoying the facilities or appreciating the special features of any stretch of coast when arriving from the sea. Until I read the relevant section in *Cruising Ireland*, I thought that I possessed a fair degree of "local knowledge" about the headlands, harbours and history of the coast of County Cork where I live. Clearly I've overlooked all manner of diversions and attractions. Now, thanks to *Cruising Ireland*, I'll take a second or third look at familiar places and find a new, unexpected dimension. So imagine how much more of an eye-opener it will be for readers when we are venturing into unfamiliar territory.

Tim Severin

West Cork, May 2012

Tim Severin's replica 6th-century currach **Brendan** *leaves Brandon Creek in Kerry in 1976 for the Faroe Islands, Iceland and ultimately Newfoundland*

Opposite: *Despite all the wisdom written in pilot books, there are still many little harbours in Connemara that are not to be attempted without local knowledge*

Preface

The whole coast of Ireland is stunningly beautiful, a cruising ground to match any in the world. But think of tourist Ireland and you may think first of the Burren of Clare, the Lakes of Killarney, the Vale of Avoca: all lovely, but all inland. Granted, the famous Giant's Causeway and Cliffs of Moher are on the coast, but from a sailor's point of view they are awkward of access, with no harbours nearby. There is, however, also a Maritime Top Twenty, of awe-inspiring places such as Skellig Michael, the Blaskets, Inishmurray and Clare Island. Inishmore's prehistoric fortress of Dun Aengus is perhaps the only site near the top of *both* lists. But once you have sailed West Cork, Strangford Lough or the Rosses of Donegal, you wouldn't go out of your way to kiss the Blarney Stone; while the Ring of Kerry looks even better from the outside.

The task of an Editor of Sailing Directions is a bit of a balancing act. What to include, and what to leave out. On the one hand, the need for the pilot book to be concise and relevant to the task in hand. On the other, the fact that this means omitting so much that might enrich the experience of the reader cruising the coast. Why are there two lighthouse towers on Slyne Head? Where are we most likely to see puffins? Who built those drystone huts, and when? None of these questions need to be answered when the paramount need is to bring the good ship safely into harbour on a darkening evening; what is wanted then is text, chart and photographs on the same or facing pages, and those photographs to be of navigational value. And no nonsense. So the beauty and fascination of the coast of Ireland is but briefly and hastily described in the Pilot.

Hence this book, written by sailors, principally for sailors, and aiming to provide in words and pictures the flavour of cruising the coasts of Ireland, with just enough pilotage information to glue it together, and no more. The scenery, history, culture, wildlife, economy, geology, ancient monuments and trivia of the coast, from a sailor's point of view. The "nonsense", if you like, that doesn't belong in the Sailing Directions, but which might make a good read of a winter's evening, or at the cabin table when planning the next day's voyage.

The stimulus to set it down on paper was provided by *Cruising Scotland*, written by Mike Balmforth my co-author and Edward Mason my counterpart as Editor of the Clyde Cruising Club's excellent *Sailing Directions and Anchorages*. *Cruising Scotland* was published in 2010 by our sister organisation the CCC, and following its success, many people suggested we do likewise for Ireland. Mike (who like me has one foot on either side of the Irish Sea) provided the vital contribution by offering to write the bulk of the main text. As compiler, editor and designer I took the word "likewise" quite literally, for with Edward's blessing, I have unashamedly designed a sister volume. I owe Edward a special debt of gratitude for his advice readily given, and the benefit of his experience and talents.

My thanks to Tim Severin for his generous Foreword, and his picture of *Brendan's* historic departure from Kerry in 1976.

Finally my thanks go again to my wife Geraldine Hennigan for multi-tasking as photographer, information technologist, office manager, sailor and soulmate.

Norman Kean

The cliffs of Clare Island tower over Achill Sound, Co. Mayo

Inishmurray, Co. Sligo, renowned for its ancient monastic remains, and – until the last of its people left in 1948 – for its illicit whiskey

Bofin Harbour, Co.Galway

Carnlough Harbour, Co.Antrim

To be invited by the Irish Cruising Club to co-author *Cruising Ireland* is not only a great honour, but also a considerable source of satisfaction to someone who has spent much of his life exploring and enjoying the Irish coast; a coast that offers such a variety of sailing waters, pleasures, and challenges to the cruising sailor.

I hope that my memories of cruises in Irish waters, mixed with those of others, will encourage the reader to venture west – for the places and the people have changed but little over recent decades. There are few areas left on the European coast where the cruising sailor can roam as nature intended, have sole occupancy of anchorages, enjoy spectacular scenery, and have a unique story to tell afterwards. Ireland's north and west coast between Mizen Head and Malin Head is one of them.

The south and east coasts have a different appeal. These are the business coasts of Ireland, where commercial and cultural influence is stronger, and boating facilities are more highly developed. They are no less enjoyable for that.

The ICC *Sailing Directions* are comprehensive, and essential for cruising the coast of Ireland, but they can cover only the essential navigational details. Norman and I have set out to describe the ambience, the enjoyment, the challenges, and the satisfaction that cruising Irish waters can bring. *Cruising Ireland*, as a result, is unashamedly enthusiastic, and we hope that our enthusiasm will prove infectious.

One of the most enjoyable things about writing this kind of book is the research one must do, which often throws up fascinating information. It makes the task a stimulating one. As a result, *Cruising Ireland* is much more than a tourist guide from a seaward perspective: we hope the reader finds our excursions into history, folklore, maritime events, and the lives of interesting people help bring the book, and the coast, to life.

We hope you enjoy *Cruising Ireland*, but – more important – we hope you enjoy cruising Ireland!

Barloge, Co. Cork

Mike Balmforth

Introduction

There is ample evidence that the earliest inhabitants of Ireland were skilled seafarers. Seven or eight thousand years ago the North Channel was being crossed routinely in dugout canoes and skin boats, and sea fishing was well developed. The port town in County Antrim has given its name to the ancient Larnian people who traded by sea with Scotland and the Isle of Man, and made their way by lakes and rivers to the west coast.

Successive waves of invaders over several millennia arrived by sea, and the sea offered a highway for the exchange of goods and technology. Ancient monuments in Scandinavia, Scotland, Ireland, France and Spain show a remarkable similarity in design. As for the boats, their development must have been, by our standards, extremely slow. We do not know when the sail first made its appearance, but the design of today's *curach* in its various local forms may be traced directly back to pre-Christian times. The early peoples had a marked predilection for small islands, which would have provided added security, but only for those who could build and handle seaworthy boats.

Among the first Irish sailors of historical times were the monks, the most celebrated of these Patrick, Columba and Brendan, and the *Navigatio Sancti Brendani Abbatis,* "The Voyage of Saint Brendan the Abbot", written perhaps 500 years after the event and semi-mythical, is Ireland's oldest surviving account of an expedition by sea.

In later centuries, the seafaring Celts established clan fiefdoms that extended as naturally across the sea as the land, and cultural links between – for example – Argyll and Antrim were much closer in the 16th century than they are today.

The earliest to cruise the coast for recreation, in the 19th century, were few in number, and were hardy souls. Indeed they had to be, for they had none of the refined equipment of today. They had a fisherman anchor, no winches, primitive cooking arrangements, and of course no engines and no weather forecasts. GPS, radio, radar, the diesel engine, the mobile phone and much else on the modern yacht would have been a source of wonder. Richard Turrell McMullen has left us an account of *Orion's* cruise to the south-west coast in 1869, and in 1937 Eric Hiscock said of Dunbeacon Cove in County Cork that "The late Claud Worth's *Foam* is the only other yacht ever to have put in here, and that was as long ago as 1889."

The coast of Ireland is a little busier today. But there are still many places where the cruising yacht will have an anchorage to herself, and long stretches of the coast call for a degree of self-reliance which, in more highly-developed cruising grounds, has been forgotten.

About 1910, Harry Donegan, a lawyer from Cork and a keen sailor, began gathering pilotage information on the south and south-west coasts, and in 1929, as a founder member of the newly-formed Irish Cruising Club, he set about publishing it. Donegan's *Sailing Directions* were at first reproduced on the office copiers of the time and made available only to Club members, as were their counterpart for the east coast, researched and compiled by Billy Mooney. The

The Baily of Howth, one of Ireland's best-known lighthouses, guards Dublin Bay

Opposite: *The classic Galway hooker* **Naomh Crónán**

Bushe's pub in Baltimore. Arrive in this port, and you might never want to leave.

accomplished Eric Hiscock meanwhile authored a slim volume entitled "South West Irish Harbours and Bays", which was published by Imrays in 1937; Imrays had previously published a pilot book for the Irish coast in 1906. But it was the Irish Cruising Club *Sailing Directions* that were to become the standard work on small-craft pilotage of the coast, in the decades after they were made available to the public with their second editions in 1946.

In the 1950s, trojan work by Billy Mooney, Bob Berridge, Paul Campbell, Roger Bourke, Wallace Clark and others extended the coverage to the entire coast of Ireland, and the Directions took on the shape that they have to this day, with the South and West Coasts described clockwise from Carnsore Point by way of Mizen Head to Bloody Foreland, and the East and North Coasts anticlockwise between the same two points by way of Fair Head. That is the format that has been followed in this Companion.

Today, the Irish Cruising Club's *Sailing Directions* are carried by the ships of the Irish Naval Service, the Irish Lights Vessel *Granuaile*, and the inshore survey vessels of the Geological Survey of Ireland. They are used by the Irish Coast Guard to assist in search and rescue work, and they are valued and respected by the UK Hydrographic Office. They strive to describe every feasible port, harbour and anchorage on the coast, a long list becoming continually longer as new technologies in navigation and pilotage make access by a stranger possible to

High Stool Days

Ireland is a country in which small things can assume absurdly large proportions, while major matters are quietly taken in one's stride with a shrug and the comment that it could be worse. That said, for the benefit of cruising visitors the local headland is always the most dangerous on the entire coast, a place of disaster and heroics. Yet people cruising from afar, anticipating such rocky outcrops with trepidation, will find that when rounding in average summer weather, the seas about these neighbourhood Cape Horns are dotted with tiny local fishing craft going blithely about their business.

Along the west coast – which is really a frame of mind, but might be defined as the Atlantic seaboard southward from Bloody Foreland in Donegal to the Blasket Islands – few locals would admit that, now and again, it rains all day. And when it does, if you suggest that in the modern world of global warming and spreading droughts such regular rainfall will soon be liquid gold, they'll respond that when that happens, the Irish for sure will be out running around trying to catch it with a fork.

As for the rangy farmer on a wet and windy morning, lingering over his pint in the classic public house which is also a grocery, newsagent, hardware shop, undertaker, post office, and animal-feed suppliers, he will simply remark that it's a high stool day and leave it at that, other than maybe adding that the great advantage of being on a high stool at a bar counter is that you dry quicker than in a rocking chair.

But as the allegedly impoverished Irish sheep farmers now drive about in top-of-the-range 4x4s , the heating and air conditioning provides drying more effectively than any high stool, while too much time atop one might cost the all-important driving licence. Today's Ireland is so unlike yesterday's that maybe you'd be better trying to find the real thing of the characterful multi-function public house in a museum. And as for picturesque ruins, in Ireland we used to be up to our tonsils in dilapidation, so we let other countries do ruins. We're happy to let places like Egypt and Rome lead the way while we get on with what passes for real life, and progressive farmers, if given half a chance, will sensibly remove ruins which old-time cruising folk have been using as leading marks for generations.

Yet tradition has its role. In the midst of the west coast, there's Connemara. It means land of the sea. They're into the traditional sailing boats, the stately Galway hookers. And along the west and north-west coasts, from Kerry to Donegal, you'll also come across many different examples of the currachs, hyper-light tarred canvas rowing craft which look frail enough, but can cope with open water and do the business lifting lobster and crab pots. Mind you, most of them are now skinned in glassfibre and have fifteen-horse outboards, but that's evolution for you and aren't they just so adaptable.

Like the west coast, the south-west coast from the Blasket Islands to Mizen Head always had a fearsome reputation among neighbouring seafarers, yet it's an enchanting and hospitable spot once you get there. But for the large sailing populations centred on the south coast, getting round Mizen Head can be quite a challenge, so no sooner have they reached the sublime coast of Kerry than they're nervously anticipating returning round the Mizen again – not the frame of mind in which to savour the Kerry delights. Take your time, for when God made time in Kerry, he made a lot of it.

The south coast from the Mizen east to Carnsore Point includes numerous gluepot ports and majestic rocks, with the Fastnet deservedly tops, while West Cork itself leads in the gluepot world – you drop by for a day or three, and are happily stuck there for weeks.

The many folk from Cork and further afield who sail from Crosshaven on Cork Harbour, or Kinsale just along the coast, will warn you that Ireland's east coast from Carnsore Point towards the majestic Fair Head is a mysterious region, a different galaxy centred about a weird place called Dublin that has notions of itself, which is patently absurd as Cork is of course the real capital of Ireland. Somewhere along that east coast, beyond Carlingford and the lovely mountains about it, multi-islanded Strangford Lough is secluded from view, and the pleasantest places are hidden unless you have the luxury of a spotter plane up ahead. If the locals take potshots at your aircraft, you'll know you're on a winner. Beyond that is Belfast Lough, described by Uffa Fox as the finest sailing water in the world. He said it of many places, but don't let that put you off.

Outside the lough, the tides of the North Channel sluice you in forceful style back towards the Atlantic. Ireland's north coast is our shortest seaboard, but it's impressive in its variety, and beyond Malin Head the majestic cliffs and intricate inlets of north-west Donegal offer cruising on a scale to rival anywhere else in this intriguing island.

W.M.Nixon

Opposite: *The classic yawl* **Ainmara***, designed by ICC founder member J.B.Kearney and built by him at Murphy's boatyard at Ringsend in Dublin in 1912.* **Ainmara** *was chartered in 1964 by William Nixon, Ed Wheeler and the late Russell O'Neill, all of the ICC, for a fortnight's cruise round Ireland. Only two miles from Bangor her engine seized solid, and the cruise was – perforce – made entirely under sail, mostly in foul weather, in 13 days and 18 hours, because the crew couldn't afford another £20 for a third week's charter. The fourth crew member, John Bailey, left at Crosshaven. They were blissfully unaware until the mid-70s that they had actually broken the round Ireland record and then held it for about ten years.*

The previous record holders were also ICC members – brothers Kevin and Colm McLaverty, and Mick Clarke, who sailed the 18-foot half-decked Waverley **Durward** *round Ireland in three weeks in 1959.*

Ainmara *has recently been carefully restored by ICC member Richard (Dickie) Gomes as she goes back to sea for her second century. She is pictured under full sail in Strangford Lough in 2011.*

On Skellig Michael

Opposite: *(top) Detail from chart 2442 of Mutton Island, County Clare, surveyed by Captain Bedford in 1850 and published in 1856.*

(bottom) View of the Blasket Islands from the south-west, from chart 2789, surveyed by Commander Edye in 1858 and published in 1861.

places where once it had to be said "local knowledge is required." A steady stream of new information arrives for the Directions, and is immediately written in to the master copies on computer, while the important points are included in the frequent Amendments on www.irishcruisingclub.com. It is well worth referring to the website before planning a cruise.

Passage Planning

On most parts of the coast of Ireland, harbours are plentiful and distances between them short. The east coast, and most of the south, are thoroughly marked by navigational aids; the west coast has so many hazards that marking to such a standard would be well-nigh impossible. The east and south coasts are relatively less exposed, less challenging, safer and more accessible to visiting boats, both from the large population centres of Ireland and from Great Britain, France and further afield. These coasts have more than twenty full-service marinas, but even so the infrastructure is far from fully developed.

The west and north coasts, on the other hand, are exposed to the full rigours of ocean weather. There are fabulous natural harbours, but some of the challenging headlands and passages may present barriers to the less experienced sailor. These coasts are further from the cities and from most of our neighbour countries. Their attraction is different – they offer wilderness cruising in remote, unspoiled and beautiful places, with, as one writer has put it, an "edge of the world" feel – somewhat higher on the scale of adventure travel.

The Charting of Ireland

The first proper Admiralty survey of Ireland was carried out from 1750 by the pioneering Scottish hydrographer Murdoch MacKenzie. The charts were published in 1776. MacKenzie's surveys were notable for their rigorous use of the latest technologies, and his charts raised standards of accuracy and detail to new levels.

A new and even more thorough survey was conducted by the Admiralty between about 1840 and 1860, largely under the direction of Francis Beaufort as Hydrographer of the Navy until 1855. Much of the data on today's charts dates back to the work of Captain George Bedford, Commanders A.G.Edye and James Wolfe, and Richard Hoskyn, Master RN, in those years. Hoskyn was also the author of the early editions of the Admiralty Irish Coast Pilot. They are commemorated by two widely separated Edye Rocks, Hoskyn's Shoal (Strangford Lough), the Hoskyn Bank (off Lambay) and the Hoskyn Channel (Carlingford Lough).

After the partition of Ireland in 1921, the new Free State government elected not to set up its own Hydrographic Office but to leave the charting of Ireland to (as the Act put it) "the Admiralty in London". The continuing validity of this was to be tested in an Irish court many years later, the case (which was ultimately rejected) being that the UKHO had upped sticks, moved to Taunton and changed its name. But for a century and a half most of the Irish coast away from the major ports was charted solely on the basis of the Victorian surveys.

Despite the quality of these, there were still opportunities for improvement. The Irish Naval Service sometimes found it difficult to enforce the 200-mile fishery limit when the courts determined that in point of fact the country didn't know where its coastline was, at least not to 21st-century standards. The advent of GPS, the prospect of joining the International Hydrographic Organisation, and the need to produce vector electronic charts first for high-speed and ultimately for all large ships, combined with a growing awareness of the vast potential of the seabed, led to the setting up of the Irish National Seabed Survey of 1999-2005 and (closer to shore) the INFOMAR programme begun in 2006 and expected to take 20 years to complete. The results, using multibeam sonar in deep water to provide full seabed coverage, are stunning. Close inshore, the task has proved challenging since the sonar footprint in the shallows is narrow, and expensive underwater instruments and rock-strewn bays do not mix. One solution has been the use of LIDAR, twin laser beams directed downwards from an aircraft in level flight, but the technique has some specific shortcomings and so the latest chart editions are based on a combination of multibeam sonar, laser, and the 160-year-old but apparently immortal leadline observations of Beaufort's surveyors.

Two possibly apocryphal but delightful stories are told of Commander Edye. Off Dinish Island in Kilkieran Bay is Bruiser Rock, marked "Existence Doubtful" on the charts. It is said that Edye charted Dinish Shoals one day and hit them the next. This was (and still is) frowned upon in the Royal Navy, but striking *un*charted rocks was looked upon as a regrettable but inevitable occupational hazard for surveyors. So Edye (allegedly) marked a previously uncharted "Bruiser Rock" on the chart. On another occasion the surveyor was presented to Queen Victoria, and the Queen, clearly well-briefed, greeted him with "Ah, Edye, so you're the man who knows where all the rocks are." To which Edye replied, "I fear not, Ma'am, but I do know where they aren't."

Which is an important distinction to make, and a very perceptive comment on the business of hydrographic surveying.

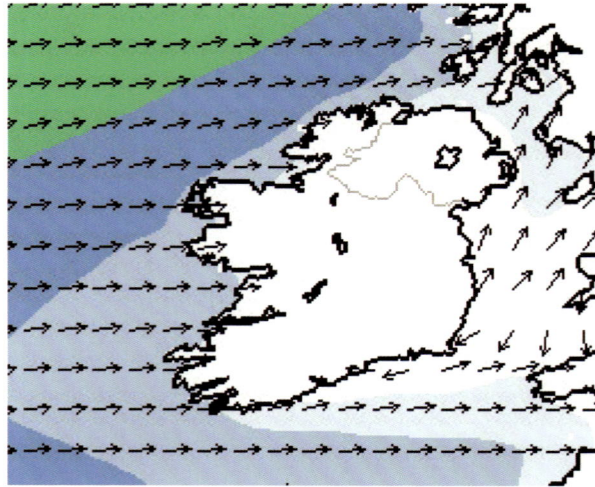

Typical summer swell pattern around Ireland (as depicted on a popular forecast website) showing the prevailing ocean swell direction, from the west. The colours represent the wave height: white less than 0.5m, green 3 to 4m. Note how the regime changes at Malin and Mizen Heads, how west Mayo and north-west Donegal have the biggest waves, and how the south coast, despite being exposed to the south-west, is shielded from the prevailing swell.

- chart by courtesy of Passageweather.com

On most of the east coast between Malin Head at Ireland's northern tip and Carnsore Point at its south-eastern corner, the tidal stream is a primary consideration in passage planning, since the tide fairly rushes in and out of the Irish Sea through both its openings to the ocean. Elsewhere, with the exception of some headlands and narrow channels, the tidal stream is not so important. In Ireland, in contrast to western England, Wales and northern France, most harbours are accessible at all states of the tide.

Ireland is conveniently-sized for a circumnavigation, and a book like this would be incomplete without addressing the perennial question: which way round? In terms of the weather a case can be made for anticlockwise, but it's marginal and other factors may prevail. The argument is set out on page 236, together with details of logistics and infrastructure. More detailed passage planning advice is given at the start of each chapter, but for serious planners the *Sailing Directions* are essential.

Weather

Irish weather is typified by its official description: Cool Temperate Maritime, which is technical-speak for seldom too hot; seldom too cold; and sometimes wet and windy. There is a slightly greater occurrence of winds of Force 7 than in, say, the English Channel, but no greater incidence of gales — one gale day per summer month, on average, is typical. Fog is relatively unusual, but what in

Amphidromic Points

If you take a blank chart and draw lines connecting places with the same tidal constant, and another set connecting places with the same rise and fall of tide, you produce what is called a "co-tidal and co-range" chart. Official versions are available from the UKHO. Here and there on these charts are patterns that look just like spiders' webs – the co-tidal lines radiate from a point, and the co-range lines form concentric circles round the point. At that central point, there is no rise and fall. The tidal "wave" appears to rotate round the point once every twelve and a half hours, while at the centre it's half tide all the time. These are called amphidromic points, and the closer you are to one, the less the range of the tide – very handy if you want to build, for example, a RoRo link span. There are two of these points in Irish waters: one off the coast near Cahore Point in Co.Wexford, and one between Rathlin Island and Islay. As a result, the tidal range at Rosslare, Arklow, Ballycastle, Rathlin and Portrush (and also Port Ellen) is remarkably small. Since it's high tide on one side of an amphidromic point when it's low tide on the other, these localities also feature very fast tidal streams – they are, as it were, the fulcrum of the tidal see-saw.

The existence of amphidromic points was discovered in 1836 by William Whewell, a polymath of astounding versatility who became Master of Trinity College Cambridge in 1841. Whewell is credited with coining the terms "scientist" and "physicist" and has a crater on the moon named after him. In keeping with his classical background the name he gave his tidal points derives from the Amphidromia, an ancient Greek naming ceremony. The newborn child was carried in a circle round the central hearth of the house by each member of the extended family in turn; just like the stately twice-daily progression of the tide-wave.

Rear-Admiral Sir Francis Beaufort

Ireland is termed a 'soft day' – warm air, high humidity and poor visibility – will often be encountered, particularly in the south-west.

Ireland gets its weather at first-hand from the Atlantic, and the only weather system that tends to persist is the large anticyclone, bringing blue skies, sunshine and calm seas. Typically, depressions give Ireland a swipe on the way past, and head off north-east towards Scotland and Norway. If you don't like the weather, wait five minutes.

The British forecasts reach well out into the Atlantic, but Met Éireann, blessed with a relatively small patch of the globe to cover, gives a very high standard of forecast that is also orientated towards smaller craft – fishing boats and yachts.

Self-sufficiency

The marine infrastructure of Ireland ranges from the five-gold-anchor marinas of Crosshaven, Dun Laoghaire and Bangor to the ancient drying stone quays of Connemara, and it cannot be said to support marina-hopping. On long stretches of the coast, there are no visitors' moorings or alongside berths, so cruising in

The Beaufort Scale

The global standard marine scale of wind strength was devised by an Irishman. Francis Beaufort, son of a Church of Ireland clergyman and distinguished academician, was born in Navan, County Meath, in 1774. He served with distinction in the Royal Navy in the Napoleonic War, and in 1829 was appointed Hydrographer of the Navy. His wind scale was adopted about the same time. Admiral Beaufort held his post until he was 80, and set new standards in hydrography. The Beaufort Sea, north of Canada and Alaska, is named after him. He died in 1857.

The Islands of Ireland

Ireland has 26 islands with year-round communities, if an island is defined as a piece of land entirely surrounded by water (even if only at high tide), and without bridge or causeway. Their total population in 2006 was approximately 2,918, although several have only a single family or even a single inhabitant. There are perhaps less than 20 reasonably robust and sustainable island communities, the largest being on Inishmore of the Aran Islands. Seasonally or occasionally occupied islands number another 60 or so (and growing), and it is difficult to estimate populations but they don't amount to many, perhaps 300 people in total. After that it all goes a bit fuzzy at the edges. Seasonally-inhabited islands may happen to be unoccupied on census day, but the converse is also true; in 2006 seven people materialised out of the blue on the rather bleak Inishkeeragh in Donegal, deserted since the 1950s but now with a new house, while on nearby Owey (evacuated in 1977) they managed to organise a census-night party for 27, after six zero returns in succession.

A study of successive censuses on the islands is revealing, and the data is available from as far back as 1841, when almost every island had a numerous population. The famine of the 1840s had different consequences on the islands; many of them *increased* their populations between 1841 and 1851, possibly because the spread of potato blight was inhibited by the water gap. But tellingly the island with the greatest population growth in that period was Spike Island in Cork Harbour, most of whose inhabitants were convicts.

Common dolphins

The Old Head of Kinsale

Dingle marina

out-of-the-way places requires good anchoring equipment, and the knowledge to use it effectively. By and large, anchoring around the coast of Ireland is not particularly difficult. Every kind of seabed will be encountered. Good anchorages here, like anywhere else, have a mud or sand bottom, but a few others will offer a greater challenge on rock, loose shingle, or kelp – the last prevalent in cooler northern waters. The more remote anchorages are seldom crowded, only a few have significant currents, and the tidal range is not large. Many are vulnerable to winds from a certain direction, so having a good weather forecast is essential when selecting the best place for a peaceful night. In bad weather the surrounding land can also affect matters: anchorages near hills and mountains may seem sheltered, but once the wind gets up they can create gusts many times stronger than the general wind speed.

The selection of gear involves the usual compromise between weight and ease of handling. A heavier anchor and chain will give better holding and peace of

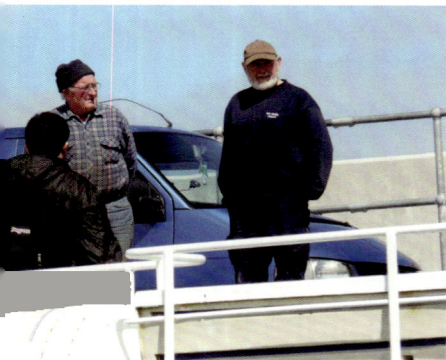

Meeting the ferry at Inishmaan

Vivace racing at Lough Swilly

mind, but above a certain weight a windlass is highly desirable. This is not a matter of being work-shy: it is a safety item that will enable you to re-anchor when you don't feel like it, but know you should, and more easily to enjoy short stops en route. Finally, have a second anchor and rode on board, and also an anchor buoy and tripping line. As for which designs of anchor to carry, take as many well-informed opinions as possible before buying.

The ICC *Sailing Directions* give comprehensive details of 400 anchorages around Ireland, as well as all the ports and harbours with more developed infrastructure. A brief summary is given in the chapters which follow. For the north coasts between Sligo and Ardglass, the free annual publication *Welcome Anchorages* also provides a handy and up-to-date guide to facilities ashore.

In the remoter places, self-sufficiency is also called for in respect of services and repairs, and sources of resupply may be few and far between. The opportunity to replenish fuel and fresh water should never be missed.

The head of Oyster Haven

Search and Rescue

The Royal National Lifeboat Institution operates seamlessly throughout Ireland, with 23 all-weather lifeboats, and a further 19 stations operating inshore boats. Search and rescue operations are co-ordinated in the Republic by the Irish Coast Guard, with its MRCC in Dublin and Sub-Centres at Valentia (Co. Kerry) and Malin Head (Co. Donegal). In Northern Ireland that rôle is filled by the UK's Maritime and Coastguard Agency, operating from Belfast MRCC at Bangor. Coastguard helicopters are based at five airports. All the agencies work in complete co-operation regardless of national boundaries.

The Garvan Isles and Malin Head

Communications

Mobile phone coverage (at the time of writing), by and large, varies with population density; best in the south, east and north, less good in the west. There may be local blank spots, so check with providers' websites for coverage maps. Wifi availability is rapidly extending to every pub and restaurant. VHF (and some MF) radio services are provided by the Coastguard stations in both jurisdictions. Full details are in the Sailing Directions.

Getting there and getting around

Ireland has ten airports offering connections to Britain and Europe, and the same number of ferry routes from eastern and southern ports. The road network has been steadily improved, and motorways now connect most of the major cities and towns. Rail services connect Dublin and Belfast with Derry and the north coast and with Rosslare, Waterford, Cork, Tralee, Limerick, Westport and Sligo. Bus networks extend into remote rural areas and good ferry services operate to all the inhabited islands. Some more details are given in the following chapters and a summary appears on page 239.

Blacksod Point: Achill Island in the distance

Opposite: *(top) the rock stacks of Rathlin Island*

(bottom) North Harbour, Cape Clear Island

Glengarriff

1 The South Coast
Carnsore Point to Mizen Head

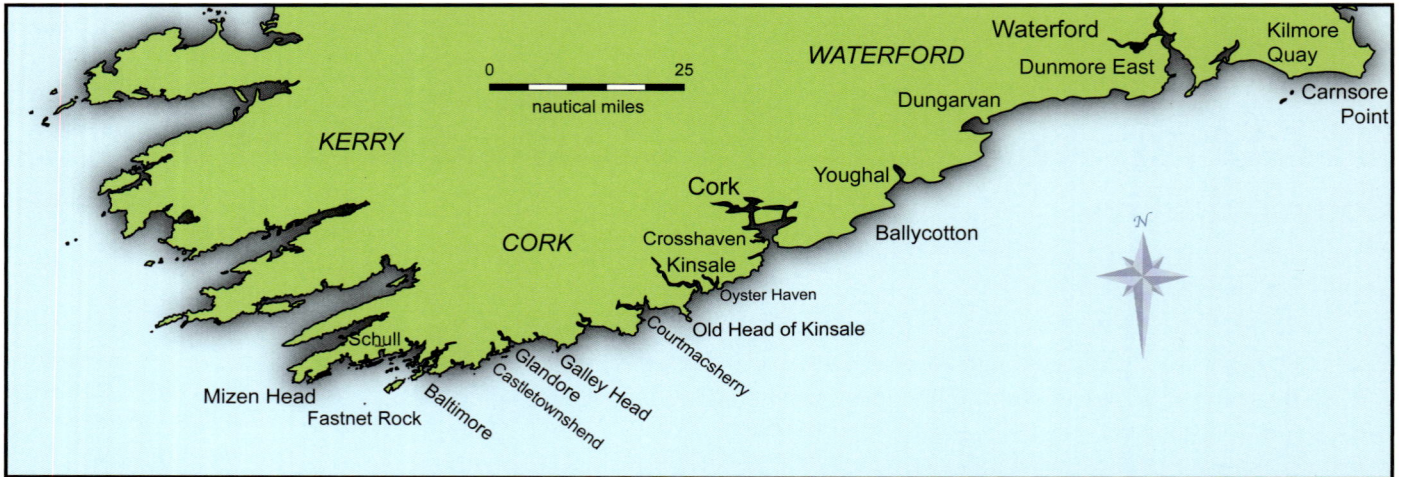

This is a coast of contrasts. Largely cliffbound, and apparently exposed for 140 miles to the Atlantic Ocean to the southwest, it is nevertheless a benign and comely coastline. It is shielded from the prevailing westerly swell, it has many closely-spaced and sheltered bays and inlets, its climate is soft and its tides moderate. Most of its havens are river estuaries, rocky in their approaches and gentler within, while further west the coast begins to assume the more rugged and dramatic character typical of the wilder shores beyond the Mizen.

Castletownshend (left) and East Ferry

For many cruising sailors those shores are their objective; for others the attraction is the regattas at the major sailing centres of Crosshaven, Kinsale, Glandore, Baltimore and Schull – of these places more later – but the south coast itself is a beautiful cruising ground.

The sailor heading westwards can be a hostage to fortune on a coast that trends a little south of west – inconveniently close to the prevailing wind – but the famous capriciousness of Ireland's weather can be an ally. If you don't like the weather, as they say, wait five minutes. The coast has much in common with Devon and Cornwall – the hinterland hilly, but not mountainous; the headlands bold and spectacular; and the havens within winding rias, affording easy entry in difficult conditions, and good shelter once inside. Towns and villages at almost every one of these inlets offer good facilities as well as Ireland's legendary welcome and creature comforts. The watering holes range from the fishing village of Kilmore Quay in the east, through the splendid harbour and city of Cork and tourist magnets like Kinsale, to the sailing-mad holiday villages of Baltimore and Schull in the west. Cork Harbour is the cradle of yachting as a sport, and west Cork is Ireland's busiest marine playground, attracting visiting craft from all around Europe and across the ocean.

Opposite: *The Fastnet Rock*

The beautiful and historic natural harbour of Kinsale

Passage Planning

Except for those fortunate enough to be based on this coast, the first consideration is getting to it, and for most that will involve crossing the Celtic Sea from Cornwall, or Saint George's Channel from Wales, or making the southward passage down the Irish Sea.

The crossing from Land's End or the Scillies to Carnsore Point is 130 miles, to Kinsale just five miles more, and (further west) to Baltimore 155 miles. The courses are all across tide, so the weather is the main consideration, and it may be wise to hedge bets and aim as far west as possible to begin with. From Wales, the strong tides of St George's Channel will govern passage planning, but even if making from South Wales for Cork or points west, it is often wise to close the Irish coast further east, to stay out of the swell further offshore. From the east coast of Ireland, the tide is even more critical.

West of Cork, the coastwise tidal streams are noticeable but not strong, except locally at the headlands, and there are no tidal gates. In the middle section of the coast the streams are insignificant. Going west in unsettled weather, the plan of

Dunworley Bay, west of the Seven Heads

A yacht noses up to the cliffs of Great Saltee Island, white with seabirds and guano

The low clay cliffs of Carnsore Point are unimposing from seaward, but its exposed position makes it an ideal place for a wind farm. It was also the proposed site in the 1970s for Ireland's only nuclear power station, which never got off the drawing board.

campaign might be to make westing in the south-easterly wind in advance of a depression, sit out the south-westerly in a cosy hostelry somewhere, and then resume the passage in the north-westerly that will surely follow. That, at least, is the theory. Needless to say, heading east is generally a good deal less weather-dependent.

Carnsore Point and the Saltees to Kilmore Quay

Carnsore Point is low, but conspicuous by virtue of its wind turbines. This corner of Ireland is adorned with a good sprinkling of rocks and islands, guarded by the Barrels, Bore Rocks and Red Bank buoys, with the Coningbeg buoy furthest to seaward. These marks guide larger vessels clear offshore of all the dangers but since the Coningbeg buoy is a full eight miles off the coast, most yachts take a short cut around or between the islands.

There are fair-weather anchorages around the Saltees. The islands only occasionally have human residents, but are a renowned bird sanctuary, home to over 300 species, and Great Saltee has a grey seal colony. The Sound between the two islands is passable with care, but the seasonally-buoyed gap in St Patrick's Bridge, a shallow ridge of rock joining Little Saltee with the mainland, is the passage of choice. Along the way the abundant bird life of Tacumshin and Lady's Island Lakes, just over the dunes, may add interest, and as this shore is now a kitesurfing destination, that is something else to look out for on the way to Kilmore Quay or Hook Head.

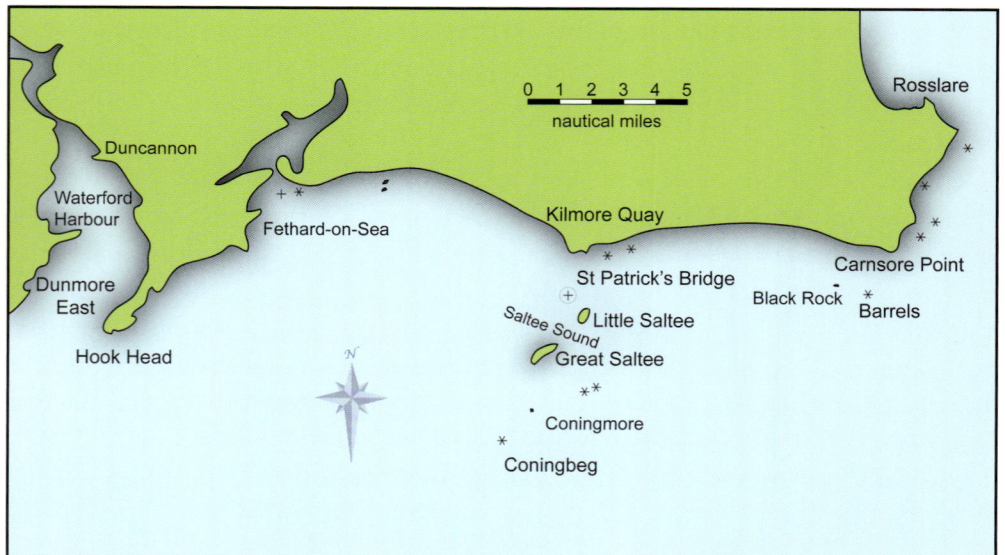

Kilmore Quay marina and the museum-lightship *Guillemot*

The distance from Carnsore Point to St Patrick's Bridge is less than nine miles, and it is a further 13 to the Hook. **Kilmore Quay** is a picture-postcard heritage village with one foot in the sea, and has been a fishing harbour since time immemorial. Its drying quay was made into a deep-water harbour in the 1990s, and that improvement included a small marina, making it a favourite staging post for yachts on passage around Ireland's south-east corner and an ideal landfall for those arriving from south and east. It's a busy place, but the 55-berth marina is suitably separated from the harbour's commercial activity, which now includes a thriving sea angling and diving scene. The 1923-built lightship *Guillemot*, permanently set in concrete beside the harbour, is a splendid Maritime Museum. The ship is complete with her generators, and all her cabins contain the original furniture and fittings.

St Patrick's Bridge

"The marks for St Patrick's Bridge are singular. A row of old men are always to be seen on the quay at Kilmore smoking. You head for the middle of the sound and watch their movements. As long as they continue smoking peacefully you are safe. If they stand up and take their pipes out of their mouths, you are too near to the island. If they get up and run forward to the edge of the quay, you are about to go aground on the mainland. At any rate it seems a much better indication than the rule given to a yachtsman about to enter Malahide, 'Keep the red cow and the brown cow in line'."

Wallace Clark, Sailing Round Ireland, *1976*

[due to the decline in the popularity of pipe smoking and the reconstruction of Kilmore Quay harbour it should be noted that these directions no longer apply – Ed]

The Princes of Saltee

In 1943 the Great Saltee was bought by Michael Neale, a colourful character who had himself crowned Prince of Saltee in 1956. Prince Michael I died in 1998 and was succeeded by his son Michael II. The Saltee family, as they are styled, have never opposed access to the island so long as visitors do not disturb its wildlife and leave it as they found it; a commendable and enlightened policy that deserves respect.

THE SALTEE ISLANDS
AND THE WATERS SURROUNDING THEM ARE AN ABSO-
LUTE POSSESSION OF THE PRINCE OF THE SALTEES
AND HIS HEIRS.

NO MAN OR ASSEMBLY OF MEN HAS ANY RIGHT
WHATSOEVER TO INTERFERE IN THE AFFAIRS OF THE
SALTEE ISLANDS

ALL DECISIONS AFFECTING THE ISLANDS ARE
MADE BY THE PRINCE OF THE SALTEES AND HIS
HEIRS, BOTH OF THE MALE AND FEMALE LINE.

ANY DECISION NOT UNANIMOUS CAN BE
BROUGHT BEFORE "THE ABSENT TWELVE"
AND THEIR DECISION IS FINAL.

THE "ABSENT TWELVE" WILL CONSIST OF
TWELVE FISHERMEN ONLY, WHO CAN COME FROM
ANY PART OF THE EARTH.

ALL PEOPLE, YOUNG AND OLD, ARE WELCOME
TO COME, SEE AND ENJOY THE ISLANDS, AND
LEAVE THEM AS THEY FOUND THEM FOR THE
UNBORN GENERATIONS TO COME, SEE
AND ENJOY.

MICHAEL THE FIRST

THE FAMILY NAME
NEALE OF THE
SALTEE ISLANDS
SHALL BE KNOWN
HENCEFORWARD AS SALTEES
THE NAME SALTEES
TOGETHER WITH TITLE
LEGALIZED 1954.

MICHAEL THE FIRST

Visitor information in Princely style, on Great Saltee

The streets are lined with thatched houses, there are several excellent places to eat and drink, and the Stella Maris Community and Tourist Centre provides showers and snacks to visiting sailors.

Waterford Harbour

Before Kilmore Quay marina was built, **Dunmore East** was the favoured port of call before or after rounding Carnsore Point, and it is still a more accessible port in a storm. Situated just two and a half miles north-west of Hook Head, it always was, and still is, a busy fishing harbour, and since it has no specific accommodation for yachts, no assumptions about mooring or berthing space should be made!

An alternative is to seek the use of a mooring in the bay just north of the harbour where members of Waterford Harbour Sailing Club keep their boats, or to anchor in the next bay north again. The club is very hospitable, welcomes visitors, and is open seven days through July and August, and the harbour has diesel on tap.

The village straggles up the hill behind the harbour, with its overlooking cliff which is home to many nesting kittiwakes. 'Wake' is the operative word, for they squabble all night, constantly screaming their name – 'kitt-i-*waaaake*'!

There is a choice of pubs and restaurants, and shops including food stores and a pharmacy.

Waterford began as a Viking settlement, became the first Norman town in Ireland, and has grown to be the principal city and port in the south-east of the country. The River Suir is busy with container ship traffic, but there is room for leisure craft as well. The estuary passage is scenic and straightforward: first the ten-mile stretch to Cheek Point and the confluence with the River Barrow (of which more later), then a final five miles winding into Waterford City. There are some quiet anchorages off the main channel.

Kilmore Quay

(below) Hook Head lighthouse

(bottom) This humpback whale was photographed breaching off Hook Head in 2010

The Hook

Hook Head lighthouse is among the oldest in the world. There has probably been a lighthouse here since the time of St Dubhán in the 5th century. The present one is founded on a Norman tower, built probably in 1245, with a spiral staircase in the wall cavity, and the lantern dates from 1864. The lighthouse now accommodates a heritage centre and visitors are welcome. See http:\\hookheritage.ie.

A Dunmore East kittiwake

Dunmore East

There is a 100-berth marina on the south bank, right by the city centre, which is perfect for a city visit. The berths are secure, and very suitable for leaving a boat for a spell if required. Waterford also has a small airport nearby with connections to destinations in the UK and further afield.

Waterford is a lively city, with its medieval character still evident amongst its Georgian and more modern buildings, including arts centres and galleries, museums, and many hotels, bars and restaurants. The 800-year-old Reginald's Tower, right beside the marina, is the oldest urban structure in Ireland and houses a Viking Treasures exhibition.

An alternative destination to Waterford is **New Ross,** ten miles up the peaceful River Barrow from the railway bridge opposite Cheek Point. Although the rail service was discontinued in 2011, arrangements for bridge opening are unchanged since New Ross is a minor commercial port. It also has a 66-berth marina and a Tall Ship museum to visit. The replica emigrant ship *Dunbrody* was built as a training project, and although the 176-foot three-masted barque is not currently in seagoing trim, she has many sea miles to her credit and she is a fine visitor

Duncannon Rear

The rear leading light at Duncannon, in the entrance to Waterford Harbour, is the only navigation light in Ireland shown from a private house. In 1991, after the ship channel was dredged, and improved marks were established, the Port of Waterford shut down the old rear mark and sold the property, a little lighthouse with attached dwellings. A few years later they thought better of it and applied to re-establish the light. The Port now maintains the light itself, and pays an annual rent to the owner of the building.

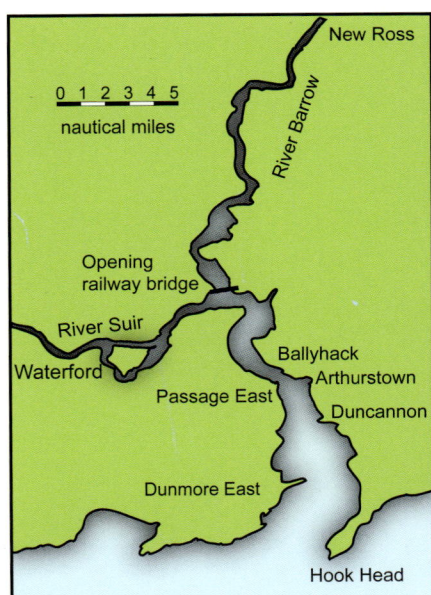

*The **Dunbrody** at New Ross*

Waterford

The German schooner **Undine** *at Waterford City Marina*

Three Sisters Marina, New Ross. The sisters in question are the rivers Suir, Barrow and Nore, which together drain almost a fifth of Ireland.

experience. New Ross is a busy country town which makes much of its claim to fame as the ancestral home of John F. Kennedy.

The Copper Coast

From Waterford Harbour to the wide, sandy, east-facing Dungarvan Harbour there extends a twenty-mile stretch of cliff coast. It is broken by the exposed Tramore Bay, which claimed many ships and many lives in the past by being mistaken in bad weather for its safe neighbour Waterford to the east. As a result, 200 years ago, the distinctive towers on either headland were built to warn mariners.

This is known as the Copper Coast, from the days when the metal ore was mined here. **Dungarvan**, the county town of County Waterford and birthplace of Ireland's only Nobel prize-winning scientist Ernest Walton, is a lovely town

The three towers on Great Newtown Head – the centre one is topped by the Metal Man, a 4-metre cast-iron statue of a sailor in naval uniform of Napoleonic times. His twin brother guards the entrance to Sligo harbour

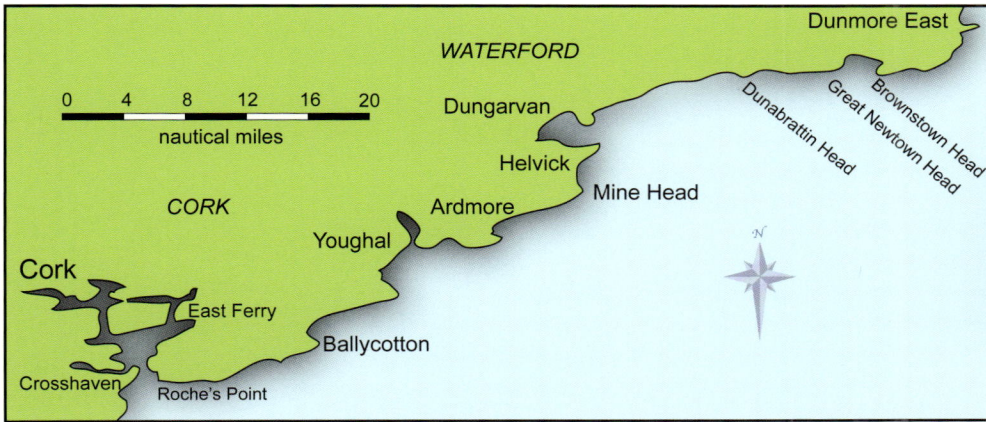

Mine pump-house on the Copper Coast

and historic port. Its drying harbour lies at the head of a winding but well-marked channel, navigable with sufficient rise of tide, with anchorages in the entrance and drying berths in the town. A more convenient passage anchorage is at Helvick, on the south side of Dungarvan Harbour, half a mile west of Helvick Head and just north of the little fishing harbour.

The cliffs continue to Ardmore Bay, five miles west of Mine Head. The bay is sheltered from winds between south-west and north, and the small village ashore is picturesque, with thatched roofs and a fine round tower. It also boasts an hotel with a Michelin-starred restaurant.

The Copper Coast

At the villages of Knockmahon and Tankardstown, on the coast between Tramore and Dungarvan, there were mines which produced 10,000 tons of copper ore in each of their peak years of 1840 and 1865. The tunnels extended out under the seabed, and relics including a preserved pumping house may be seen close to the little harbour at Boatstrand, east of Dunabrattin Head.

A raft-up of Dungarvan Harbour SC yachts on the Copper Coast; (right) Dungarvan Harbour

The cliffs of the Copper Coast, between Tramore and Dungarvan

The Leaning Tower of Ardmore

The Round Tower at Ardmore (which has a jaunty tilt) is one of about forty similar towers of a design almost unique to Ireland, 18 to 40 metres in height and with a conical stone cap. Most are situated inland, and the Ardmore tower (and those on Scattery Island in the Shannon and at Killala, Co.Mayo) are among the few that are both complete and on the coast. The lower section of one on Tory Island also survives. The towers date from some time between the 9th and 12th centuries, and their original function is uncertain – some features of their design, such as doors high on the walls, would suggest a defensive purpose, but they are not generally sited strategically. They may have simply been bell-towers, and have survived because their shape fortuitously made them exceptionally weather-resistant.

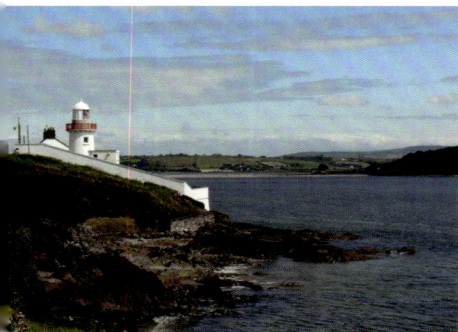

Youghal lighthouse on Moll Goggin's Corner

Youghal Harbour and Ferry Point

Opposite: *Ballycotton by day and dusk*

Youghal's Clock Gate dates from 1777

Youghal to Cork Harbour

The historic town of **Youghal**, at the mouth of the River Blackwater, was one of the main medieval ports in Ireland, having received its charter around 1209 not long after the Norman invasion, although the settlement goes back long before that. Later, one of the principal landowners of the area was Sir Walter Raleigh, who was granted estates by Queen Elizabeth I for his part in suppressing an Irish rebellion in 1579. Sir Walter is of course credited with introducing the potato from the New World to Ireland.

The estuary has a swift tide that sweeps past the town quays, making anchoring difficult. However there are visitors' moorings, or the option of anchoring in quieter water north of Ferry Point on the opposite shore. At the Town Quay a pontoon berth for charter boats can be used on occasions for loading, and obtaining water.

Youghal is a tourist town steeped in history, with many restaurants, shops, and other amenities.

The coast west of Youghal is characterised by two prominent headlands, each with a small offlying island. Knockadoon Head and Capel Island are four miles to the south-west, and Ballycotton Island, with its prominent lighthouse, is another seven miles to the west. The small village of **Ballycotton** has a snug harbour tucked inside the point; a yacht might find a berth here, or take a visitor's mooring in the sheltered bay north of the harbour.

Ashore, apart from (a claimed) ten golf courses – and the renowned Ballymaloe restaurant and cookery school – within ten miles, there are good hotels and

Capel Island Tower

The conspicuous tower on Capel Island, at the west end of Youghal Bay, was the result of a classic planning U-turn. After 19 years of lobbying, the merchants and shipowners of Cork succeeded in 1847 in getting the Ballast Board, against its better judgement and the advice of its own Inspector, to start building a lighthouse on the island. But in the same year, the *Sirius*, famous as the first ship to cross the Atlantic entirely under steam, was wrecked on the Smiths rocks at Ballycotton. The same Cork merchants and shipowners now petitioned for lights on Ballycotton Island and Mine Head, which was the scheme the Ballast Board had wanted to build in the first place. The works at Capel Island were suspended and the tower was capped at two storeys high, as it remains to this day.

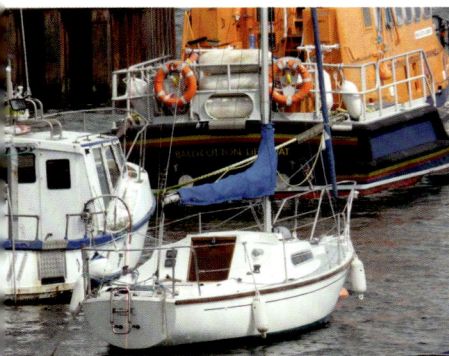

restaurants, and one or two small shops. Needless to say, as Ballycotton is both a fishing community and a sea angling centre, the seafood available locally, either cooked or fresh, is exceptional. Ballycotton's finest hour was in February 1936 when its lifeboat rescued the crew of the Daunt Rock lightship in a rescue operation 79 hours in duration (see page 193).

Cork Harbour would warrant a book on its own, as one of the finest and largest inland seaways in Ireland; perhaps excelled for completely sheltered-water sailing only by Strangford Lough. Deep channels extend up the Owenboy River past Crosshaven, round both sides of Great Island and ten miles up the estuary and the River Lee to the heart of the city of Cork. The Harbour also has extensive shallows and drying banks, and twelve islands. Haulbowline Island is the Headquarters base of the Irish Naval Service, and Spike Island has been home to residents from early monks through Vikings to 19th and 20th-century convicts. Its prison buildings were in use until recent times. All the islands, except Spike, are now bridged to the shore.

This is Ireland's second busiest port, with installations all around its shores, but they do not spoil the scenery and tranquillity. The mudflats habitat is important for many bird species, and the harbour is a Special Protection Area.

The cruising sailor has a wide choice of ports of call here, depending on time and inclinations, and apart from the main centres, there are many anchorages in quiet corners.

Cork Harbour is known worldwide as a yachting centre. The Royal Cork Yacht Club was formed in Cobh in 1720 as the Water Club of Cork, and is the oldest in the world. Today, the epicentre of activity is **Crosshaven**, where the RCYC – located here since 1966 – is the venue for world-class championship events including Cork Week, held in July of alternate (even-numbered) years. Crosshaven offers three marinas, a boatyard, riggers, sailmakers, diesel on tap, the hospitable RCYC, and good shops and pub grub.

Just over a mile up the Owenboy River is the peaceful **Drake's Pool**, a gorgeous and wonderfully sheltered anchorage – although due to the number of moorings,

Roche's Point, at the entrance to Cork Harbour

Action at Cobh; the American yacht **Pyewacket** *races at Cork Week*

The Irish Naval Service's 50th anniversary in 1996. LÉ **Ciara** *(left) and LÉ* **Eithne**

*Seven ships of the Irish Naval Service in line ahead: LÉ **Emer** (P21) is followed by LÉ **Orla** (P41) and her sistership LÉ **Ciara** (P42), then LÉ **Niamh** (P52) and her sistership LÉ **Roisin** (P51). Bringing up the rear are the Emer's sisterships LÉ **Aisling** (P23) and LÉ **Aoife** (P22). The photograph is taken from the eighth ship, the flagship LÉ **Eithne** (P31).*

The abbreviation stands for Long Éireannach, *Irish Ship. The ships are named after heroines of Irish mythology and legend.*

(bottom) Drake's Pool

The Irish Naval Service

A visiting yacht in Irish waters is quite likely to meet, or at least see, one of the ships of the Naval Service. The Republic's 200-mile limit encloses 130,000 square miles of ocean – five times the land area of the state, and 14% of all EU waters – rich in fish, hydrocarbons and priceless ecosystems. Ireland's long coastline presents a tempting prospect for smugglers as well as a formidable hazard to shipping. EU Fisheries Policy, unpopular and much derided, has nevertheless to be enforced. Marine accidents must be dealt with, and search and rescue provided, especially outside the range of lifeboats or Coastguard helicopters; all this in addition to maritime defence requirements and the need to support Irish forces on UN peacekeeping missions around the world.

To cover this, the Irish Naval Service currently (2012) deploys eight ships, with a total force afloat and ashore of around 1,000 men and women, and aims to have two or three ships on patrol at any one time. Endurance, toughness and seakeeping qualities are paramount – for ships and crew alike. Patrolling the north Atlantic off the west coast of Ireland in all weathers and all seasons, and boarding rolling and pitching fishing vessels from a RIB, is not a trivial task!

The INS was formally established in 1946 as a permanent component of the Defence Forces, although during the Second World War the State had deployed six ex-British motor torpedo-boats. These vessels were quite unsuited for any kind of patrol task, but the new INS acquired three much more appropriate ocean-going *Flower* class corvettes. They were succeeded in 1971 by ex-*Ton* class minesweepers which served until the late 1970's, when a start was made on creating a modern and appropriate fleet of all-weather patrol vessels.

Small as it is, the INS is a highly professional force with many successful operations to its credit, including some high-profile drug and arms smuggling interdictions, together with routine fishery protection work. The ships are controlled from Naval HQ at Haulbowline in Cork Harbour. Some fine old Napoleonic War-era buildings are still in use at the base, bearing names redolent of their Royal Navy history. The well-equipped operations room keeps tabs on all fishing vessels in Irish waters, and participates with other European navies in monitoring suspect vessels all over the Atlantic.

The INS upholds the tradition of the dipped-ensign salute, long discontinued by the Royal Navy. When you meet one of these ships at sea, haul your ensign to half mast and wait. The ship will return the salute; when she has re-hoisted her ensign, hoist yours, put down your camera, and wave. If she does send over a RIB for a look, its crew will be unfailingly courteous.

Ed Wheeler

East Ferry

A session at Cronin's pub, Crosshaven

Opposite: *Crosshaven*

anchoring may be something of a challenge! The old Cork to Crosshaven roadside railway track is now an attractive riverside path, and affords fine views of this pretty estuary.

The new **Monkstown** Marina is situated just south of the narrows between Great Island and the mainland. The dredged and buoyed ship channel continues up-river through Lough Mahon and past the container terminal at Tivoli to the city centre, where **Cork City** Marina – at the eastern tip of the island in the River Lee upon which the city was founded – comprises a visitors' pontoon with 150 metres of secure berthing. It is just 500 metres from Patrick Street, the main thoroughfare, so is ideal for a city visit. A good starting point is the Cork City Tourist Information Centre, on Grand Parade, for the low-down on what to see and do. Cork is an attractive and lively place, so beware entrapment: your stay at the pontoon is restricted to six nights!

East Ferry is at the quiet end of the Harbour. East Passage, between the eastern end of Great Island and the mainland, is untouched by industry; its banks are wooded and its ambience is rural and scenic. The 80-berth East Ferry Marina is on the island side.

Cork City Marina

Racing in West Cork, 1949 style

"The party went to Royal Munster Yacht Club at Crosshaven about 5 p.m. 3rd July so that the owner might attend a Meeting called to consider the vile weather prevailing. General opinion was that the race [to Schull] would be postponed.

"6 p.m. Lighthouse keepers along the course all reported very heavy seas, impractical for sailing craft. Air-met. reported wind S.W., veering later to West 20-25 m.p.h. Sailing committee decided to postpone start until 5 a.m. following morning.

"6.5 p.m. Paddy O'Keefe, owner of the modern ocean racer "JOHN DORY" 16 tons whose home port is Bantry, decided he wants to go home and announced belligerently that he will sail to-night, race or no race, at the advertised time of the start – 8 p.m. It is clearly understood that in his view all the rest of us are a bunch of cissies. Paddy, of course, has certain advantages apart from his ship. His crew are almost professional – Peter Brett, Pierce, two bearded Frenchmen borrowed off Sergeant Sullivan, and a Clear Islander. No particular reason why he should be cissie: he wants to go home!

"However, Sullivan, owner of "MARCHWOOD MAID" a modern 13 ton cutter, decides that Paddy cannot be allowed to get away with this sort of thing. "OSPREY" decides ditto and the race is on. Hectic rush to feed and get aboard. All mothers of young in considerable state of emotion at brutal fathers risking lives of children in useless exhibition of bravado. Children, all twenty years of age or thereabouts, rather over excited."

....

- *twelve hours later:*

"6.30 a.m. Weather topmast shroud parted at bottle screw.
Went about briefly to repair it and then again stood in to the land.
6.45 a.m. Out whisky bottle.
6.55 a.m. Watch on deck begins to feel much better."

....

"Soon afterwards we were first shaken rigid and then delighted to see the mythical "Albert", the grampus of Baltimore. A grampus is a killer whale and according to my encyclopaedia reaches 20 ft. in length. We thought he looked longer than that. "Albert" gave a splendid display of jumps, always a cable to weather of us on each tack. Presumably he hoped that we were going in to Schull as we had passed Baltimore. At both places he likes to rub the lice off his backside on the bottom or cables of visiting ships. "Albert" is a popular fellow locally, but apparently visiting yachtsmen do not appreciate his sense of humour. Evidently he thought we were going to New York, as after we made out to the Fastnet from Cape Clear we saw no more of him."

James Crosbie, log of "Osprey", ICC Annual, 1949

Cork Harbour to Kinsale and Glandore Bay

Oyster Haven and Kinsale are ten and twelve miles, respectively, from Cork Harbour entrance along a cliffbound coast backed by rolling farmland. The more exposed **Oyster Haven** is entirely rural, and a pleasant stop in settled weather, with the sailing, sailboarding and holiday Oysterhaven Centre, one of the first of its kind in Ireland, as its main focus of activity.

Ireland's gourmet capital **Kinsale** is busy with tourists from all over the world. Its magnificent sheltered natural harbour is well endowed with three marinas and a boatyard. The biggest and most central marina is owned by Kinsale Yacht Club, and its visitors have the use of the club's bar and dining facilities overlooking the quay. It goes without saying that the town also has an unparalleled choice of restaurants to suit all tastes; while art galleries and the town's very own

Oyster Haven

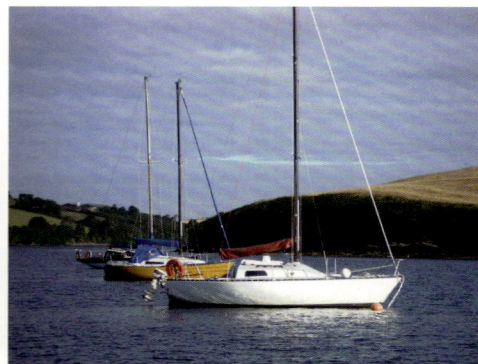

Kinsale YC Marina

microbrewery add to its attractions.

There is a lot more to do, however, than eating, drinking and shopping. Kinsale is steeped in history, and whether you take a guided tour of its narrow winding streets, or follow the signposted tourist trail for yourself, you can while away several days with ease. The Tourist Office, a suggested first point of call, is centrally situated. Here you can choose between the many attractions. For forward planning, the town's tourism website – www.kinsale.ie – is comprehensive.

The massive Charles Fort, dating from 1670 and overlooking the harbour

Kinsale town museum (left)

A yacht makes her way into Kinsale beneath the ancient walls of Charles Fort

Charles Fort

Kinsale and the Robinson Crusoe Connection

In 1703, the galley *Cinque Ports* left Kinsale for a privateering voyage in the Pacific. One of her crew, a Scot called Alexander Selkirk, was later marooned (for incitement to mutiny against the villainous captain William Dampier) on Más a Tierra, one of the uninhabited Juan Fernández islands off the Chilean coast, and remained alone there for over four years before being picked up. Daniel Defoe, who had been a government agent in Kinsale in 1690, later met Selkirk, who (with some added licence and plagiarism by Defoe) became the hero of *Robinson Crusoe*. The character of Man Friday in the novel was based on a native South American who had previously been marooned on the same island, but had left it several years before Selkirk arrived. Selkirk later became a naval officer, and died, probably of yellow fever, in 1721. The Chilean authorities have renamed the island Robinson Crusoe in the interests of its tourist industry, while its neighbour Más a Fuego is now Alejandro Selkirk, although Selkirk never set foot on it.

And that is why there is a Man Friday Restaurant in Kinsale.

Opposite: *Trident Marina and the Town Quay, Kinsale*

The narrow streets of Kinsale are lined with restaurants, craft shops and galleries

entrance, is Kinsale's most impressive historic site. The Battle of Kinsale, fought in 1601 between a combined Spanish and Irish force and the English armies of Queen Elizabeth I, established English rule in Ireland for the next 300 years, and first James Fort on the west side of the estuary, and later Charles Fort on the east, were built to defend the port. Upriver of James Fort and opposite the town is Castlepark Marina, a quieter spot away from the bustle of the port, and with a wider range of services and facilities. James Fort can be conveniently explored from the marina, and offers fine views of the town and the estuary. Kinsale has several golf courses including the spectacular Old Head course, on the tip of the promontory.

In fine weather, **Summer Cove**, close north of Charles Fort, is a delightful stopover, and the pub usually has a visitors' mooring available.

Westward Ho!

The coast to the west is a succession of bold headlands – the Old Head of Kinsale, Seven Heads, Galley Head and Toe Head – and beautiful bays open to the south. Sheltered inlets, some navigable and some almost entirely drying, open off these bays, and there are many little coves for short-stay anchorage. There are a few pontoons but no more large marinas west of Kinsale, and to enjoy the coast to the full the visitor should be confident in using a good anchor or a harbour wall.

Lusitania

The Cunarder *Lusitania* was torpedoed by U-20 ten miles south of the Old Head of Kinsale on 15th May 1915, and sank with the loss of 1,198 lives. Among the casualties were the American millionaire Alfred Vanderbilt, the writer and philosopher Elbert Hubbard and his wife Alice, and Sir Hugh Lane, Irish art collector and founder of the Hugh Lane Gallery in Dublin. There were 761 survivors, but Courtmacsherry lifeboat, arriving under oars three and a half hours later, found only floating bodies and wreckage.

Conspiracy theorists have had a field day with the sinking; intending passengers were warned by the German consulate that the *Lusitania* was (in their view) carrying munitions, thus forfeiting her right as a passenger ship to immunity from attack. It has been claimed that she was sunk by a second, *internal*, explosion, and it has even been suggested that she was "trailed" across the path of the U-boat. But what is not in dispute is that public reaction all over the world caused a change in German U-boat tactics, and ensured that American policy was, from then on, firmly in favour of the Allies.

Kinsale museum has an excellent exhibit describing the disaster. The wreck lies in 51° 24′·73N, 8° 32′·84W. Every five years, on the anniversary of the sinking, the present Courtmacsherry lifeboat goes out to lay a wreath over the spot. It takes her not quite half an hour to get there.

The Old Head of Kinsale

Opposite: *Courtmacsherry*

Courtmacsherry, seven miles west of the Old Head, is the nearest of the navigable inlets and home to one of Ireland's longest-established lifeboat stations. The village is a small fishing port and sea angling centre, with pubs, pub grub and music ashore, and an annual horse-race meeting which takes place on the drying sandbanks at low tide. The wooded slopes behind the village offer perfect shelter from even the heaviest weather from south and south-west, and a pontoon at the pier provides a convenient alongside berth. In all these coastal villages, most of the houses are second homes, and populations double or triple in summer.

Clonakilty Bay to the west has no good harbours – the channel leading to the lively little town almost dries and the entrance is exposed to the south. The same is true of Rosscarbery, in Glandore Bay to the west of Galley Head. But of the many delightful sailing haunts along this coast, **Glandore** ranks among the most attractive and picturesque. The tiny village overlooks the historic harbour, where

Courtmacsherry

The Caves of the Old Head of Kinsale

At the narrow neck of the peninsula, the Old Head is penetrated right through by several caves, which are navigable by dinghy in very settled weather, taking care to shelter from the shrieking kittiwakes. It is thus possible to circumnavigate the lighthouse. The story is told that – based on this – the keepers once petitioned for the island allowance. The bays on either side of the isthmus are called Holeopen Bay, East and West.

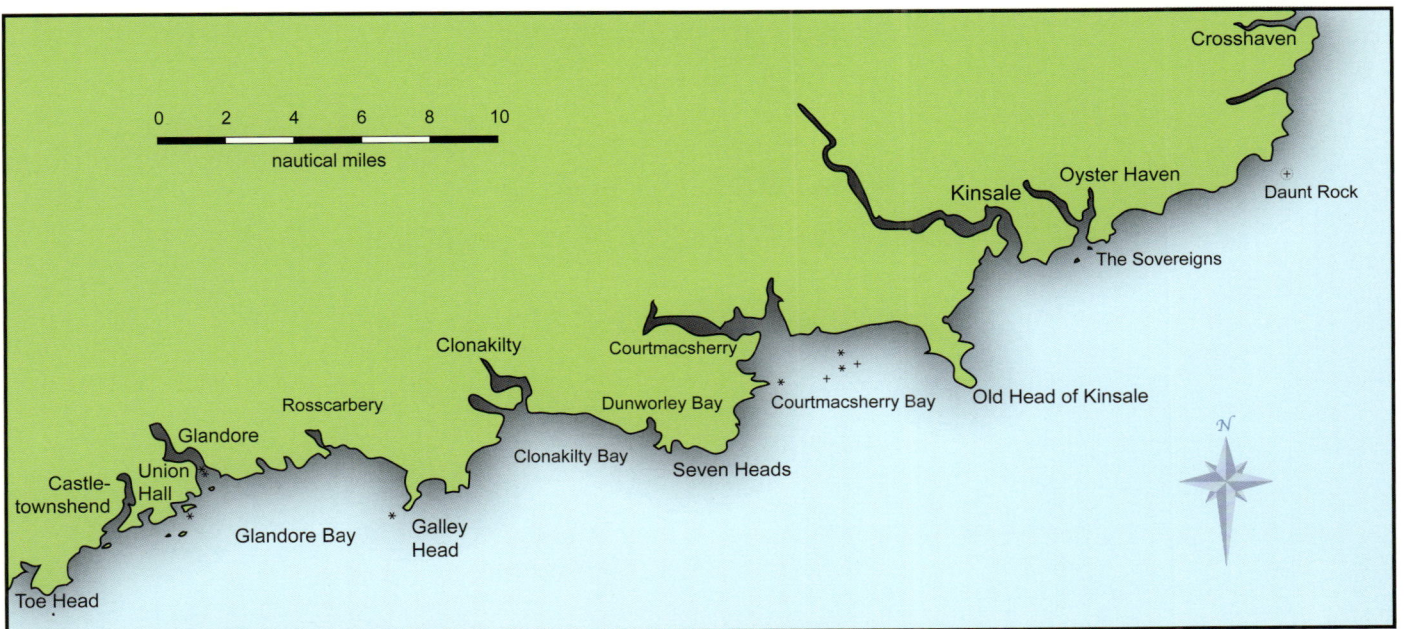

Glandore, with Union Hall across the harbour

Otters are common in west Cork and may often be glimpsed along the shore

the first regatta was held in 1830. Since 1992 the Glandore Classic Regatta, a splendid spectacle held in even-numbered years, has attracted scores of traditional boats.

Glandore hamlet itself has a couple of restaurants and a pub, but **Union Hall,** just over half a mile away on the west side of the creek, is a bigger village and a major fishing port, with more amenities including (at the time of writing) an outstanding seafood shop; and it also has a quirky museum and a whiskey distillery. Choose your anchorage with care if the visitors' moorings at Glandore are full, because the big trawlers, drawing three or four metres or more, must take the deep mid-channel.

Opposite: *(top) Galley Head*

(bottom) The coast west of Glandore Harbour, with Castle Haven and Castletownshend in the middle distance

Glandore

Union Hall

Drombeg Stone Circle

About 2km east of Glandore and not far off the main road is a Megalithic stone circle dating from about 900 BC. It has 17 stones and two "portal stones", and in the centre was found a pot containing the cremated remains of a young person. Nearby are the foundations of two stone huts, and a *fulacht fia*, an outdoor cooking trough. Water was boiled by adding hot stones, and the heat generated was enough to cook an entire deer carcase (it has been tested). Drombeg is one of the best-preserved and most-visited Megalithic sites in Ireland, and the most accessible for anyone cruising the coast.

Castle Haven

A few miles to the west lies Castle Haven, also sheltered and snug. The village of **Castletownshend** is centred on one long, narrow and steep street, a test for seafarers' legs, but halfway up, for rest and refreshment, is an outstanding pub and restaurant. The beautiful old church of St Barrahane, overlooking the harbour, is the venue for five classical concerts in July and August each year. The village was named after Richard Townsend, a Cromwellian soldier who was granted the estate in the 1650s (the extra "h" was a Victorian embellishment). The castellated building beside the harbour is not the castle of the name; that is a much older and now ruinous tower south of the village.

(Right) Edith Somerville's memorial in St Barrahane's Church

(Far right) Castletownshend's steep main street

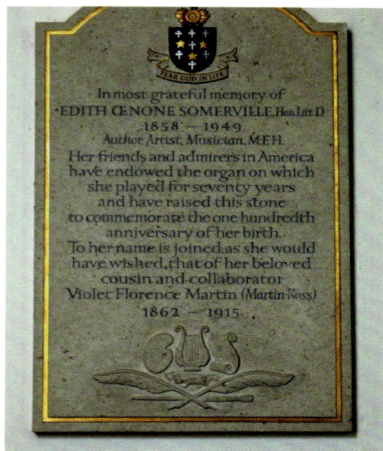

Edith Somerville

Edith Œnone Somerville grew up in Castletownshend as a member of one of the three Anglo-Irish "big house" families of the village. With her cousin Violet Martin, she began a literary partnership in 1887 which lasted until Violet's death in 1915, Violet writing under the pseudonym "Martin Ross". Somerville and Ross's most famous work is *Some Experiences of an Irish RM*, dramatised by the BBC in 1983 with Peter Bowles as the hapless Major Yeates, sent to Ireland as a Resident Magistrate to dispense justice to a people who had their own unique definition of what the term meant.

Castletownshend retained its "Irish RM" ambience for many years after independence in 1922. Edith Somerville was also an accomplished painter, a campaigner for women's rights, a master of foxhounds and for seventy years the organist of St Barrahane's Church; she died, aged 91, in 1949.

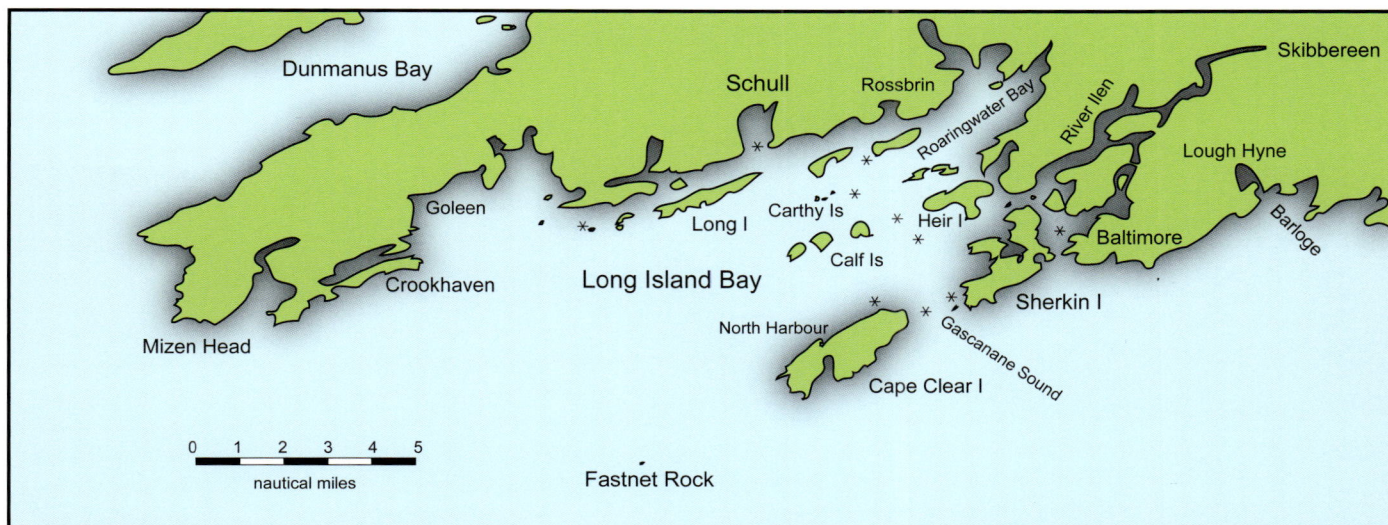

Whale-watching around Ireland

Whether you sail inshore or offshore around Ireland – and particularly off the south coast – there are plenty of opportunities for some of the best whale-watching in European Atlantic waters. Which species you see will very much depend on your location and timing, and of course your experience and interest. As whales and dolphins are highly mobile mammals, there will always be an element of luck underpinning each encounter.

Observing cetaceans from sailing boats isn't without its difficulties. Good sailing conditions generally make for difficult whale-watching! The tell-tale signs are diving seabirds, surface disturbances in calm water, or the sight and smell of hanging vapour plumes.

The very latest sightings (and strandings) are validated and made available online on www.iwdg.ie, the Irish Whale and Dolphin Group website. This unique resource is updated daily and enables online interrogation of almost 20,000 sighting records (as of 2012) by species, location and time frame. So when planning a route, you can map the most recent sightings in the area of interest, thus increasing your chances of finding the activity "hotspots" en route.

The eight species encountered most consistently each year, in rough order of frequency, are the harbour porpoise, bottlenose dolphin, common dolphin, minke whale, fin whale, Risso's dolphin, humpback whale and killer whale. These species comprise 99% of all sightings submitted to the IWDG and are based on a sample size of 1,500-1,800 records reported annually from land, sea and air. The first five of these species are common, the remaining three infrequently seen. There is of course a bias in these figures towards inshore species (within eleven miles of the coast).

Padraig Whooley, IWDG Sightings Co-ordinator

(left) Fin whales off Galley Head. These are the second largest animals on Earth, the adults 20m in length and weighing 60 tonnes. Live strandings of these majestic animals are unusual, but invariably fatal. One such, of an adult female, happened in Courtmacsherry harbour in January 2009 (below)

Castle Haven to Baltimore and the islands

The tiny creek of **Barloge**, a cosy anchorage in settled weather, is hidden behind Bullock Island, two and a half miles west of Toe Head. It is a wonderful place to explore by dinghy, especially to shoot the rapids that partially fill and empty **Lough Hyne** on every tide, but also for exploring the caves and cliffs of the island.

Lough Hyne is a unique habitat, a deep lake refreshed by the sea, but only above half tide. Its unusual biodiversity made it Ireland's first Marine Nature Reserve. For scientists, it is fascinating. For scientists and non-scientists of all ages, negotiating the rapids by dinghy provides endless fun.

The entrance to **Baltimore** harbour, a wide and sheltered stretch of water, is marked by a gleaming white stone tower, named Lot's Wife after that ill-fated lady of the Book of Genesis. Baltimore is very much a recreational boating centre; a venue for dinghy championships and (at the end of May) an annual Wooden Boat Festival. It is a lively and energetic place, with excellent pubs and restaurants. Les

The rapids of Lough Hyne at low tide: towards high tide they run the other way

Opposite: *(top) Barloge*

(bottom) Lough Hyne

Lot's Wife guards the entrance to Baltimore; Sherkin Island, beyond

The Wreck of the *Kowloon Bridge*

The largest shipwreck in the world occurred on the Stags Rocks off Toe Head in November 1986. The ore, bulk and oil carrier *Kowloon Bridge*, with a cargo of 165,000 tonnes of iron ore from Quebec to Hunterston in the Clyde, had previously put into Bantry Bay with cracks appearing in her deck after her Atlantic crossing in heavy weather. Having broken an anchor chain in continuing storm force winds she put back to sea, only to have her steering gear fail. She drifted helplessly in 15-metre swells and struck the Stags in the early hours of 24 November, breaking in two later that day. Efforts to tow her off failed and she slipped into deeper water and sank on 3 December. She has been a magnet (in more ways than one) for divers ever since, and the wreck is marked by a south cardinal buoy.

The *Kowloon Bridge* was one of six sister ships, all of which suffered structural cracking at various times. One of them, the *Derbyshire*, disappeared with all hands in a typhoon off Okinawa in 1980.

The Stags

Heir Island

Glénans sailing school has one of its two Irish centres here, and ferries run from the harbour to Sherkin, Cape Clear and Heir Islands.

Protecting Baltimore Harbour is **Sherkin Island**, home to 120 people including artists of many nationalities, a remarkable marine biology station and a ruined 12th-century Franciscan abbey. Sherkin has pontoon berthing, and a couple of pubs. The North Passage from the Harbour leads to the Ilen River, which is navigable with care and suitable rise of tide to Oldcourt Quay. This is about two miles short of **Skibbereen**, the busy and cosmopolitan chief town of west Cork, which is accessible by dinghy (or taxi) and has – among many other shops – a comprehensive chandlery. At Oldcourt are two of Ireland's most capable boatyards.

North-west of Baltimore and the mouth of the Ilen lie Heir Island and the rest of Carbery's Hundred Isles. This is a wild and unspoiled playground

Baltimore and its busy sailing club

Sherkin pontoon

The Sack of Baltimore

In the early 1600s Baltimore, like many other places in Ireland, accumulated a small colony of English settlers. In 1631, North African pirates, led by a Dutch captain and piloted by a captive Irish fisherman, entered the harbour, raided the village and took over 100 prisoners, few of whom ever saw Ireland, or England, again. The raid is commemorated in the name of the Algerine pub in the village.

Manx shearwaters migrate daily past Cape Clear

for the cruising yacht with time to spare, but apart from the islands there are rocks aplenty, and very few navigational aids, so it also calls for sharp pilotage. Baltimore's lifeboat is often the busiest in Ireland.

However, from Baltimore some kind of course can be shaped almost regardless of wind direction, and the inner islands offer good shelter. **Heir Island** (population 27) has a renowned if quirky restaurant where booking months in advance is advised.

Cape Clear, the southernmost inhabited part of Ireland, lies across the rock-strewn and tidal Gascanane Sound from Sherkin, its North and South Harbours just six miles from Baltimore. Cape (as it is known), almost treeless and more rugged and exposed than Sherkin, has like many other offshore islands a special atmosphere, an intense social life, and an important religious history. It is just three miles long and a mile across, so is ideal for walking and exploring. It is part of the Gaeltacht, areas where Irish is given a special status, and an important

West Cork Food

The artisan food producers of West Cork have an outstanding reputation. The local cheeses, smoked fish and poultry, breads and pastries, meats and seafood are all mouthwatering, and the black pudding is famous. The supermarket in Skibbereen stocks them all and delivers to the pier at Baltimore. See www.westcorkfood.com for more details.

North Harbour, Cape Clear

Dún an Oir, Cape Clear. The Fastnet Rock is just visible on the horizon at extreme left

North Harbour, Cape Clear

Distinctly not racing round the Fastnet Rock

part of the island economy is the annual hosting of students on residential summer language schools. The island, with a population of 130, is a magnet for birdwatchers, since it lies on important daily and annual migration routes.

North Harbour is the ferry port, built into a narrow and spectacular cove in the cliffs but (at the time of writing) somewhat in need of structural repairs and dredging. A yacht which can dry out alongside the inner harbour walls will have no trouble finding a berth. South Harbour, across a narrow isthmus, is a spacious anchorage, although exposed to the south.

The **Fastnet Rock**, four miles to the south-west, needs no introduction to sailors. Lit since 1854, and automated since 1989, its lighthouse is a first landfall for transatlantic shipping, and the rock is the turning mark for the 608-mile Fastnet Race from Cowes to Plymouth.

Baltimore and Cape Clear to Mizen Head

The beaten path leads from Baltimore's south entrance through Gascanane Sound to Cape Clear and **Schull**, while the tortuous routes south or east of Heir give more sheltered, if trickier, passages. Roaringwater Bay (which does not roar, the name is that of the river at its head) is sadly encumbered with mussel rafts, but it is possible to squeeze past them to the head of the bay at **Ballydehob. Rossbrin**, north of Horse Island, has a useful boatyard, and the channels among the islands make for fascinating day-sailing, with a lovely remote anchorage at

The Fastnet Race

The RORC's Fastnet Race has been a classic of the offshore calendar since its inception in 1925. The 28th Race, with 306 competitors, was struck by a storm of unusual ferocity on 14 August 1979. A depression of 979 hPa passed over south-west Ireland, with secondaries in its southern quadrant, and rapidly-changing wind directions and contrary local gusts raised extraordinarily confused and violent seas. 23 yachts were lost or abandoned and 19 people died. Four lifeboats from Ireland – Dunmore East, Ballycotton, Courtmacsherry and Baltimore – and all the ships of the Irish Naval Service, participated in what was then the largest search and rescue operation ever mounted in peacetime. The lifeboats were at sea for almost 24 hours. The Watson class lifeboat *Sir Samuel Kelly*, on relief duty at Courtmacsherry, was the same boat that had rescued 31 people from the sinking *Princess Victoria* off Belfast Lough in 1953. In 1979 she towed in the stricken yacht *Casse Tete V* and rescued her crew of ten.

During the 2011 Race, the 30m yacht *Rambler 100* suffered the loss of her keel soon after rounding the Rock, and immediately capsized. All 21 members of her crew were rescued, 16 by Baltimore lifeboat and five, after a two-hour search, by the sea angling boat *Wave Chieftain*.

South Harbour, Cape Clear

The Tower Houses of West Cork

Many old castles and tower houses are landmarks on the West Cork coast. Most of these are 15th-century constructions by the Gaelic clan chiefs of the time – the O'Driscolls built Rincolisky, Dún na Sead at Baltimore, Dunalong on Sherkin, Dún an Oir on Cape Clear, and the castle from which Castle Haven took its name. On the Mizen peninsula the O'Mahonys built Dunbeacon and Dunmanus, Leamcon and Rossbrin, and the much older Dunlough on Three Castle Head. Kilcoe was a MacCarthy construction and the original Dunboy was built by O'Sullivan Bere.

All these castles attracted unwelcome attention in the 16th and 17th centuries, and by 1655 all of them had been either taken over by the officers of the new Ascendancy, or left in ruins. Dunboy, near Castletownbere, saw the last stand of the old Gaelic order in 1602, after the battle of Kinsale was already lost. Many are haunted – Dún an Oir has a ghost ship, and Dunlough a White Lady. Several have recently been restored as residences, including Dún na Sead and Kilcoe, the latter by the actor Jeremy Irons.

Kilcoe Castle

A dinghy race at Schull

The Loch Fyne skiff **Cruachan,** *built in 1899, beneath the ruin of Rossbrin castle, older still*

Schull

Opposite: *(top) Goleen*

Long Island and its Channel

Carthy's Island. This area epitomizes the very cosmopolitan nature of Ireland's south-west; when the Minister of Education opened the fine new Fastnet Marine and Outdoor Education Centre in Schull, she was greeted by the youthful skippers of the Optimist dinghies in each of their native languages – fourteen of them! Schull Harbour, a mile by half a mile, can be so crowded in summer that it is hard to find an anchorage, but visitors' moorings are available. Calves Week racing, held at the start of August, attracts a large fleet. Any association with Cowes Week is coincidental: the event is named for the nearby Calf Islands, and no pun intended (but of course). Schull has good shops and excellent restaurants and pubs.

Long Island, with a population of just six, is a tranquil spot, worth walking from end to end for the sheer peace of the place and the magnificent views in all directions. The west end of its channel explodes in a welter of islets and rocks, with Man O'War Sound and Barrel Sound between. **Goleen**, five miles from

Schull, is a tiny creek, steep-to, narrow and rocky, drying at its head, and with a handy quay with good depth near the entrance; a pleasant stop in quiet weather.

The fine and spacious anchorage of **Crookhaven** is sheltered from all except north-east winds. The village has good pubs and restaurants, and there are visitors' moorings. In times past Crookhaven, because of its strategic position, was a staging-post for many ships going to and from America, and shipping lines had agents here to give the ships their sailing orders. There were even plans for a major transatlantic passenger port, but the essential railway connection got no further than Schull. Crookhaven had one of Marconi's early radio stations, built to communicate with Cornwall and used to pass signals to and from shipping via the Fastnet lighthouse. A century ago 700 people lived and worked here; today

(Above) Long Island Channel

(Below) Crookhaven

there are fewer than 30 permanent residents.

Crookhaven makes an excellent point of departure for a rounding of the Mizen, but whether or not this is part of the passage plan, it is worth making the effort to visit the maritime museum at Mizen Head Visitor Centre (www. mizenhead.net), a five-mile walk or taxi ride from Crookhaven. Displays include a Navigational Aids simulator, communications for safety at sea, explanations of Marconi's wireless experiments, and of the more modern Racon, GPS and DGPS navaids.

And the views, of course, are simply stunning.

(Above and right) Crookhaven

Mizen Head

The Great Hunger

West Cork has been described as the epicentre of the Potato Famine; Skibbereen has a museum devoted to it, and a mass grave of 9,000 of its victims.

In 1844, Benjamin Disraeli described Ireland as having "a starving population, an absentee aristocracy, an alien church, and the weakest executive in the world". The country's production of beef and cereals was increasingly being sent for export, and a rapidly-expanding peasant population had turned to the potato to such an extent that millions of people ate little else. It was the only crop that could feed a family who had to live off the produce of less – often a lot less – than 15 acres (as two thirds of Irish tenant farmers did). It was however a disease-prone plant, and there were frequent failures.

In that year 1844, Ireland grew almost 15 million tons of potatoes. But in 1845, a new and devastating organism, *phytophthera infestans*, attacked the crop. More than a third of it was destroyed. The blight attacked potato crops in many other countries, but it was in Ireland that it was to have the most disastrous consequences. Crop failures recurred in each of the four following years. The response of the Government was mired in political issues and ultimately inadequate. Sir Charles Trevelyan, the Chief Secretary for Ireland, was even quoted as saying that the famine was the judgement of God sent to teach the Irish a lesson. One author reports that the Government allocated £100,000 in relief and at the same time allocated twice that to the beautification of Battersea Park. As the same author also ironically commented, anyone who knew Battersea Park would agree that that was not nearly enough. But famine-relief schemes were set up in Ireland, and much of the basic infrastructure of the country, especially in the south and west – minor roads, bridges, piers, causeways – owes its origins to the Famine years, when destitute men were paid in food for a day's work.

The response of the big landowners was mixed. Some went to extraordinary lengths to relieve the suffering of their tenants, and many bankrupted themselves in the process. But many did nothing, and some used it as an excuse to evict an unwanted peasantry. The churches offered relief, but sometimes on condition of religious conversion.

An estimated one million people died from starvation and disease, and hundreds of thousands emigrated, aggravating an already-established pattern that was to persist for another century and a half. In ten years the population fell from over eight million to six and a half; by 1890 it was down to five million and by 1950 to four, all this in spite of an above-average birth rate. It did not begin to rise until 1970.

The political consequences were far-reaching. The Famine gave a new impetus to Irish nationalism, and created a huge diaspora with folk memories of oppression and suffering, memories which influence political and economic decisions worldwide to this day.

The potato still grows well in Ireland, although *phytophthera* remains endemic. Growing crops used to be treated with copper sulphate to kill the blight, but now the choice is between synthetic fungicides and planting newer blight-resistant or GM varieties. Blight warnings are issued on radio and television in warm humid summer weather. To ignore them is to lose your potato crop.

Lazybeds were built up by hand, using sand and seaweed, to enable potatoes to be grown on otherwise thin and barren soil, or even bare rock. These are on Clare Island, Co.Mayo, but traces of old lazybeds may be seen all around the coast.

On Long Island

Barley Cove, between Crookhaven and Mizen Head

The South-West Coast
Mizen Head to Loop Head

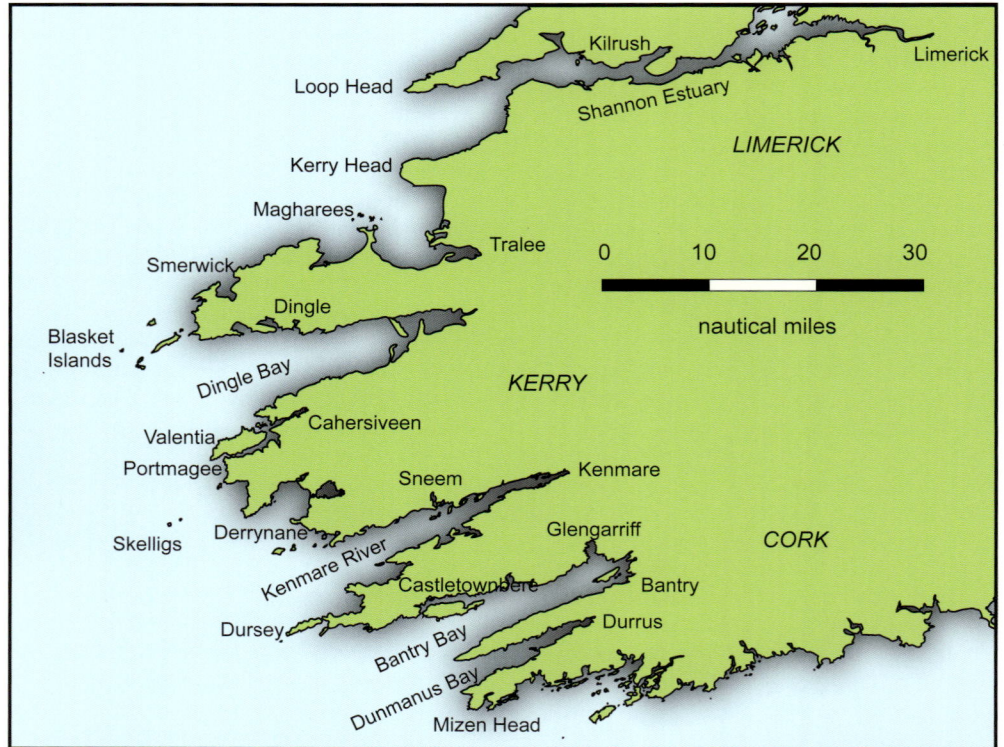

The south-west of Ireland is one of the world's classic cruising grounds, and well worth the slight effort of rounding Mizen Head to get there from the south coast. One reason is the changing scale of the land and seascape. The mountains are higher, the bays bigger and deeper, the offlying rocks and islands more dramatic, and the anchorages more numerous. There are scores of them around this coast, offering seclusion, magnificent scenery, and fascinating pilotage, and they draw cruising folk back year after year. Marinas at Bere Island, Cahersiveen, Dingle, Fenit and Kilrush have added a useful dimension to this cruising ground. But the crowds have been left astern.

The feel of the sea changes as well, as the transition from the Celtic Sea to the Atlantic brings the first sensations of ocean swell. A seakindly yacht smoothly rises to these long waves – much more comfortable than a short sea – and they have a rhythm that seems to bring a good boat alive. The cliff scenery,

The Blasket Islands, rugged, remote and mystical

Durrus pier, at the head of Dunmanus Bay

Sunset at Dunboy

meanwhile, is awesome. This coast is, of course, also a major stamping ground for land-based tourists, which means that the towns and villages are relatively well furnished with creature comforts. For crew changing, Shannon and Kerry airports are within easy reach, and the railway links Dublin with Killarney and Tralee.

Passage Planning

Mizen Head is not challenging, as exposed headlands go, and with a little tidal planning the passage is straightforward. From there to the Blaskets is about 45 miles, and from there directly to Kilrush in the Shannon, the same again. The tides in general are not strong, although the salient points and the narrow channels – Dursey Head, Bolus Head, Bray Head, Dunmore Head and Sybil Point, and Dursey and Blasket Sounds – accelerate the tide and raise the sea, while the same is true in the narrower reaches of the Shannon estuary. But only those with a strict timetable or a poor sense of priorities would sail *past* this coast. The four rias offer magnificent and relaxed sailing, with each one different in its ambience. Dunmanus Bay, just 12 miles to its head from the open sea, is the

Common seals, with their dog-like faces, are numerous in the inlets of the south-west

Derrynane, one of Ireland's classic anchorages

The ancient beehive huts on Skellig Michael

least-travelled. Larger and offering wider choices is Bantry Bay, 30 miles in length from Dursey Island, its western limit. The Kenmare River is similar in size but different in character, more remote and secret. Dingle Bay is wide, with fewer anchorages, and (unlike the others) not navigable quite to its head. In all these, the ocean swell quickly dissipates inside the entrances.

Derrynane is one of Ireland's classic anchorages. Valentia Island is bridged to the shore, but the harbours east and south of it are splendid. With settled weather, the opportunity to explore the spellbinding offshore islands – the Skelligs and the Blaskets – is not to be missed.

Most yachts heading north from Dingle are bound for Connemara or the Aran Islands, an 80-mile offshore passage, but Tralee Bay and the Shannon offer a less daunting alternative. Coastwise, Smerwick Harbour, Brandon Bay, Magharee Sound and Fenit Marina successively provide shelter, each no more than ten miles apart.

The 50-mile Shannon estuary offers excellent sailing waters, although the lack of good shelter near its mouth means that coasting yachts tend to pass it by, which is a pity. At Limerick the estuary connects with the Shannon Navigation, allowing suitable craft – those with limited air and water draft – to gain access to the extensive inland waterway network of Ireland.

For supplies, Castletownbere and Dingle offer ease of access and good facilities, while Bantry, Kenmare, Cahersiveen and Kilrush are equally capable but not quite so handy.

Castletownbere, 1937 and 2000

"Mrs O'Shea, who keeps a clean little "pub" in the square, is kindness itself, and as soon as she realises that you are a yachtsman, will do or get anything for you. She will also let you fill your water-breakers there.

"A circus in the summer and an occasional travelling film show are the only forms of "popular" amusement.

"A steamer, *Princess Beara*, connects Castletown with Adrigole, Glengarriff and Bantry twice a week; and a 'bus does the same thing every day, return fare 10/-."

Eric Hiscock, South West Irish Harbours and Bays, *1937*

"The dense, luxuriantly-sculpted pint of stout is five minutes in the pouring, the precise amount of time needed to confess your entire life history to the skilled Irish bar person."

Pete McCarthy, McCarthy's Bar, *2000*

Dunmanus Harbour

Kilcrohane, on Dunmanus Bay

Dunmanus Bay

Most yachts pass by this little gem of an inlet in their haste to get to Glengarriff or Derrynane, which is their loss. The shores are rugged and beautiful, and Kitchen Cove, at the hamlet of Ahakista, is a lovely anchorage. Other possibilities are Dunmanus Harbour on the south shore, or Dunbeacon Harbour at the head, where the charming village of Durrus is a brisk walk from the pier.

Kitchen Cove (below left)

Lord Bandon's Tower looks across Dunmanus Bay to Mount Gabriel; the tower is neither an ancient fortress nor a Napoleonic signal tower, but a Victorian folly

The Air India Disaster

A little way east along the road from Kitchen Cove is a memorial garden to the Air India disaster of 1985. In June that year a Boeing 747, eastbound from Montreal to London and Delhi, was blown up in mid-air. The aircraft crashed in Irish territorial waters 180 miles west-south-west of Dursey Head, and LÉ *Aisling*, which was among the first ships on the scene, co-ordinated the recovery of bodies. The death toll was 329, the worst loss of life in a single terrorist incident until the attack on New York's World Trade Center in 2001.

The memorial incorporates a sundial whose shadow is said to fall in the direction of the crash at the time of the anniversary each year: that is approximately true, but much more accurate is the shadow, 13 miles to the south, of the Fastnet lighthouse.

Ardnakinna lighthouse guards Pipers Sound

Sheep's Head (above); Dunboy Bay (right)

Berehaven and Bere Island

It is just five miles from Sheep's Head across Bantry Bay to Pipers Sound, the cliffbound western entrance to Berehaven. For centuries a strategic naval anchorage, its deep water sheltered by Bere Island, Berehaven has three very different harbours in Dunboy Bay, Castletownbere and Lawrence Cove. **Dunboy** is a quiet, pretty and atmospheric anchorage, overlooked by the restored but – for its first 128 years to the present, at least – luckless and empty Dunboy House. The grass-grown ruins of Donal Cam O'Sullivan Bere's more ancient castle, now all but invisible from seaward, are nearby.

Dunboy, 1937

"When, in the stilly watches of the night, you hear a strange bubbling noise along the shore, remember that it is only the ghost of Puxley who was murdered nearby. Although he is quite harmless, there are but few people at Castletown who would care to venture there by night."

Eric Hiscock, South West Irish Harbours and Bays, *1937*

(above and below) Castletownbere

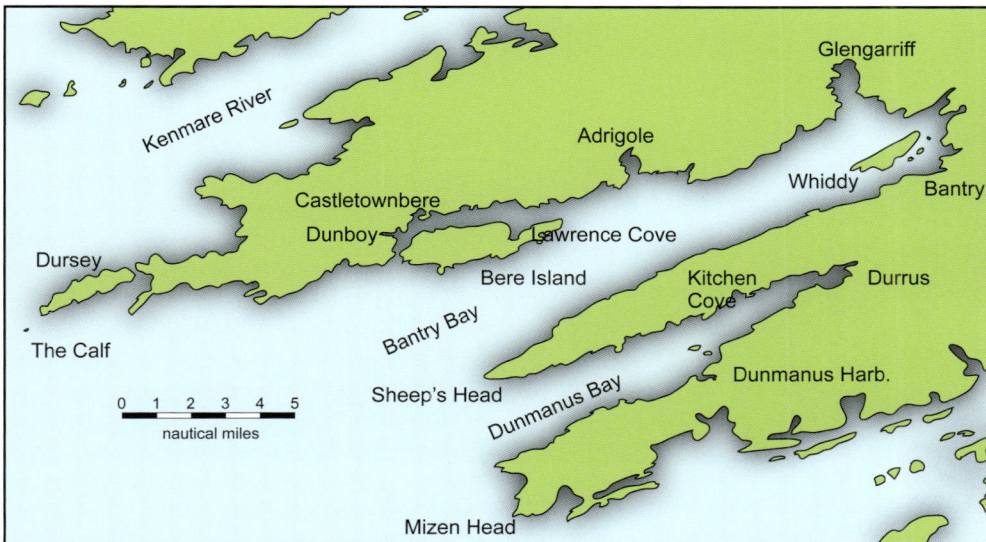

The village-town of **Castletownbere** is Ireland's second fishing port, and with a good supermarket next to the quay, is the handiest place on this coast for stores. Although there is normally room to anchor out of the traffic, an alongside berth is a privilege granted to very few. A pint of the black stuff in the original MacCarthy's Bar – which was justly famous even before Pete McCarthy wrote his bestseller – is an essential part of the Castletownbere experience.

At the head of a creek on the north shore of Bere Island, the compact and family-run **Lawrence Cove Marina** enjoys the best shelter of any on the coast. The Cove was a favourite anchorage for many years, and the nearby village of Rerrin has pub and shop. Bere Island, with a population of 180, is a place redolent with history. Its relics date from the Bronze Age to the first World War and they include ring forts, standing stones, wedge tombs, burial sites, Martello Towers, and a battery with two six-inch guns. The island was a key part of the British naval base here until 1937.

Lawrence Cove Marina

Adrigole

Lonehort

Opposite: (top) Leaving Lawrence Cove, in the shadow of Hungry Hill

(bottom) The gardens at Illnacullen

Lonehort Harbour, on the south side of the island, is a secluded anchorage with an entrance that requires careful pilotage, but it is as snug as they come. There are no facilities nearby, but Rerrin village is a pleasant mile's walk.

Ferries run from Lawrence Cove to Pontoon Pier, a few miles from Castletownbere, and from the west end of Bere Island to Castletownbere itself.

Adrigole, Glengarriff and Bantry

The spectacularly beautiful natural harbour of **Adrigole** is overlooked by the bare rocky ridges of Hungry Hill, at 685 metres (2,247ft) the highest summit on the Beara peninsula. The anchorage commands views over low shores to the towering and barren hills, a perfect panorama.

Glengarriff harbour nestles in the innermost part of Bantry Bay, and is studded with wooded islands, the largest of which is Illnacullen or Garnish Island. Its remarkable botanical garden is open to the public from March to October. The Irish Cruising Club was founded at Glengarriff in 1929, and cruising sailors still love its perfect shelter and scenery. Traditionally one of the boxes to be ticked on the whistle-stop road tour of Ireland, Glengarriff village is a popular tourist centre with shops, art galleries, pubs and restaurants, and good transport links through Bantry to Cork. There is a remarkable outdoor museum of zany and hilarious sculptures. The bay is home to a colony of unusually tame common seals.

The Treaty Ports

The Royal Navy, at its zenith before and during the First World War, enjoyed the use of three excellent natural harbours in what was later to become the Republic: Cork Harbour, Berehaven and Lough Swilly. The Treaty of 1921, setting up the Irish Free State, guaranteed the continued availability of these to Britain, and in the three harbours the military establishments at Haulbowline, Bere Island and Dunree continued to fly the British flag. The government of Eamon de Valera negotiated their handover to the Irish defence forces in 1938, although at that time Ireland owned no naval vessels. Winston Churchill, almost a lone voice, expressed himself "surprised" by the concession, in the light of the growing threat from Germany; but from de Valera's point of view the same threat meant that British use of the ports would no longer be a mere formality, and Irish neutrality would therefore be compromised.

Fort Dunree on Lough Swilly was the last to be formally handed over, in October 1938, the Union flag being hauled down by a British NCO and the Tricolour raised by an Irish one. The two men were brothers-in-law. That fort is now a museum, and the Irish Army uses some of the old facilities on Bere Island as a training camp. The dock and magnificent 200-year-old buildings on Haulbowline Island in Cork Harbour are now the headquarters of the Irish Naval Service.

Adrigole

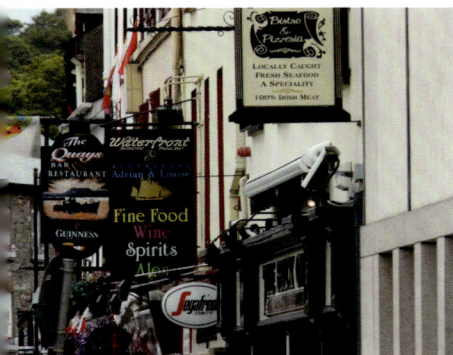

Bantry

Bantry is the region's principal town. Bantry Harbour, sheltered by Whiddy Island, is largely given over to mussel farming, but there are anchorages either in the lee of Whiddy, or within a few hundred metres of the town. Bantry is a lively place with many restaurants, bars, and shopping opportunities, and the splendid and historic Bantry House is open to the public. Each summer Bantry hosts the West Cork Chamber Music Festival in late June/early July, immediately followed by the West Cork Literary Festival, with musicians and writers of international stature, in Bantry House and at other venues in town.

Whiddy, like Bere Island, has ancient monuments and military relics, and today houses the national strategic oil reserves. Tankers discharge their cargoes from the mooring buoy north of the island. The installation was built in the 1960's as a storage and transhipment depot. In January 1979 the French tanker *Betelgeuse* exploded and sank at the jetty, killing 51 people, the worst maritime accident in recent Irish history. The wreck was removed, but the jetty was not used again.

Glengarriff

Glengarriff, 1937

"This is, of course, what everyone comes to S.W. Ireland to see, and it certainly is a very lovely place, although a little spoilt by motor launches and charabancs...Large cruising liners sometimes anchor S. of the island while their passengers go ashore to see the 'sights', and are usually rushed off to Killarney....A visit to Glengarriff would be quite wasted without paying a visit to Mrs. Flynn of Roche's Hotel – better known to the navy and yachtsmen as 'Auntie May'."

Eric Hiscock, South West Irish Harbours and Bays, *1937*

Glengarriff

The French Invasion of Bantry Bay

In 1796 the United Irishmen, under the leadership of the 33-year-old lawyer Theobald Wolfe Tone, persuaded the revolutionary government of France to mount an invasion of Ireland in support of the group's aims for Irish independence. In mid-December, 43 ships carrying 15,000 men sailed from Brest. They were fortunate in evading heavy units of the Royal Navy, but communication errors and the weather scattered the fleet and only 15 ships and 6,400 men reached Bantry Bay. The flagship carrying the French commander General Hoche was among the 28 which failed to make the rendezvous. In strong easterly winds and foul weather it took the depleted fleet several days of hard beating from Mizen Head to reach anchorage off Whiddy Island. With his forces weakened, and convinced that a large British force awaited him on shore, the senior French officer decided to abort the expedition, and having scuttled the leaking and unseaworthy 32-gun frigate *La Surveillante* north of Whiddy, put to sea and headed home. Overall losses were seven ships to the weather and six to the Royal Navy's guns, in addition to *La Surveillante*.

In fact there had been almost no defending force on shore. Most of the few available militiamen deserted when they saw the size of the French force, although a small French shore party was arrested and its boat seized. Richard White of Bantry House was created Lord Bantry and later Earl of Bantry in recognition of his contribution to the successful intelligence and disinformation campaign which defeated the invasion. Bantry House, still owned by his descendants the Shelswell-White family, has a fascinating museum devoted to the episode, including recovered artifacts from *La Surveillante* and other ships. Bantry also has a statue of Wolfe Tone.

It might have turned out differently. The best of the French Navy's officers had been aristocrats, and those who avoided the guillotine were disillusioned, and unimpressed by the quality of new recruits. The navy was in poor shape after years of neglect. General Hoche (who was just 29) was chosen for command of the expedition in preference to a promising 27-year-old Corsican officer who was considered for the post but was preoccupied in the Italian campaign at the time. His name was Napoleon Bonaparte.

Wolfe Tone's statue in Bantry, with the salvaged anchor of La Surveillante *behind*

Bantry House

Garnish Bay, Dursey Sound and Dursey Island, with the Cow and the Bull beyond

Not precisely like those to be seen in ski resorts...

Kenmare River

The shortest route from Bantry Bay to the Kenmare River is through **Dursey Sound**, something of a rite of passage for cruising sailors. Dursey is connected to the shore by a cable car (with an overhead clearance of 21 metres) spanning a Sound with a couple of inconvenient rocks and a tide of up to four knots. Rounding Dursey Head is the alternative, affording a closer look at the highest cliffs in County Cork and the impressive maritime farmyard of the Bull, the Cow, the Calf and the Heifer. The 62m (200 ft) high and precipitous Bull Rock is a spectacular seamark, although dwarfed by the Skelligs 14 miles to the north-west.

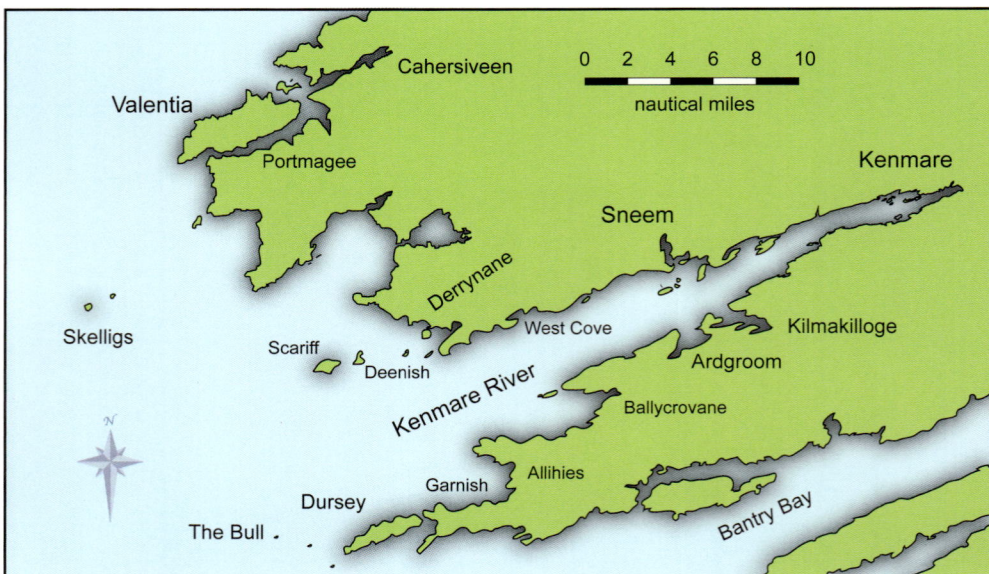

Old cable cars never die, they just retire and become henhouses

Ballydonegan Bay, with the old mining village of Allihies clinging to the hillside above

Dursey itself, with just six full-time residents, has no secure anchorage and is awkward of access to the cruising sailor, but rewards the effort in settled weather. The Kenmare River, becoming progressively more sheltered as it extends eastward, has many more anchorages than its neighbours and in itself is a cruising ground in miniature. Apart from Kenmare at its head, there is nowhere on its shores that could be termed a town.

Three of its outstanding natural harbours, on the south side, have fish cages and mussel rafts, but only at Cleanderry, smallest of these three, does fish farming virtually preclude anchoring. Thanks to the County Council there are a few more navigational aids than in R.T. McMullen's day, but still not many, and the lush greenery of Kerry will always strive to hide the elusive leading marks at Ardgroom.

Garnish Island (not to be confused with its namesake at Glengarriff) provides a bolthole just east of Dursey Sound while **Ballycrovane** offers better shelter, with the colourful village of Eyeries a mile's walk away.

Ruined mine pumphouse on the hill above Allihies

The Copper Mines of the South-west

Copper was mined on the slopes of Mount Gabriel, near Schull in west Cork, 3,800 years ago, and mining there ceased only in the 19th century. Mining at Allihies, south of Cod's Head on the Kenmare River, began in 1813, and by 1842 employed 1,600 men. In the peak year of 1863, the mine produced over 8,000 tons of ore. Its owner Henry Puxley began building a grand mansion at Dunboy in 1866, but the price of copper fell, Puxley sold the business, and by 1884 there were only ten employees left. Dunboy House was completed, but Puxley never lived in it, and it was burned by the IRA in 1920. Throughout the period, many miners emigrated, most of them to copper mining towns such as Butte, Montana, where the West Cork names Healey and O'Sullivan are still among the commonest.

The Allihies mine inspired Daphne Du Maurier's novel *Hungry Hill*, which is set against a dramatised and very thinly disguised backdrop of actual events at Allihies and Dunboy (the novelist was a friend of the Puxley family). Dunboy House was restored in 2005-7 and briefly opened as an hotel.

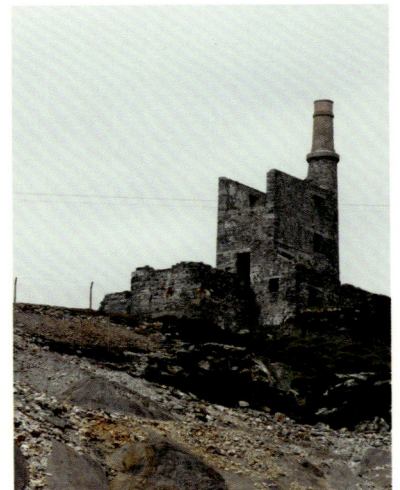

R.T.McMullen on the South-West

Richard Turrell McMullen was a pioneer of short-handed cruising, and his 1869 book *Down Channel* has been a classic ever since. Arthur Ransome wrote the foreword to the 1931 edition, and said: "…a book not easily to be obtained. Private owners of it do not lend it."

McMullen cruised round Britain in 1863 in the 32-foot *Sirius*, and two years later built the 42-foot cutter *Orion*.

The *Orion* to Bantry, 1869:

"For the information of anyone who wishes to know something of the general character of the south-west coast of Ireland, I may say that it is very wild and pretty, with many fine natural harbours. The scenery in some of them is magnificent, especially in Glengarriff, Ardgroom, and Kilmakilloge — the former in Bantry Bay, the two latter in Kenmare River. Fish of all sorts is very plentiful, and can be bought for very little if you are too idle, or, as in my case, have not the time, to catch it.

"The climate is mild, humid, and much subject to haze, particularly in wet weather, when the coast is so densely shrouded in mist that navigation is extremely dangerous. According to the book of sailing directions, all the harbours are easily distinguished by certain features of the landscape or conspicuous old towers and beacons; but to render the instructions complete there should be added 'weather permitting', for as a rule in wet weather the leading marks are in the clouds.

"To sail this coast with any comfort, the largest-scale Admiralty Charts are indispensable, as the rocks are numerous, and buoys and beacons very scarce.

"On all the rocks in Kenmare river there is only one small beacon.

"In choosing open anchorages on this coast in stormy weather from the south and west, it is important to bear in mind that the wind often veers suddenly to the northward, and blows frightfully.

"I will close these remarks by saying that provisions are good and abundant at the chief towns, and the people generally so civil and obliging that it is pleasant to deal with them."

The anchorages further east are all notable for their tree-clad shores. The beautiful **Ardgroom** offers intricate pilotage, while **Kilmakilloge,** better marked, has a renowned pub and the splendid Derreen gardens on its shores. On the north side, **Sneem** harbour is snug and pretty, and has visitors' moorings. The village of Sneem is a two-mile walk or a mile and a half by dinghy towards high tide; a pretty place with good pub grub, but a little given over to the tourist traffic on the busy Ring of Kerry road.

Teddy O'Sullivan's bar at Bunaw Pier on Kilmakilloge Harbour

Opposite: *Sneem*

Kilmakilloge

Sneem, Aran sweater capital of the world

Derreen (left) and Sneem

Sneem

Lehid, **Ormond's**, **Dinish**, **Coongar**, **Blackwater** and **Dunkerron;** the upper stretch of the bay is a maze of wooded creeks and little rocky islands, a splendid playground particularly for a shallow-draft boat or a cruising dinghy. **Kenmare** itself is an affluent and cosmopolitan place, and the wide choice of restaurants, bars and shops in the town reflects that.

Kenmare rock group

Derrynane and the Skelligs

The coast from Lamb's Head to Valentia, with its craggy islands and towering cliffs, is simply magnificent, and **Derrynane** is a classic anchorage below rugged hills. In the eighteenth century it was a nest of smugglers but today it is a favourite stopping point on passage, offering good shelter and holding ground. Moorings are provided, and nearby is a superb beach and a homely pub, with more facilities at Caherdaniel, a leafy two-mile walk past the historic Derrynane House. Derrynane's entrance between the rocks is deep and well-marked, but no less thrilling for that. The tidal Abbey Island, accessible on foot, has the

Derrynane House

Daniel O'Connell of Derrynane

Daniel O'Connell "The Liberator" was born into a minor landowning family in Kerry in 1775. He became a barrister but as a Catholic he was disqualified from standing for Parliament and from holding many other important public offices, which at that time were open only to members of the established Anglican Church. Catholic emancipation was the first great crusade of his life, and in 1829 he succeeded, the new law entitling not only Catholics but Presbyterians and many others to enter Parliament. O'Connell then turned his attention to the question of Irish independence. As a dedicated supporter of constitutional politics (among his most often-quoted statements was "The altar of liberty totters when it is cemented only with blood") he was careful not to indulge in rabble-rousing, but he was a powerful orator. Literally as well as metaphorically, it seems, because his rallies, called "monster meetings", were attended by up to 100,000 people, and there was of course no such thing as a public-address system. But when Peel, the Prime Minister, banned a rally at Clontarf in 1843, O'Connell's respect for the law made him call it off. His campaign fizzled out, but his leadership and oratory were to inspire many others including Ghandi and Martin Luther King.

He is regarded today as one of the fathers of his country, and Dublin's grand thoroughfare O'Connell Street is only one of many named in his honour. His family home at Derrynane, a lovely old Georgian house with beautiful gardens, is open to the public and is only a short walk from the magnificent anchorage there.

(above and left) Derrynane

Ogham

The Ogham alphabet was used by the Celtic languages of Ireland, Wales and Scotland about the 5th century AD. It has much in common with Runic and its 25 letters were named after trees. Surviving Ogham inscriptions are usually on memorial stones, many of them in south-west Ireland. Most Ogham letters consist of a vertical stroke with different numbers of horizontal strokes to right or left, and the script is read from the bottom of a pillar up the left hand side and down the right.

The Skelligs on the horizon from Derrynane

remains of a tenth-century abbey, and an important Ogham Stone stands beside the Caherdaniel road. The harbour is also home to a busy watersports centre.

Deenish Island, a couple of miles from Lamb's Head and Derrynane, has a sheltered bay and stunning panoramic views from its 141m (460ft) summit.

All along this coast the towering pinnacles of the **Skelligs** serve as dramatic punctuation marks on the horizon. There is no anchorage at either island, and only the Great Skellig – Skellig Michael – offers a landing. **Little Skellig**, the inner of the pair, 130m (425ft) high, is the second largest gannet colony in the world, with 30,000 pairs breeding each summer. **Great Skellig** is a UNESCO World Heritage Site, on account of its astonishing sixth-century monastery

Opposite: (top) Derrynane (bottom) the view from the summit of Deenish

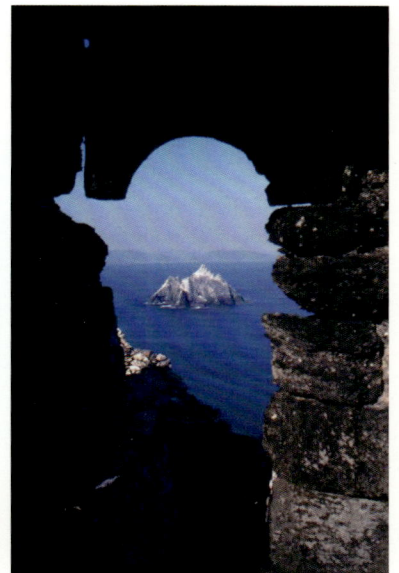

(left and above) The Skelligs

The lighthouse on the Great Skellig was one of a pair built originally in 1836. The upper light was discontinued 30 years later, and the lower light was replaced in 1966

clinging to a ledge 160 metres above the sea. The twin-peaked island is 215m (705ft) high, and no wider than that at its narrowest point. Sailing close by makes a profound impression! Great Skellig's bird life is different from that of its smaller neighbour, for gannets shun human company and there are none here, but the island has breeding colonies of shearwaters, guillemots, kittiwakes, fulmars and storm petrels, and 2,000 pairs of puffins, so tame that one can almost touch them. Boat trips run from Portmagee, Ballinskelligs and Derrynane when the weather is suitable, and the jetty in the tiny creek at the north-east corner can be used to land by dinghy. A team of guides and caretakers live on the island in summer, and cruising sailors are requested to visit only during the working day. The ancient stone beehive huts and monastic buildings, and the remains of the monks' garden, leave a lifelong impression on visitors. The climb up the steps to the monastery, on the saddle between the two summits, is not unduly dizzying, but a further and steeper climb leads to a lonely and awe-inspiring hermitage on the very pinnacle of the island.

The Skellig Lists

Skellig Michael was for many years a place of pilgrimage. In 1752, nobody told the small monastic community that the Gregorian calendar had been adopted, and for some time the notional offset of eleven days was used as a loophole when couples who wished to get married during Lent could achieve their purpose on the Skellig. The requirement to spend time in contemplation and prayer there beforehand degenerated into an excuse for much partying. There then arose the custom of the "Skellig Lists", ribald publications in which the fancies and clandestine relationships of the people of Kerry were laid bare, often in verse. The Lists continued to appear right through the nineteenth century and well into the twentieth.

A beehive hut on the Great Skellig

Hopelessly addicted

"Once you have crept up on Bolus Head in the mist, hung off Great Skellig in a cloud of gannets or rounded the Mizen in dolphin company with the *Granuaile Suite* playing loudly and the sun glittering under scudding clouds, you always want that moment again. And like any addict, you are prepared to put up with no end of humiliation, disappointment, expense and diminishing returns. Face it. Irish weather comes raw off the Atlantic and can be many degrees beyond vile. You can spend two weeks of westerly gales hoping for a chance to get out of some wicked inlet which tempted you in on that one spinnaker-day. You can live in full oilskins for an entire cruise, until the smell of your clothes becomes so unbearable that you are embarrassed even to throw them into the harbour skip. If there is a harbour skip.

"And then the sun comes out and you are in the cockpit looking out at the nearest landscape to Paradise that earth holds: distant blue mountains, a symphony of grass and granite and cottages and sheep all washed clean to a sparkle by the great rains, the lane winds up to a pub from which floats music, erratic and live, carried on the perfumed honeysuckle breeze. And you are the only boat in the anchorage, except perhaps an old Galway hooker on which someone is lovingly playing *The Queen of Connemara* on the whistle…

"So you're back in your opium-eater daze again. It is, obviously, the last day of your cruise so now you have to flog back home. But Ireland has got its rocky claws in you, and you're doomed."

Libby Purves, Confessions of a craic addict

Opposite: *The path winds its way up the cliff to the monastery*

Portmagee

In very settled weather, a yacht heads for the narrow Puffin Sound, south of Portmagee. Bray Head beyond

Valentia Slate

The slate quarry on Valentia Island operated for almost a century, employing up to 400 men, but closed in 1911. The stone is very strong and particularly suitable for use in thick flat slabs, and the Public Records Office in London has 21 miles of shelving made of Valentia slate, weighing almost 20,000 tonnes. It was much in demand for roofing as well, and covers the Houses of Parliament in Westminster. The quarry re-opened in the 1990s, and today manufactures a wide range of products from garden furniture to worktops and fireplaces.

The slate quarry overlooks Cromwell Point, at the entrance to Valentia harbour

Valentia and Cahersiveen

For most cruising yachts, the low bridge across Portmagee Sound precludes direct access to Valentia Harbour. Even so, **Portmagee** is a well sheltered bolt-hole if the passage round Bray Head does not appeal, and it has visitors' moorings too. The pier is used by fishing boats and trip-boats to the Skelligs. Ashore, Portmagee village has a post office, general store, coffee shop, and a bar and restaurant.

The formidable Bray Head, its cliffs rising to 240m (787ft), forms the south-west extremity of **Valentia Island**. Valentia is perhaps best known for its rôle in communications, as the site of the first transatlantic telegraph station, established

in 1866 and operational until 1966, and the home of one of Ireland's Coast Radio stations, now also a Coast Guard MRSC. For 24 years from 1868 it also had a weather station, still reporting as Valentia even though it has been on the mainland for over a century, since the wife of its chief scientist announced in 1892 that she wouldn't go on living on then-remote Valentia. The island's Heritage Centre chronicles all these developments in fascinating style, and is well worth a visit. The principal village of **Knightstown** owes its name and its oddly Victorian-seaside style of architecture to its foundation as a planned settlement by the landowner, the Knight of Kerry, in the 1830s. At the time of writing a 200-berth marina project has stalled with its floating breakwaters in position, but no pontoons; nevertheless it provides shelter and a handy alongside berth.

Two miles up the well-marked Fertha River from Valentia harbour is the little town of **Cahersiveen**, notable for its connections with Daniel O'Connell and its extraordinary Barracks building, erected for the Royal Irish Constabulary in

(Top) Valentia Harbour, before the breakwaters at Knightstown were installed; (centre) Valentia MRSC looks north to Dunmore Head and the Blaskets; (bottom) Knightstown

Valentia's Tetrapods

In 1993, a geology student discovered fossilised tetrapod trackways, footprints in mud preserved in Devonian rocks on the north coast of the island. About 385 million years ago a primitive vertebrate ancestor to the dinosaurs passed along a muddy shoreline in the equatorial swampland that is now south-western Ireland and left prints as if in wet concrete. The prints were preserved by silt overlying them, and were converted to rock over the ages. The Valentia Island trackways are among the oldest signs of vertebrate life on land.

Chris Stillman

Cahersiveen, with its marina and its extraordinary, almost Disneyworld, Barracks, built in 1870 for the Royal Irish Constabulary

1870. On the Ring of Kerry tourist route and as the main business centre of the Iveragh peninsula, Cahersiveen punches above its weight for a town of just 1,300 people. Its 105-berth marina, opened in 2003, was a community project and offers a secure berth, close to the town with its supermarkets, shops, banks, library and information centre. A choice of restaurants, and almost twenty pubs, will ensure that the inner sailor will be well catered for! The old Barracks houses a good Heritage Centre and the Met Éireann Valentia Observatory is situated nearby.

Emigration from Ireland

The Irish have been emigrating for centuries. The first to leave in significant numbers were those soldiers who found themselves on the losing side in the religious wars of the 17th century – the so-called "Wild Geese" who became mercenaries in foreign armies. It was from one of these that Napoleon's Marshal MacMahon got his name. In the 18th century, about 200,000 of the emigrants were the Scotch-Irish, whose forebears had come from Scotland to Ulster a hundred years before, and whose descendants would play a key role in the shaping of the United States of America. These would include 17 Presidents, men like Jackson, Polk, Buchanan, Grant, two Harrisons, Wilson and Clinton.

Mass emigration resumed after the Napoleonic Wars. Between then and the Famine in 1845, a further 200,000 left, mainly from the poorer areas of the south and west. These were the times of the "coffin ships", when thousands died of disease before reaching their destination. The Famine resulted in as many as a million leaving in ten years, and the trend continued. Poor Irish families began to take it for granted that many of their children would leave as soon as they could, never to return, and for much of the nineteenth and twentieth centuries remittances from families abroad were a major factor sustaining the economy of Ireland. The custom of the "American wake" grew up, where the departure of an emigrant was marked as though it were a death.

For at least sixty years, in the poorer counties of the west, over 35% of teens and twenties emigrated. Only in Dublin and Antrim was the number under 20%. The same pattern of rural depopulation was repeated in many other countries, but in Ireland – with the sole exception of Belfast – there were no burgeoning industrial cities in which to find work. Ireland, it could reasonably be said, was raising children for export. The United States was the destination that first springs to mind today, but millions moved to Britain. The Irish diaspora continued to spread worldwide; Che Guevara's mother's maiden name was Lynch. Irish emigrants and their descendants, such as William Brown and Bernardo O'Higgins, played a key role in achieving South American independence. Newfoundland has a large Irish population, and St Patrick's Day has long been celebrated in Montserrat.

The flow was briefly reversed in the Celtic Tiger years between 1995 and 2008, but emigration has resumed, with most of the new emigrants being not only young but now also well-qualified.

Dingle Bay and the Blaskets

Dingle Bay – although spectacularly scenic – differs from its southern neighbours in having no worthwhile and accessible harbours in its upper reaches. The picturesque village-town of **Dingle** became famous as the setting for the 1970 film *Ryan's Daughter*, and with a little help from Ireland's most celebrated cetacean and its own enterprising citizens, has thrived mightily. It was the first harbour in south-west Ireland to develop a marina, in 1996, within its spacious and well sheltered harbour, and it is now the most popular port of call for yachts cruising this coast. Dingle buzzes with life in the summer, and has an indefinable 'end of the road' atmosphere. This is one of Ireland's chief fishing ports, with a sizeable trawler fleet, and has gained for itself a reputation for seafood cuisine to rival that of Kinsale.

Dingle

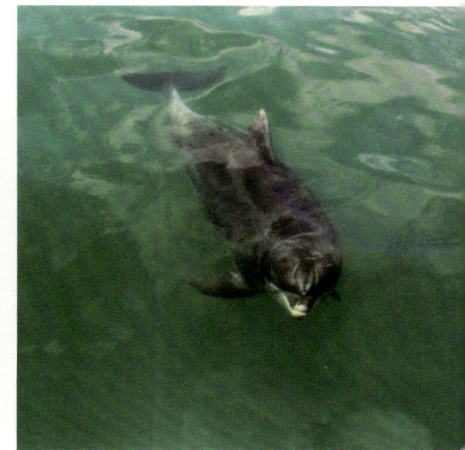

Fungie the Dingle Dolphin

Fungie is a male bottlenose dolphin which has lived in the approaches to Dingle harbour since 1984. Why he chose to do this, as a solitary animal, is unknown, but dolphins may mate for life, and around the time he appeared, a young female bottlenose was washed up dead nearby. If Fungie is indeed a widower, he is certainly a merry one, and enjoys playing with humans. He has been intensively studied over the years and much has been learned from his behaviour. Many ingenious games have been devised for him; Fungie greets each new game with enthusiasm, but typically tires of it fairly quickly. But like all of his kind, he has a *joie de vivre* that is consistent and infectious.

Not everybody loves him, though:

"The bicycle shop that is a pub also sells vegetable seeds and items of hardware. I go inside for an inner tube and some cabbage seeds, but I don't really need them, so I have a pint instead. I take a seat at the tiny bar, on a stool next to two conspicuously-veined old Kerrymen.
'How are ye enjoying yer holiday?' one of them asks me.
'It's grand, thanks. I'd say the town's changed since I was last here though.'
'Sure, it has,' He takes a sip of his whiskey. "I blame that feckin' dolphin.' "

Pete McCarthy, McCarthy's Bar

In contrast to the bustle of Dingle, the wide bay of **Ventry Harbour** is far from the madding crowd, but it has some visitors' moorings convenient for the pub.

The west and north-west facing coasts of the peninsula have magnificent cliffs and golden sandy beaches, and across a tideswept sound lie the fabulous Blasket Islands. **Great Blasket** offers anchorage and a landing place at its eastern end. The island was inhabited until 1953 and is celebrated for the literary output, originally in Irish, of its natives Peig Sayers, Tomás O'Crohan and Muiris O'Sullivan during the 1920s and 30s. Knowing that its days were numbered, these unschooled authors told of a close-knit community on the very edge of Europe with a unique, ancient and fragile culture. Peig Sayers could neither read

The Literature of Great Blasket

"I have written minutely of much that we did, for it was my wish that somewhere there should be a memorial of it all, and I have done my best to set down the character of the people about me so that some record of us might live after us, for the like of us will never be again."

Tomás O'Crohan, An t-Oileánach

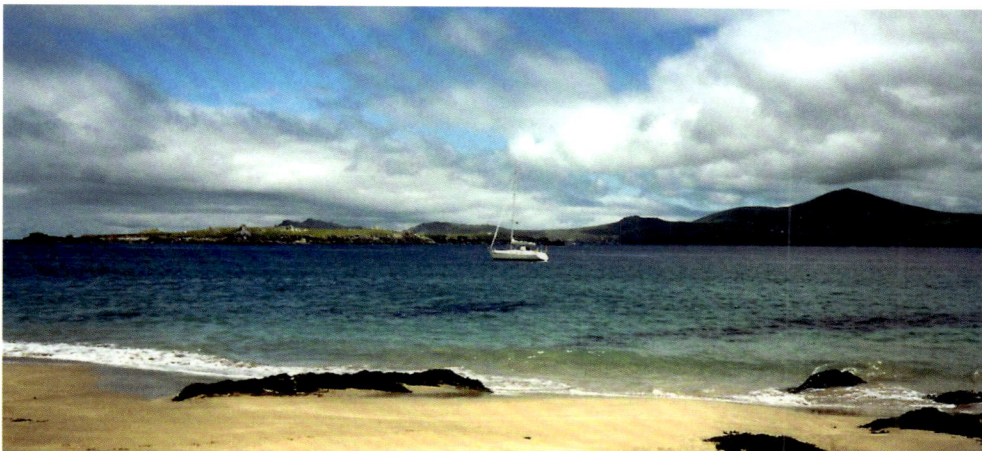

The Blaskets (top)

Great Blasket Island (left and below)

Opposite: *Dingle*

The Spanish Armada

After the defeat of the Armada in 1588 by the English navy, its remaining ships made their way ponderously round the north of Scotland. Their orders were to head out into the Atlantic with the objective of sighting Rockall before turning south, which – considering that Rockall is about the size of a self-respecting oak tree and nobody in those days had much idea where it was – represented quite a navigational challenge. Hampered by adverse weather and poor charts, the ships that found themselves close to the Scottish and Irish coasts, by and large, came to a sticky end. About 20 ships were lost on the coast of Ireland. Sometimes the survivors found shelter and support, but most of them were either murdered for their valuables or put to death by the authorities.

Perhaps the most dramatic sequence of events occurred around the Blasket Islands, where a squadron of three ships made its way (possibly with prior local knowledge, but beyond doubt with astonishing luck) between Great Blasket and Beginish, and found shelter and anchorage. A shore party from the flotilla was promptly taken into custody. A fourth ship, arriving later, dragged her anchor and was lost on Stromboli Rock, and a further two came in afterwards. One of these sank, leaving four ships which – having by then only to make a good offing and head due south – made their way safely home.

The greatest loss of life from Armada wrecks occurred on the north coast of Ireland, described in Chapter 7.

Dunmore Head, the western point of mainland Ireland. looks across at Great Blasket and Inishtooskert

The westernmost of all, the Great Foze Rock

Opposite: *(top) the Blaskets, seen from Dunquin on the mainland (bottom) the anchorage at Inishvickillane*

Peig Sayers, the revered storyteller of Great Blasket

nor write, but others faithfully recorded her stories, including some that were considered a little too earthy for the delicate sensibilities of citizens of the new Irish State and lay unpublished until 2009.

Great Blasket is a place of great atmosphere and stark beauty, and has one seasonal resident, the handloom weaver Sue Redican, who has lived there every summer since 1985.

The other islands, with their fantastically splintered and castellated cliffs, have no easy landing places, and in the case of **Inishnabro**, **Inishtooskert** and the lighthouse island of **Tearaght,** are usually inaccessible. Inishnabro and **Inishvickillane** huddle together to provide an anchorage of sorts; Inishvickillane has a single house, once the holiday retreat of Taoiseach Charles Haughey. **Beginish**, with a cluster of islets and drying rocks, lies to the north of Great Blasket. In settled weather a twenty-mile cruise among these islands will reward with spectacular scenery and breathtaking wildness, but beware the tidal currents, which run at up to three knots around and between the islands.

The Great Foze Rock, 27 metres high, off the Blaskets in 10°41·4' west, is Ireland's westernmost point.

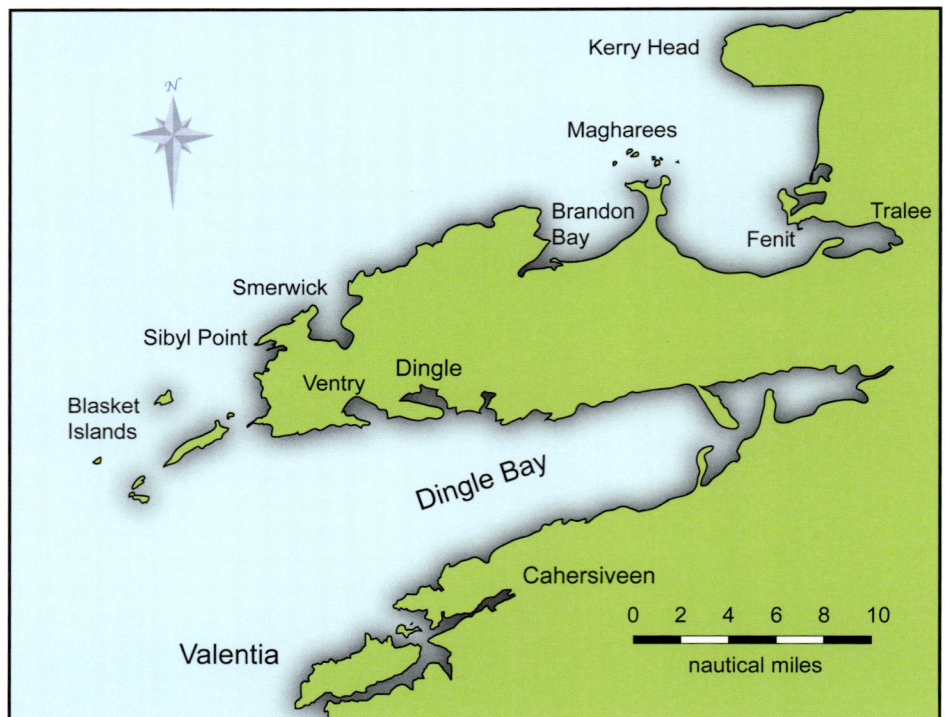

The coast from Sybil Point to Ballydavid Head, with the Three Sisters

The third of the Three Sisters, at the entrance to Smerwick

The coast east of the 250m cliffs of Ballydavid Head

Blasket Sound to Tralee Bay

Battered and hewn by the worst the Atlantic can throw at it, this is a dramatic stretch of coast. Sybil Point is succeeded by the Three Sisters, their sweeping slopes truncated to sheer and uncannily similar cliffs. Beyond the wide bay of Smerwick looms Brandon Mountain, its 950m (3,120ft) twin peaked massif dominating the approaches to Tralee Bay and the Shannon, and the cliffs continue unbroken until Brandon Bay opens to the south. But not quite; for two miles east of Ballydavid Head, exposed to the north-west, is the tiny and barely navigable Brandon Creek, from where Saint Brendan the Navigator left on his great voyage of discovery. Although the mountains of the Dingle Peninsula march on eastward, the coast beyond Brandon Point becomes more gentle, leading to the sheltered confines of Tralee Bay.

Smerwick Harbour – although a little open and subject to swell – has some visitors' moorings, and offers a means of shortening the long day's sail to or from the Aran Islands. Also prone to swell, Brandon Bay has a hamlet tucked into its western corner, with the atmospheric Nora Murphy's pub a few hundred yards from the quay. Brandon Mountain to the west, and the 823m (2,700ft) Beenoskee

Dún an Oir, Smerwick Harbour

In 1578 the English adventurer Martin Frobisher led an expedition to Greenland and returned with the holds of his ships filled with what was believed to be gold ore, but was in fact just worthless rock. On the return voyage one of the ships, the storm-damaged *Emanuel of Bridgwater*, was run ashore in Smerwick Harbour, and 100 tons of the "ore" was salvaged before the ship broke up. John Fitzgerald, Earl of Desmond, was in rebellion against the Crown at this time and was building a fortress on a small peninsula nearby. His men built the *Emanuel*'s cargo into the walls of the structure, which became known as Dún an Oir, the Golden Fort. The fate of the *Emanuel*'s crew is not recorded.

The fort's future was to be anything but golden. Just two years later its Irish garrison was reinforced by 600 Spanish and Italian troops who arrived by sea. English forces surrounded them and blockaded the ships in the bay, the fort surrendered after two days of bombardment and the garrison of 700 was massacred. The grass-covered outline of Dún an Oir may still be seen.

Smerwick Harbour from the site of Dun an Oir; Brandon Mountain beyond

to the south, dominate the bay.

The **Magharee Islands** (the Seven Hogs) provide a secluded anchorage in settled weather; the bay in the shelter of **Illauntannig** is delightful, or – to be nearer humanity – **Scraggane Bay** is a good anchorage in most conditions, with a pub and a restaurant less than a kilometre away.

Fenit Harbour is tucked into the south east corner of Tralee Bay. The harbour, constructed originally by bridging the rocky Great Samphire Island to the shore, now incorporates a 130-berth marina as well as a general cargo berth, and is the base of Tralee Sailing Club and an all-weather lifeboat. Fenit's chief claim to fame is as the birthplace of St Brendan the Navigator, who is commemorated at the Heritage Centre at the harbour. The visitor must take care to distinguish fact from legend! Fenit is just 12km from Tralee, the capital of Kerry and a lively place, especially during the annual Rose of Tralee Festival. Tralee has all the amenities of a town of 20,000 people, and good transport connections by rail and road with Dublin and Cork.

Gallarus Oratory

This little ancient building, a mile south-east from Ballydavid pier or the fair-weather anchorage at Carrigveen in Smerwick Harbour, is the most astonishing piece of drystone masonrywork in Ireland. It is 8m long, 5m wide and 5m high, a tiny sacred building with a door at one end and a minuscule window at the other. Scholars consider that it dates from some time between the 8th and 12th centuries, the sole evidence for the later date being the engineering design of the window. It is hard to believe, given its immaculate condition, and surrounded as it now is by a neatly-maintained gravel path and manicured lawns, that it was not built yesterday.

Illauntannig anchorage

Fenit Harbour

Saint Brendan

Brendan the Navigator was born about 480 AD, and (possibly when he was in his thirties) made a voyage westwards in search of the Isles of the Blest. This is recorded in the *Navigatio Sancti Brendani Abbatis,* "The Voyage of Saint Brendan the abbot", dating from perhaps the tenth century. While much of it could be dismissed as mythology, the researches and subsequent epic voyages of Tim Severin, partly described in his book *The Brendan Voyage*, clearly demonstrated that the undoubtedly historical Brendan could have, and indeed probably did, voyage far out into the Atlantic and discovered lands and creatures hitherto unknown, including at least Newfoundland and possibly the mainland of North America, which Columbus, a thousand years later, never did. The ancient description of the sea monster Jasconius will ring true with anyone who has ever met a drowsy fin whale, while the aggressive behaviour of the Roc has uncanny similarities to that of an offended great skua. Brendan's Islands of Sheep bear a remarkable resemblance to the Faroes (which name, indeed, means just that.) The historian Dicuil, writing in 825 AD, said of the Faroes that "There is another set of small islands, nearly all separated by narrow stretches of water; in these, for nearly a hundred years, hermits from our country, Ireland, have lived." Brendan spent time at Iona and sailed the coast of Scotland. The hamlet of Brandarsvik on the Faroese island of Streymoy is locally understood to owe its name to the saintly Navigator, as also may the parish of Kilbrandon near Oban, and Kilbrannan Sound in the Firth of Clyde.

Statues of Brendan may be found at Fenit and in the square in Bantry, County Cork. Brandon Mountain and Brandon Creek are also named after him.

James Joyce neatly summed it up when he said "Christopher Columbus is best remembered as the last man who discovered America."

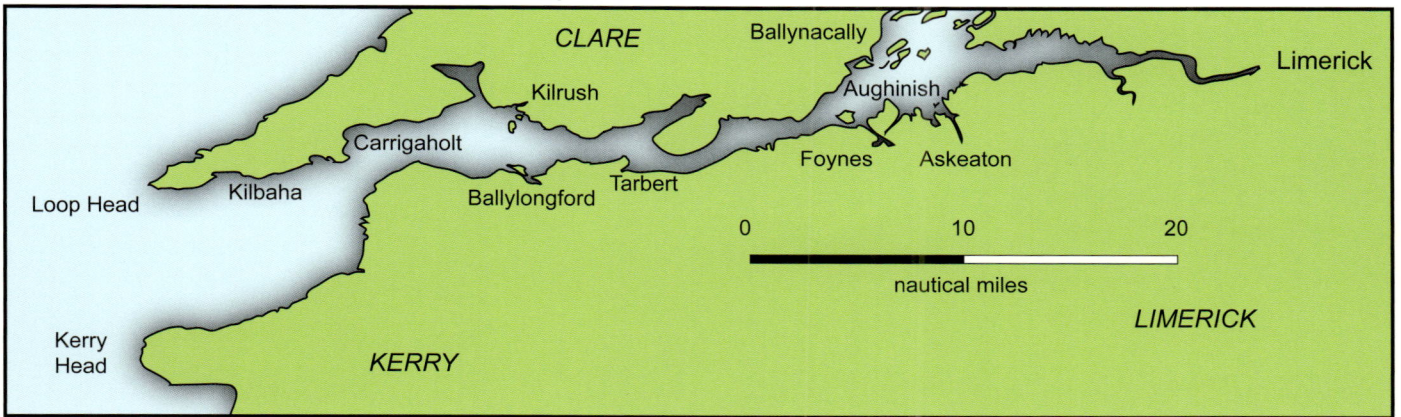

The Swiss topsail schooner **Salomon** at Carrigaholt

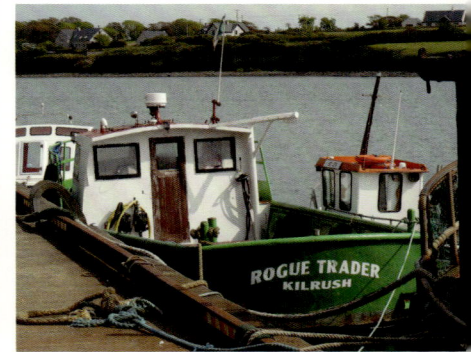

The Shannon Estuary

From the open sea to Limerick is fully 50 miles, but the estuary provides passage anchorages at Kilbaha and Carrigaholt, a marina at Kilrush, and a sheltered cruising area extending for thirty miles from Carrigaholt to the confluence with the Fergus. In settled weather **Kilbaha** Bay, just three miles from Loop Head, offers a stopover not too far out of the way on the otherwise long voyage up the cliffbound west coast of Clare, while **Carrigaholt**, seven miles further, is

The lower Shannon estuary has a resident pod of bottlenose dolphins

The cross-Shannon car ferry approaches Tarbert slipway on a misty July morning

Kilrush

Kilrush Marina

Galatea (left) and **Mayflower**

more sheltered. **Kilrush,** 16 miles from Loop Head, is the principal town on the estuary, and its marina, secure from all weather behind a lock gate, offers perfect shelter. Scattery Island, in the approaches to Kilrush, has 6th century monastic ruins including a well-preserved round tower. Shannon Airport is less than 30km by road from Kilrush, making this a good place for crew changing, or for a mid-cruise lay-up. The Shannon has relatively strong tides, which can raise a steep chop against the wind in its narrows, but its middle portion is a lovely cruising ground between rural shores. It is also an important commercial port, but ships carrying bauxite ore to the refinery at Aughinish, fuel to the power station and cargoes to the port at Foynes scarcely disturb its peace.

There are many anchorages along the shores, and opportunities for poking into the muddy creeks of the tributary rivers. Above the head of navigation at

Paradise Lost – the ruins of Paradise House

Paradise

Near Ballynacally and overlooking the estuary of the River Fergus two miles above its confluence with the Shannon are the ruins of Paradise House, built in 1685, rebuilt in 1863, accidentally burned down in 1970 and now completely overgrown and quite hard to find. It was the home of the Henns, an Anglo-Irish family well-respected in County Clare.

Lieutenant William Henn raced his cutter Galatea for the America's Cup in 1886. The yacht was built of steel, 31 metres (102 feet) overall with a draft of 4.16m (13 feet 8 inches), a displacement of 158 tons, and 7,300 square feet of sail. William and his wife Susan both sailed on her to New York (with, of course, a numerous crew) for the race series. The saloon was filled with valuable furnishings, leopard-skin rugs and potted plants, and Mrs Henn (who was by all accounts the perfect hostess ashore and afloat) kept on board several dogs and a pet monkey called Peggy. It is not clear whether Mrs Henn, or indeed Peggy, were aboard when Galatea was soundly defeated by General Charles Paine's Mayflower in two races.

The Henns remained in the States for another year, then returned to Ireland and continued to live aboard the yacht until his death in 1894 and hers in 1911. On one occasion Henn sailed Galatea up to the anchorage at Paradise, no mean feat considering her draft and lack of mechanical power, and the fact that the channel has only 0·6m at LAT at its narrowest point. Galatea was broken up in 1912.

Paradise remained occupied until 1936, and was sold by the Henn family in 1960.

Paradise

King John's Castle and the rapids of the Shannon at Limerick

Limerick the river falls 33m from Lough Derg in fifteen miles, and is harnessed for power generation at Ardnacrusha. Access to the extensive inland waterway network (for boats of limited air and water draft) involves using a bypass canal through Limerick city, the tail race of the power station, and the Ardnacrusha lock. About 250 boats make the challenging transit each year.

Reaching towards Loop Head from the south – the Aran Islands on the horizon and the fabulous cruising grounds of Connemara beyond.

3 The West Coast
Loop Head to Erris Head

Aquamarine water over white coral sand at Omey Island

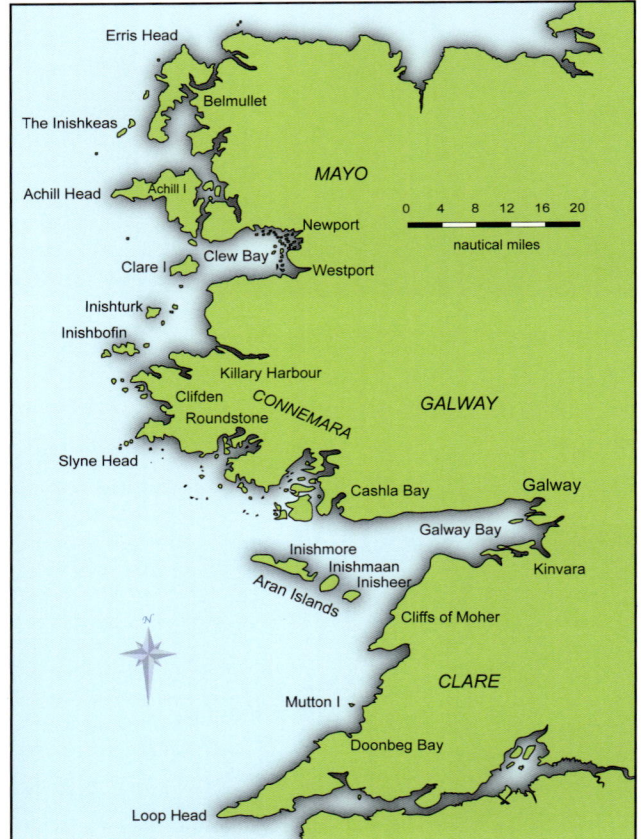

Loop Head lighthouse, built by George Halpin Senior in 1852

This is Ireland's coast of islands, for between Loop Head and Erris Head are around 160, large and small, about twenty of them inhabited at least seasonally and nine of those with permanent populations ranging from one (in the case of Omey and Inishbarra) to eight hundred (on Inishmore). Many others on the south Connemara coast are bridged to the shore, as is Achill, often called Ireland's largest island but a true island no longer. Many now-deserted islands are crowded with ruins, for the islands once supported a much greater population, but the briefest study of the census data here reveals the ironic truth that the surest way to retain a community on an island is to bridge it to the shore.

The coast is breathtaking in the variety of its beauty: sheer cliffs give way to low, rock-strewn shores backed by bare and gaunt mountains, then to steep-sided inlets, Clew Bay's maze of drumlin islets, the awe-inspiring cliffs of Clare and Achill and the wild oceanic shores of the Mullet and the lonely Inishkeas. The geological foundations of this dramatic scenery also give rise to the rare and precious *karst* landscapes of the Burren and the Aran Islands, with their unique flora. But almost anywhere on this coast, the salient feature of the view is *rock*.

Traditionally a poor part of Ireland – and legendary for the poverty of its soils – the west has prospered from land-based tourism and (in the particular

The cliffs of Loop Head

A curach adhmaid *moored among the skerries inside Slyne Head. The adjective, simply meaning "wooden", is approximately pronounced "aye-mid".*

case of its principal city of Galway) a remarkable flowering of sophisticated and technological industries. The larger villages and towns of the coast – Roundstone, Clifden, Louisburgh, Westport, and Belmullet – are all planned settlements dating from the late 18th and early 19th centuries, and now important tourist centres. The Aran Islands, although well endowed with antiquities including the remarkable ancient fort of Dún Aengus, have created for themselves a huge tourist industry essentially seeded from one iconic Hollywood film, the 1934 *Man of Aran*.

The coast abounds with traditional boats, ranging from the 40-foot *bád mór*, the "big boat" or Galway hooker, to the light *curach* with its unmistakeable upswept bow, and its heavy wooden cousin the carvel-built *curach adhmaid*. The inshore fishermen of this coast, for the most part, eschew modern designs of open

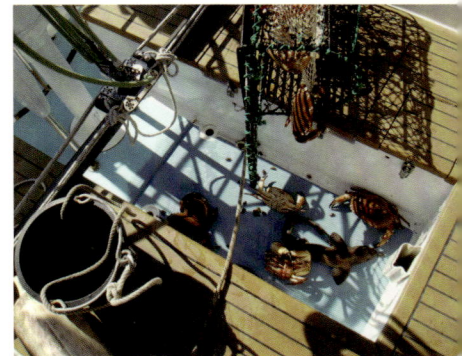

Collecting seaweed for fertiliser, Connemara

The 200m Cliffs of Moher, perhaps Ireland's most recognisable stretch of coast, are by no means its highest cliffs

Galway Hookers in Greatman's Bay

Opposite: *(top) Kinvara*

(bottom) Anchor Beach, near Cleggan

boat in favour of the *curach*, invariably with outboard motor, while the hookers and their smaller versions the *leathbhád*, *gleoiteog* and *púcán*, take part in a keenly-contested racing scene.

Although they are only two of seven designated *Gaeltachtaí* in Ireland, Connemara and west Mayo are the places where Irish is most often used as a language of first choice.

Passage Planning

The coast from Loop Head to Galway Bay offers little in the way of shelter. Anchorages at Doonbeg Bay and nearby Mutton Island are tenable in settled weather, but generally the passage has to be planned as non-stop, as also does the longer crossing from Dingle or Smerwick to the Aran Islands. Galway Bay has few deep-water harbours but the coast from Cashla Bay west and north is broken and indented and offers an unparalleled cruising ground, best taken as slowly as time permits. Tides are generally not strong, although close around Slyne Head they may reach three or four knots, less further offshore. Slyne Head, and Achill Head to the north, are considerable projections, and although its tides are moderate, Achill Head can raise a lumpy sea. The rounding of Slyne Head conveys an agreeable feeling of having passed into a whole new realm of the

The Cliffs of Moher

Sailing past these famous cliffs on this exposed coast it is difficult to approach them closely enough to appreciate their spectacular nature. They are perhaps more breathtaking when viewed from the land than the sea, and if time permits, a visit is well worthwhile. Approaching across a featureless plateau of meadowland, the visitor is abruptly faced with an awesome precipice more than 600 feet high and extending for five miles. Though not the highest, nowhere else in Ireland are the cliffs so vertical and overhanging. All of the rocks are of Upper Carboniferous age – they are about 300 million years old – and the base of the cliffs is of dark-coloured shales with thin beds of flaggy sandstone. In places it is possible to see what appear to be channels cut into these by rivers 300 million years ago. Above rise hundreds of feet of stratified flagstones topped by a thick yellowish sandstone. The top 40 feet are composed of black shales, which weather into a black muddy soil which provides a rather dangerous footing to observers wishing to approach the very lip of the cliff.

The cliffs are also deservedly famous for their bird life – some 30,000 birds from more than 20 species.

Chris Stillman

The traditional oars of a curach are pivoted on thole pins, and have no blades, so reducing wind resistance and avoiding the risk of capsize by 'catching a crab'. The light craft are easily propelled by the bladeless oar (although an outboard is much more effective).

coast, and the harbours of Roundstone to the east and Clifden to the north are only ten miles' sail each way. Although the bridge at Achill Sound was replaced in 2008 and is capable of opening, the shallow and winding Sound and the logistical difficulties combine to make that passage impractical.

The Aran Islands provide Galway Bay with effective shelter but the rest of the coast is exposed to the ocean swell, in places the governing factor in passage planning. On the west coast a yacht is often "west of the weather" and can enjoy sunshine and blue skies when the mountains to the east are hidden in rainclouds, and even when Atlantic depressions assault the coast, being west of the land mass often means that low pressure systems pass on very quickly, and the cruise can be resumed after a short interruption. With good planning, this can be spent in convivial surroundings.

The cruising sailor on this coast must be prepared to be a little more self-sufficient than usual, for sources of aid and supply may be few. The larger towns, apart from Galway, are relatively difficult of access by sea and may involve a taxi ride from an anchorage, while fuel in particular requires forethought, and no opportunity to refuel should be missed. There are no fixed quayside diesel pumps, and apart from 30 berths in Galway dock, there are no marinas.

But although ATMs and supermarkets are few and far between, today's visitor is unlikely to have the experience enjoyed by Wallace Clark and his crew on *Wild Goose* many years ago, as recounted below.

Supplies in the 1950s

"We were itchy to be off, but first Henry and I rowed ashore for milk. The owner of the cottage by the water ushered us in to sit by the fireside, dusting down the seats with his cap in the traditional gesture of hospitality. A row of children sat like mice on a bench watching silently. We threw our jerseys behind us on to the double bed in the corner beside the fire. It seemed to serve as a receptacle for fishing lines, baskets, old copies of *The Western People,* and other impedimenta. The weather, the yacht and where we'd come from were slowly discussed while Herself was milking the cow. After some time the bed gave a heave and a white-haired figure sat up in the middle of it. It was like a scene from *Riders to the Sea* by Synge; I expected some remark like 'There'll be no good come out of this.' But Granny silently subsided."

Wallace Clark, Sailing Round Ireland, *1976*

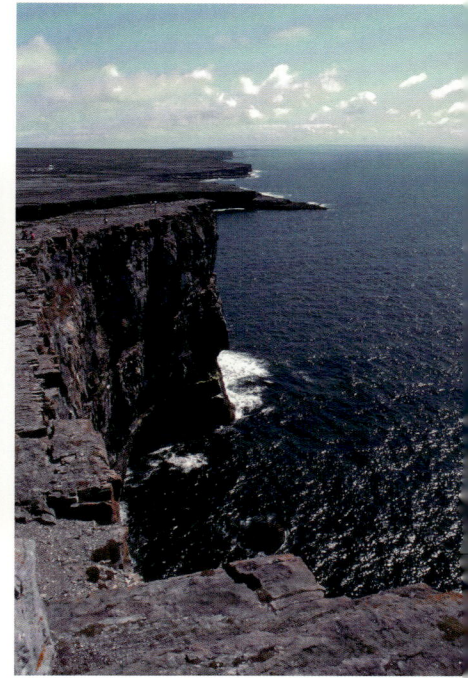

The Aran Islands

The biggest island, **Inishmore**, has a newly rebuilt harbour at Kilronan accessible by day or night in all weathers. Inishmore is a magnet for tourists, most of whom come only for the day. The island is perhaps best explored on a hired bike; alternatively, hire a jaunting car or minibus and be taken around with less effort, but also less opportunity to explore and experience the unique ambience of this unusual landscape. The World Heritage Site of Dún Aengus consists of a series of concentric semi-circular walls, the innermost enclosing an area approximately 50 metres in diameter with four-metre-thick walls of stone. These walls have been rebuilt to a height of six metres and have wall walks, chambers, and stairs. The sheer 80m cliff forms the south side of the enclosure – proof against any invader – but thanks to erosion we do not know how much larger

(from top left) Kilronan pier; the cliffs of Inishmore, from Dún Aengus; Gregory Sound and Inishmaan, from Inishmore

A land of stone: drystone walls on Inishmaan (right) and Inishmore (below)

the fort might have been when originally built at least 2,700 years ago. Nor do we know whether the site had a purely defensive purpose or if it also had ritual significance. The island's other attractions include medieval churches, a Neolithic tomb, the Megalithic fort and the heritage park at Dún Eochla, and the island's signature classic movie *Man of Aran*, played every day in the Heritage Centre. There are many pubs and restaurants, cafés and tourist shops, and a good little supermarket.

Inishmaan also has a fine new harbour, which has made access to this, the most tranquil of the three islands, much easier; while **Inisheer,** sadly, has only an open roadstead where it may be inadvisable to leave a yacht unattended.

Inishmaan harbour. It seems at first odd that on a island so well endowed with stone, the breakwater is of precast concrete blocks.

The landscape of the Aran Islands

Largely covered by thin soil, the islands' rocks are almost all white limestone, of the same formations as the Burren in Co. Clare to the east, and show the same striking surface features. The limestones formed as sediments in a tropical sea approximately 350 million years ago, and were then compressed into horizontal strata containing abundant fossils. Other rock strata were deposited on top of them, but major erosion exposed the limestones during the Ice Ages, and subsequent weathering over the last 10,000 years has produced a land surface called *karst*. The Aran Islands are one of the finest examples of such a landscape in the world. Karst is created by rainwater which – being slightly acid – dissolves limestone and widens cracks to form a pattern of gullies which shelter a rich alpine-type flora containing many rare species. These gullies or *grykes* are separated by the remaining limestone which is left as flat pavement-like slabs. The process allows water to penetrate to considerable depths, and form caves and underground galleries creating complex subterranean drainage. There is very limited surface water, hence the absence of rivers and lakes, and so water supplies are mostly taken from wells and boreholes. Unfortunately due to the limited areas of land above sea level and the open fissure nature of the groundwater supply, contamination by seawater is an ever-present problem, which, in the smaller islands, can damage the entire water supply, particularly in a dry summer.

Glacial erratics – boulders of rock from other areas, often granites – were left on the surface when the ice retreated, but a number of very large boulders have been found up to 25 metres above the sea at parts of the west-facing cliffs, which appear to be an extreme form of storm beach, thrown up by giant waves that occur on average once per century.

Chris Stillman

Karst pavement at Black Head, Co.Clare

Galway Docks and Marina

The hooker **MacDuach** *at Kinvara*

Galway Bay

The south side, and the low-lying head, of Galway Bay have shallow and rocky meandering inlets that offer some interesting pilotage but usually involve drying berths alongside the piers at **Ballyvaughan**, **Aughinish**, **Kinvara** or the **Weir**, but seriously good restaurants, certainly at the last two, may prove a sufficient attraction. Every August Kinvara hosts the *Cruinniu na mBád*, a hugely successful traditional boat festival. The energetic and hospitable Galway Bay Sailing Club has its base at **Renville** (New Harbour), where it can often find a mooring for a visitor. The historic and lively city of **Galway** itself is the centrepiece of the bay. Galway has a small marina in its wet dock, behind lock gates that open on every high tide, and there are good support facilities including sailmakers. The port was a stopover on the 2010 Volvo Round the World Race, and after providing outstanding organisation and a world-class festival, was chosen as the finish for the race in 2012; a remarkable achievement for what is, on a world scale, a modest port with an isolated sailing club and little in the way of permanent marine leisure infrastructure. But Galway can cause things to be done and it knows how to host a party.

The Spanish Arch and Nimmo's pub, Galway

It is hard to believe that several hundred people once scraped a living from the rocky soil of Inishbarra, in Kilkieran Bay

South Connemara

This coast and its islands, with the stunning backdrop of Knockmorden, the Maumturks and the Bens – the Twelve Pins of Connemara – are a wonderful place to spend time exploring. The drowned granite landscape of Cashla Bay, Greatman's Bay, Kilkieran Bay and Bertraghboy Bay is a place where land and sea interpenetrate, the coast is studded with rocks and islands and the intricate passages among them make for fascinating day-sailing. In times long gone by, more of these passages were open (all but one of them drying at low tide), but today seven causeways or bridges link islands to each other and to the mainland. Of the inlets, **Cashla Bay** is the easiest of access – and the best-marked, largely because it shelters the vital fishery harbour and ferry port of **Rossaveal**. **Greatman's Bay**, to the west, is wider, and navigable with care right to its head – and the pub – at the bridge over Bealadangan Pass, where it once gave access (and still does, for boats of low enough air draft) to the innermost recesses of Kilkieran Bay. **Kiggaul Bay,** much smaller but well enough sheltered, provides a handy passage anchorage close to the beaten track along the coast. **Kilkieran Bay** and its many

The Trading Hookers

In times past, the tan-sailed Galway hookers provided most of the transport along this coast and to the Aran Islands. They typically carried turf for fuel to Aran or the Clare coast, and returned with limestone to treat the acid soils of Connemara, an economy driven by the very different geology of the opposing coasts. Hookers and their smaller cousins were also used for fishing and carrying passengers. Nowadays they are heritage vessels, maintained and sometimes even built or rebuilt by enthusiasts. In recent years hookers have crossed the Atlantic and explored Greenland and Svalbard.

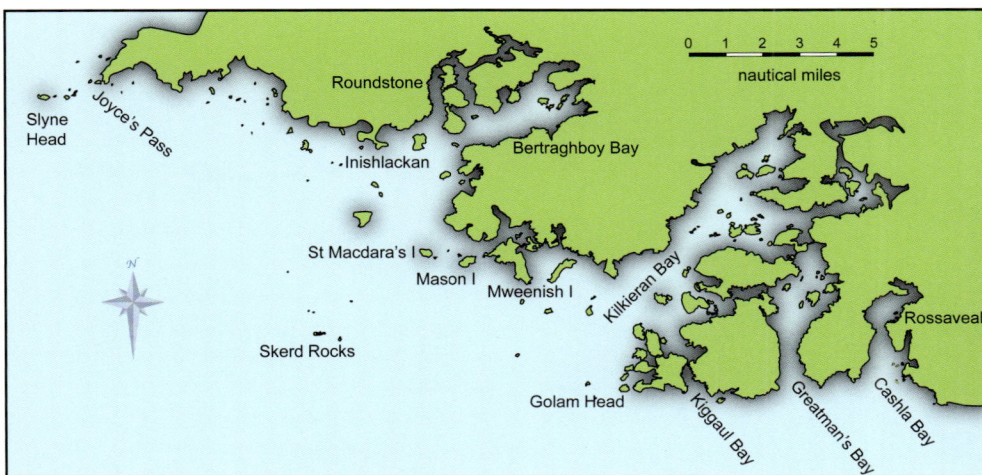

Rosmuck, in the heart of Connemara

*Early on a July morning, the fishing vessel **Skipper** heads home to Rossaveal with her catch*

The old signal tower on Golam Head is the key landmark of the south Connemara coast

The rock-strewn upper reaches of Kiggaul Bay, a typical Connemara seascape.

branches extend for miles inland, studded with rocks and constricted by tidal narrows. **Kilkieran Pier**, on the west shore of the bay, offers the only all-tide alongside berth between Rossaveal and Slyne Head, and a hospitable pub and a small supermarket are a short walk away.

Offshore are wave-battered reefs and skerries; the Namackan Rocks, the Skerds and the Mile Rocks, while the names of the Wild Bellows and the Sunk Bellows speak for themselves. The Inner Passage, between the dangerous Tonyeal Rocks and Saint Macdara's Island, offers a short cut to Roundstone. New houses mark the shore-connected islands like Mweenish and Inishnee, while the clustered ruins of Inishbarra, Illauneeragh and Finish tell of their vanished communities. The deserted islands are poignant, but at the same time a delight to explore.

Signal Towers

More than sixty square towers were built (within sight of each other) on headlands and coastal hilltops from Dublin clockwise to Malin Head, about 1806. Their purpose was to raise and pass the alarm in the event of another French incursion by sea, which had happened in 1796 at Bantry Bay and again in 1798 at Killala, and was clearly not regarded as ruled out by Nelson's then-recent victory at Trafalgar. In later years, not long before the development of radio, many of these towers were used by Lloyd's of London as a means of passing orders by flag signals to passing ships. Most are now in ruins but are still conspicuous landmarks.

While the charts here immortalise the truly heroic efforts of the Victorian surveyors, it must be borne in mind that the depths and drying heights of many hazards still provide surprises, the existence of uncharted rocks cannot be ruled out, and conversely there are some long-charted features which appear not to exist. Navigational aids are few and far between. For 160 years, a recorded depth of 2·1 metres over Trabaan Rock, in the fairway of Greatman's Bay, drew no comment; it was recently resurveyed at 0·7 – and it is not alone. Here, the best advice to the navigator is to use all available tools and give each its due and no

The ancient chapel on Saint Macdara's Island. It is traditional, when passing the island, to dip the peak of the mainsail in reverence to the saint.

Across the Sound is the lovely Mason Island, uninhabited but with a few renovated houses where adventurous tourists can be (voluntarily) marooned.

With the distinctive twin towers of Slyne Head on the horizon, a lobster fisherman tends his pots at the Skerds. Pot buoys with long floating lines are a particular hazard on this coast.

103

Roundstone

Ruined cottages on Illauneeragh

more, and to practise (above all) the ancient skill of spatial awareness – or in other words, look where he (or she) is going. The Sailing Directions strive to be accurate and comprehensive, but they too are just one of the essential tools in the box.

Bertraghboy Bay is navigable all the way inland to lovely anchorages at Cashel Bay and Cloonile Bay, and the village of **Roundstone** is a beautiful spot with the backdrop of the Bens. Roundstone has good restaurants, shops and a filling station, and its harbour affords a drying berth and its bay a sheltered anchorage.

Alexander Nimmo

Alexander Nimmo was a remarkable Scottish engineer who left an outstanding legacy of harbours, roads and bridges in Ireland. Born in 1782, he came to Ireland as Engineer with the Bog Commissioners when he was 29, and stayed for the rest of his life. He built many of the roads, and forty piers and harbours, in Counties Mayo and Galway, and also the harbour at Dunmore East in Co. Waterford. Between 1822 and 1826 he surveyed the fishery stations of Connacht, and his report makes fascinating reading. It includes, for the impoverished fishing village of the Claddagh in Galway, proposals for "a road or dyke …three hundred yards long, to be a short cut to the slate pier by near half a mile, and also an additional quay for the fishing craft." This quay is still called Nimmo's Pier. Nimmo never married, and died in 1832 at the age of 49, probably from rheumatic fever.

He is believed to be buried in the old Presbyterian cemetery at Roundstone. No trace of his grave can be identified, but the harbour and village there are among his many lasting memorials.

Roundstone

The coast continues rock-strewn to Slyne Head, actually a string of islets and rocks extending two miles from the mainland. Although the islets are low, the distinctive twin lighthouse towers on the outermost one are conspicuous for many miles. There are channels between the islands, but only one of these, called **Joyce's Pass**, can be adequately described to a stranger. It is navigable only in settled weather, and it is not for the faint hearted, but tales of a successful transit may be dined out upon for years after. It has even been done under spinnaker, but this is not recommended for a first attempt!

Seven miles north of the Head along a coast of rocks and breakers is the entrance to Clifden Bay, marked by the bold white pillars on Carrickrana and Fishing Point.

The pool between Skerdmore and Skerdbeg, south of Roundstone

The essence of Connemara cruising

The twin lighthouse towers of Slyne Head are conspicuous

Paired Lighthouses

The sailor cruising the Irish coast cannot fail to notice a number of disused towers, each one close to a present-day lighthouse, and may assume that an old building has been replaced by a newer one. True in some cases, but not all. In 1781, twin lighthouses were built on Wicklow Head, and in 1818 these were replaced by a new pair designed by Inspector George Halpin of the Ballast Board, the predecessor of the Irish Lights. Around 1830, Halpin built five more stations with twinned lights – on Skellig Michael, Slyne Head, Eagle Island, Inishowen Head and the Maidens. The intention was to provide more certain identification (there was much less scope in those days to differentiate by flash characteristics), and a position line. The idea didn't catch on, and the cost of manning and maintaining the extra lights was of course very high. Between 1865 and 1903 all these stations were reduced to a single light, in the case of Eagle Island after its east tower was all but washed away in a storm. The two old towers now conspicuous on Wicklow Head are the back towers of 1818 and 1781; the older of these two, the octagonal tower, has been converted as holiday accommodation by the Irish Landmark Trust.

The twin towers on Slyne Head were completed in 1836, and the south tower was disestablished as a lighthouse in 1898.

Opposite: (top) Inishlackan

(bottom) Dawn over Roundstone Bay

Joyce's Pass, the handy – if somewhat daunting – short cut inside Slyne Head

Clifden

Clifden to Inishbofin

The charming town of **Clifden**, 'capital of Connemara' and the region's only sizeable community, is well endowed with tourist attractions, supermarkets, restaurants and pubs. Its drying quay is difficult of access but there are visitor's moorings off the Boat Club (with its welcoming bar) on the north shore of the sheltered bay, and a very safe anchorage in its southern arm, **Ardbear Bay**. Clifden is famous on several counts. In 1919 British aviators Alcock and Brown completed the first transatlantic flight by crash-landing into Roundstone bog, south-east of Clifden. There is a memorial to their achievement four kilometres south of the town on the site of the Marconi wireless station, from which the aviators transmitted news of their successful flight. Clifden had been selected by Marconi as the site for the station, which in October 1907 was the first to establish regular transatlantic radio transmissions.

Clifden is also the venue for the international Connemara Pony Show every August.

Clifden Bay at sunset, with (right) the anchorage at the Boat Club

Guglielmo Marconi

The inventor of radio communication has multiple connections to Ireland. Marconi's grandfather was Andrew Jameson, who with his two brothers founded the whiskey distilling company. Andrew's daughter Annie was brought up in Enniscorthy, Co.Wexford, and against her parents' wishes went at the age of 20 to study music in Bologna – she was a gifted soprano. There (to her parents' horror) she met and married Guiseppe Marconi, son of a wealthy Italian family. Their second son Guglielmo, born in 1874, grew up bilingual, and fascinated by recent developments in physics. Italy showed little interest in his inventions and he continued his experiments in England. In 1898, two of Marconi's assistants conducted trials between Ballycastle and Rathlin Island, following that up with ship-to-shore radio reports of Kingstown Regatta (at Dun Laoghaire) in July that year – the first-ever example of radio reporting of a sports event. A radio station was established at Crookhaven in 1902, and Marconi then set up stations at Rosslare and at Derrygimla, south of Clifden, to act as links in a transatlantic radio chain, which operated from 1907 to 1922. All of this was of course in Morse code – voice radiotelephony would not come into general use until after the Second World War.

Awarded the Nobel prize for Physics in 1909, Marconi developed communication technology which has revolutionised our lives ashore and afloat, and the mobile phone, television, the Internet, wifi, GPS, radar and modern weather forecasting all owe their existence to his inventions.

Wild flowers grow in profusion along the boreens of Connemara

(Left) Ardbear Bay

The scatter of islands and rocks to the north west of Clifden include two, **Inishturk** and **Omey**, that have pretty anchorages, and two more, **High Island** and **Friar Island**, that have some fascinating history and ancient remains but are much more challenging of access. But **Inishbofin**, twelve miles north of Slyne Head, and a similar distance from Clifden, is directly on the rhumb line course up

(Below) The coast north of Clifden, with Carrickrana (foreground), Inishturk and Omey on the right, and Cruagh, High Island, Friar Island, Inishshark and Inishbofin in the distance.

The drying sandbar at Omey is put to good use on summer weekends

Opposite: (top and bottom) Inishbofin, right on the rhumb line and with its fine natural harbour and hearty welcome, rivals Dingle as the single most popular port of call for yachts circumnavigating Ireland

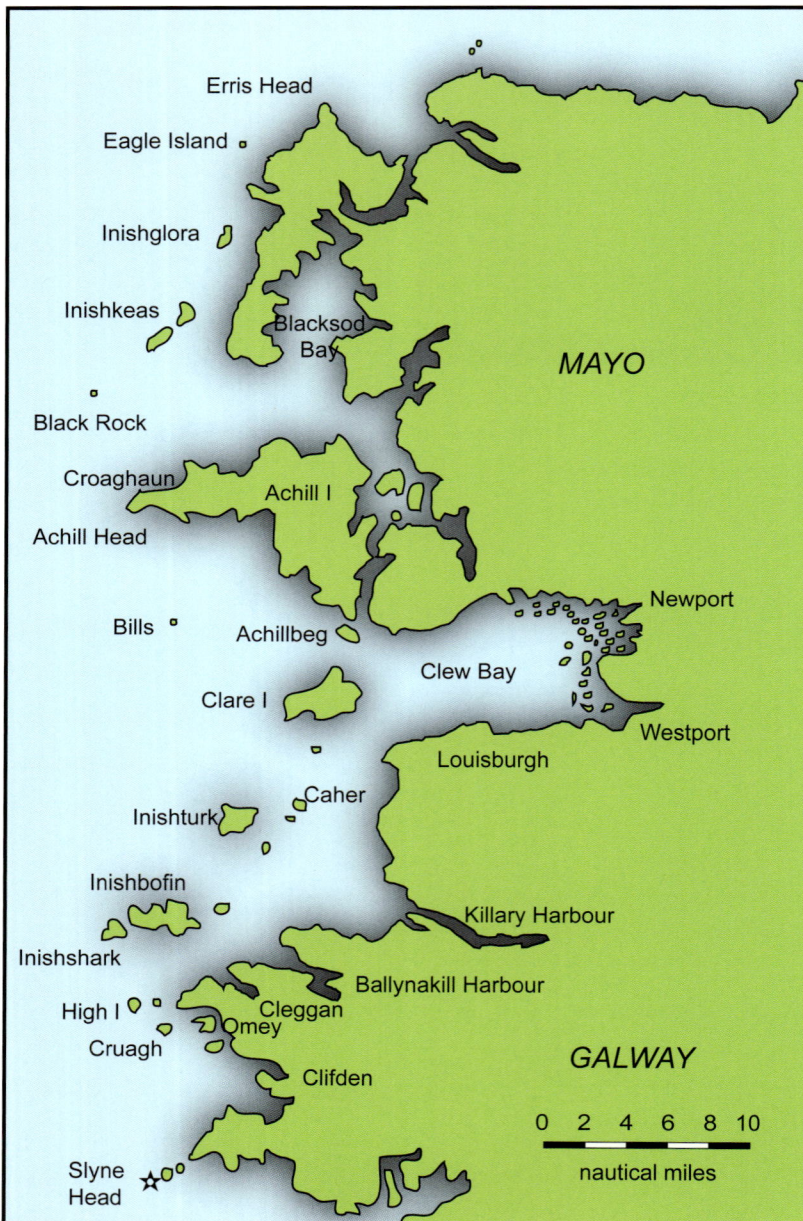

Erris Head
Eagle Island
Inishglora
Inishkeas
Blacksod Bay
MAYO
Black Rock
Croaghaun
Achill I
Achill Head
Bills
Achillbeg
Clew Bay
Newport
Clare I
Inishturk
Caher
Louisburgh
Westport
Inishbofin
Killary Harbour
Inishshark
Ballynakill Harbour
High I
Cleggan
Cruagh
Omey
GALWAY
Clifden
Slyne Head

0 2 4 6 8 10
nautical miles

The Islands of West Connemara

Tim Robinson, in his authoritative work, *Connemara: The Last Pool of Darkness*, describes how in the seventh century St Féichín founded a major monastic settlement on Omey Island, with a more penitential outpost on the much more rugged High Island, lying a little further offshore in often perilous waters. The ruins of the church named after him, and his well, still considered by many to have holy properties, can still be seen on Omey. The traveller to High Island willing to brave the swell that is there even on the calmest of days, and the scramble up a rough cliff-face to obtain a landing, is rewarded by a walk through the past, among the monks' beehive huts, ruined chapel and remains of a mill-race, as well as the most tranquil and unspoilt landscape imaginable, bounded on most sides by sheer cliffs.

But High Island, and other nearby islands such as Cruagh (known locally as "Crow") and Friar, were just too inhospitable for more modern times. With no viable landing places, and little enough land to work, they have long been abandoned. Even Omey Island, connected to the Aughrus Peninsula by Omey Strand for six or more hours per tide cycle, has proven too inconvenient for modern living commanded by the clock and the need for regular commuting. In fact, although some new construction provides hope of neighbours, Omey Island at present boasts a year-round population of just one. Pascal Whelan, ex-boxer and stuntman who once worked with the best-known names in the film industry, maintains his normally solitary habitation on Omey through summer sun and winter gales – although he is often enough joined by groups of walkers and campers and, in the summer months, by families occupying what are now comfortable holiday homes. All are attracted by the (temporary) island life, the breath-taking views, the heady scent of wild sea-thyme underfoot, and the numerous rabbits and seabirds.

Heather Greer

The Leaving of Inishshark

Just south-west of Inishbofin, almost joined to it by reefs and the tiny island of Inishskinny, lies Inishshark – not as large as Bofin, but a substantial and a fertile island nonetheless. Once it supported a large population, but the harsh and perilous life took its toll, and the numbers dwindled. In 1959, two of the last eight families remaining on Inishshark left the island for good. During that year atrocious weather cut off the island for a week, while an Inishshark man lay dying of appendicitis and no word of his plight could be got out from the island.

On Thursday, October 27th 1960, 24 of the 25 remaining inhabitants of Inishshark – members of six families – were carried ashore for the last time, together with thirteen cattle, twelve dogs, eight cats, scores of hens, and a hundred sheep, and all of the household possessions they could transport ashore with them. By Thursday night, all but one had left the island for good. The one was Thomas Lacey the elder, described in the Connacht Tribune as 'The Grand Old Man of Inishshark'. He had lost two of his sons to the sea eleven years earlier, and his wife, unable to deal with the harsh island life any longer, had gone to live on the mainland in 1959. But on that October Thursday in 1960, Thomas Lacey was not quite ready to leave. All Thursday night and Friday dawn he sat alone in his kitchen, the only human left on Inishshark. That Friday he too abandoned his life on Inishshark forever, and the island died to human habitation.

The families were resettled on the mainland, on twelve-acre holdings and houses provided by the Land Commission. They settled more or less within sight of their old homes on Inishshark, and they carried on their lives there. It is difficult to imagine the pain of a return visit – to the infants' graveyard still there, in the grassland hard by the crumbling pier, to the houses, ruined now and silent, the hearths cold and still. A return was planned, in October 2010, to commemorate the fiftieth year following the final abandonment of Inishshark; and a mass was celebrated in the Church of Our Lady Star of the Sea, in Claddaghduff. But ironically, typically, and perhaps for the survivors of that abandonment, with a tinge of relief, bad weather again foiled the plan, and that journey back in time was itself abandoned.

The island is still much used. Numerous sheep graze during the summer months on the grass growing around and through the ruined buildings, including the now roofless church and the silent National School. Fishermen occasionally take shelter on the island. On calm days tourists visit, from Inishbofin or from the mainland or from passing yachts, to walk among the ruins and wonder at the beauty of the island. The views on sunny summer days, past the small island of Inishgort towards the Aughrus Peninsula and the unmistakable silhouette of the Twelve Bens behind, are amongst the loveliest in Connemara. It is peaceful, and somehow it calms the soul, at the same time as the mind marvels at the steadfastness and stoicism of the hardy men and women who made the island their home over the centuries. But it is poignant too.

Heather Greer

(top) Cromwell's Barracks and Bofin Harbour

The Boughil, on the north coast of Inishshark

Ballynakill Harbour

the coast, and is seldom bypassed by cruising yachts. *Inis Bó Finne,* the Island of the White Cow, is many cruising sailors' favourite. It has a resident population of 200, an excellent natural harbour, a lively buzz, welcoming hostelries, a heritage museum and delightful walks to either end. Bikes can be hired – probably the best way to explore this lovely place. The island is rich in legend and has an intriguing history, since the otherwise ubiquitous standing stones and Neolithic tombs are conspicuous by their absence. Artefacts of more recent times include the ruins of a Celtic fort, and of St Colman's Monastery from 670AD. Cromwellian troops built a star fort around 1655, the ruins of whose barracks building still stand. Diving, birdwatching and sea angling are popular with visitors. At the right time of year you are likely to see and hear the corncrake, rare elsewhere, but thriving on Inishbofin. This is a centre of traditional Irish music and song, and local musicians often provide spontaneous sessions in the island's pubs.

A session at Oliver's Bar, Cleggan

Killary Harbour and Little Killary Bay

Ballynakill Harbour

Derryinver pier, in Ballynakill Harbour

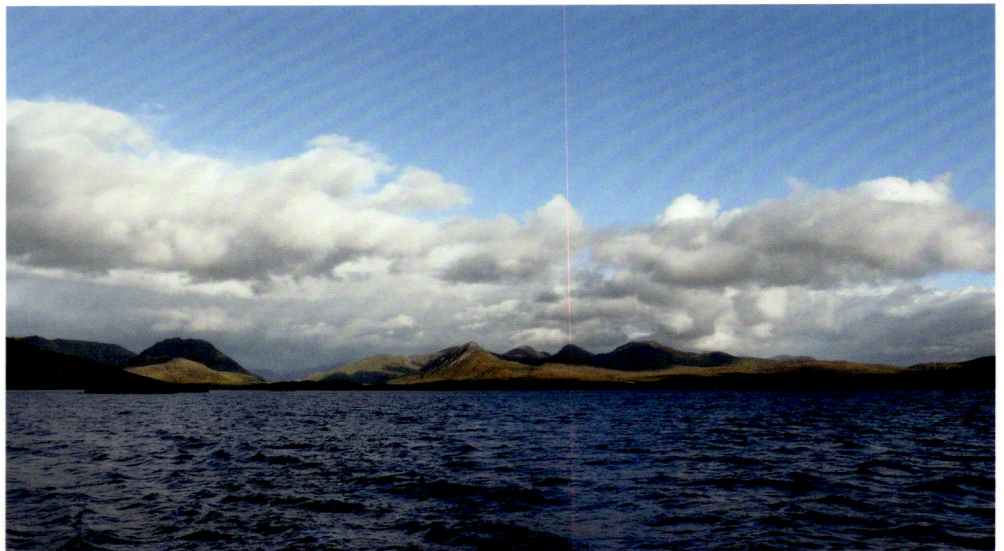

Cleggan to Clew Bay

The pier at **Cleggan**, from where ferries serve Inishbofin and Inishturk, is one of the few on the mainland of County Galway with deep water. The village has shops and pubs. The two spectacular inlets east of Cleggan Bay, approached past rocks with names like O'Malleybreaker, Blood Slate Rocks and Tom's Anchor, are very different each from the other. **Ballynakill Harbour** shallows and branches in its inner part to provide a choice of sheltered anchorages while **Killary Harbour** is a fjord, steep sided and deep and subject, like all of its kind, to fierce gusts of wind. **Little Killary Bay** is more approachable and offers better anchorage than its longer and deeper neighbour. The shores of all three are remote, but the village of Letterfrack, on the innermost recesses of Ballynakill harbour, has a shop, pub and filling station.

The delightful, unspoiled and friendly island of **Inishturk** lies nine miles offshore. Its 60 people live by a little fishing, a little sheepfarming and a little tourism. There are visitors' moorings off the harbour at Garranty on the island's east side. *Inis Toirc* is literally Wild Boar Island, although the animals are now unlikely to be met on a walk to the ruined 16th-century church, the 9th-century fort, or the 1806 signal tower. Nearby **Caher Island** is an important religious

Killary Harbour

(right and opposite): Inishturk

Clew Bay

Clew Bay, with its eighty drumlin islands, has a maze of waterways that are a delight to explore in a small boat, and offer safe anchorage for cruising yachts. Access to the tidal quay of **Westport** is easier than it used to be thanks to much improved buoyage through the maze, but the easiest place to call is **Rosmoney**, home of Mayo Sailing Club and one of the two Irish centres of Les Glénans sailing school. This sheltered haven is busy with moorings, and with tyro dinghy sailors, but there is still room to anchor. The sailing club is not open every day,

The 460m cliffs of Clare Island tower over the old lighthouse, disestablished in 1968 because, at 125m, it was too high and often disappeared in the clouds

Ancient carved stone on Caher Island

Inishturk

Opposite: *(top and bottom) Granuaile's castle on Clare Island stands guard over a scene that Granuaile herself could scarcely have imagined*

Walking is a rewarding pursuit on Clare

destination, although well-nigh inaccessible except in the most settled weather. There is no anchorage, but a landing by dinghy is possible with care. On 15th August each year, weather permitting, it is a place of pilgrimage, the main attractions being St Patrick's Oratory and the remains of a 6th- and 7th-century Christian monastery.

Guarding the entrance to Clew Bay is **Clare Island**, famous as the home of the pirate-queen Granuaile. Her castle – one of several, the rest are on the mainland – overlooks the island's anchorage at its south eastern corner. There are visitors' moorings in the bay. The north coast of the island has spectacular cliffs, 460m (1,509ft) at their peak, with a disused lighthouse at their (lower) eastern end. Walking is a rewarding pursuit on Clare, whether to the Abbey, up to the old lighthouse, the circuit of Knocknaveen, the island's central hill, or out to the ruined signal tower at the west end of the island. Guided walks and bike hire are also available. The shop is out by the Abbey, and the hotel, coffee shop and restaurant are by the harbour. The island has 140 people, and ferries run from Roonagh Quay.

Granuaile and Queen Elizabeth I

Gráinne Ní Mháille, born about 1530, was the daughter and heir of the chieftain of the O'Malleys, a notably piratical clan. As a teenager she is reputed to have cut off all her hair in protest at her father's refusal to allow her to sail offshore with him, an act which earned her the nickname of *Gráinne Mhaol* (in English, bald Grace). Gráinne was, to say the least, a feisty lady. She successfully led the defence of her first husband's castle on Lough Corrib, exacted tribute from passing ships on the west coast and conducted raids by sea as far afield as Waterford, Donegal and the coast of Scotland. In 1593 she met Queen Elizabeth of England and treated her as an equal, an approach which was surprisingly successful since the two women were of an age, had much in common and hit it off rather well; since neither spoke the other's language they conversed in Latin. Gráinne died about the same time as the Queen in 1603, having outlived her first husband and divorced her second, and she had at least two children. Her nickname *Gráinne Mhaol* is approximately pronounced "Gron-ya-Wale" with the accent on the first and third syllables. Her fortress on Clare Island is marked on the chart as "Grania Wael's Castle" and the more elegant English transliteration *Granuaile* has been the very appropriate name of three of the ships, including the present one, of the Commissioners of Irish Lights.

Clare Abbey

"Cistercian Gothic architecture in Ireland is dull, but the plain round arch leading from the roofless nave to the chancel of Clare Abbey is entrancing. It frames a green slate altar and two narrow windows behind it, and a coat of arms topped by a white seahorse over the inscription *Terra Mariq Potens O'Maille* (O'Malley powerful on land and sea). The ceiling shows traces of paintings of a hound, a stag and an animal like a dragon. There are in Ireland only two other examples of medieval fresco paintings. Clare Abbey pairs with the nunnery on Iona as the two most fascinating medieval buildings on the whole western seaboard."

Wallace Clark, Sailing Round Ireland, *1976*

Clew Bay

Clew Bay, with its eighty drumlin islands, has a maze of waterways that are a delight to explore in a small boat, and offer safe anchorage for cruising yachts. Access to the tidal quay of **Westport** is easier than it used to be thanks to much improved buoyage through the maze, but the easiest place to call is **Rosmoney**, home of Mayo Sailing Club and one of the two Irish centres of Les Glénans sailing school. This sheltered haven is busy with moorings, and with tyro dinghy sailors, but there is still room to anchor. The sailing club is not open every day,

The 460m cliffs of Clare Island tower over the old lighthouse, disestablished in 1968 because, at 125m, it was too high and often disappeared in the clouds

Westport Quay

The anchorage at Inishlyre, one of Clew Bay's 80 islands

but the bar at Les Glénans is, and welcomes visitors. The busy and prosperous town of Westport is a 20 minute taxi ride away, and well worth a visit. The channel to **Newport** in the north-east corner of the Bay is shallower, and the anchorages, tranquil and wooded, are relatively far from the village. The whole area is overlooked by the 756m (2,480ft) peak of the holy mountain Croagh Patrick, whose quartzite cone towers above the south shore of the bay. On the last Sunday of July thousands of pilgrims, some barefoot, climb to the summit. Twenty years ago a different sort of pilgrim visited the mountain – in search of gold. They found it, but were denied permission to mine in the area, which is now a Special Area of Conservation.

Overlooked by Croagh Patrick, a fisherman tends his pots from his currach

The Rocks of Galway and Mayo

Few coastlines in the world offer such variety of scenery in a short compass, and the underlying reason is the extraordinarily complex geology. The rocks are ancient – at the Inishkeas and the Mullet, as old as 1,700 million years – and of a bewildering variety. The granites of south Connemara produce a broken coastline studded with islands and rocks, overlooked by the quartzite peaks of the Twelve Bens. These conceal seams of Connemara marble, with its serpentine making it the world's only truly green variety of the stone, from creamy pale to shades of sage and moss. South of Clifden are bays of coral sand, owing their origins to modern cold-water corals offshore. Mweelrea mountain is of a relatively younger but still ancient sandstone, while Killary Harbour is one of Ireland's three true fjords (along with Lough Swilly and Carlingford Lough). The islands of Clew Bay are glacial drumlins, and the magnificent cliffs of Achill Island are quartzites, in which are occasional crystals of amethyst. The granite resurfaces here and there, such as at Omey, and Clare is (geologically and very obviously) an island of two halves.

with acknowledgements to Chris Stillman

(Below left) Inishgort lighthouse, at the entrance to Westport

(Below) The tree-lined anchorage at Burrishoole in the innermost recesses of Clew Bay

The amphitheatre anchorage at Keem Bay, Achill

The awesome cliffs of the north coast of Achill, with Croaghaun and Carrickakin in the distance

Kildavnet Castle overlooks Achill Sound

Achill Bridge, 1937 Style

"As we approached the bridge the fisherman shouted to us that there were telephone wires slung across the Sound, but added that our mast should clear them by a few feet. While we were waiting for the bridge to open, we dropped our hook and watched the crowds gathering on both sides of the bridge. When the smack had gone through we hoisted our sails and boldly sailed for the narrow gap hoping that our mast would pass clear. It didn't. There was a very high-pitched twang and the broken ends of the thick copper wire flew apart and fell among the excited crowd who were by now roaring and cheering like mad."

Iain W Rutherford, At the Tiller, *1946*

This account (from the classic log of *Suilven*) would scarcely represent best practice today, and for one thing, the cables now run underwater. The cruising sailor may be assured that if he ever breaks an overhead cable, he may get concerned gasps but he won't have a crowd cheering him on. Be that as it may, although the Sound south of the bridge has been well provided with buoys and beacons, the north Sound is tortuous and unmarked, and both are very shallow. And while the bridge was replaced with a new one in 2010, teething troubles continue – at the time of writing – to dog the installation, and the transit of Achill Sound can scarcely be regarded as a practical proposition for the sailor with finite time to spare.

Achillbeg lighthouse

The ironbound coast of Achill Island

Achill Island to Erris Head

Achill is a great – and from the sailor's point of view largely awkward and unwelcoming – lump of a thing, lovely to look upon but often hard work to get past. Not quite as high as Croagh Patrick but at least as imposing, Achill's mountains form a substantial chain, highest in the north and west, and from there falling in magnificent cliffs to the sea. The island offers fully sheltered anchorages only on its east side in **Achill Sound**, although both **Keem Bay** and **Keel Bay** on the south coast of the island are possible, but the ever-present swell may make them untenable.

Although the tides around Achill Head are not exceptionally strong, the island tends to have a disproportionate effect on the weather. The nearest anchorage on the south side is **Achillbeg**, 14 miles from the Head, and on the north side Blacksod Quay and Inishkea South are both around ten miles away. Achill Head is a long narrow ridge of rock, 111m (360ft) above sea level, with precipitous cliffs on each side and the offlying skerry of Carrickakin, and close east of it on the north side are the 661m (2,168ft) cliffs of Croaghaun, a mountain with no back to it. These are the highest sea cliffs in Ireland and this is the raw edge of Ireland's west coast. Prepare to be impressed, challenged or even (but hopefully not) a little intimidated.

Notwithstanding, for the dedicated explorer, Achill Sound is a most interesting

Achill Head

Achill Bridge

Achill north sound, and Inishbiggle

Opposite: *(top) Blacksod Bay*

(bottom) Inishkea South

Talbot's shop at Aghleam on Blacksod Bay

waterway, and the little cluster of buildings at the bridge includes a supermarket, a hardware shop and pubs. The Bull's Mouth, in the North Sound, has five-knot tides and is the only real tidal gate on the west coast.

The wide **Blacksod Bay** is sheltered from the swell by the Mullet peninsula, and offers a selection of good – if rather lonely – anchorages in this, the remotest part of mainland Ireland. The best of these anchorages is **Elly Bay,** but **Blacksod Quay** is nearer the entrance, and therefore a handier passage anchorage and an easier place to get ashore. At one time a canal was dug at Belmullet, from the head of Blacksod Bay into Broad Haven, intended to avoid the passage around Eagle Island and Erris Head. The canal is still there, but it was always too shallow to be useful, and the swing bridge in the town centre, not having been opened in living memory, was replaced long ago by a fixed bridge.

The delightful **Inishkeas** lie immediately west of the Mullet peninsula. Two main islands, Inishkea North and Inishkea South, together with a dozen outlying islets and rocks, make up the group. With their sandy beaches and (to use the Scots Gaelic term) *machair*, as well as their geology and oceanic environment, they much resemble the islands of the Outer Hebrides. Despite their remote

Basking sharks are showing a marked recovery in numbers

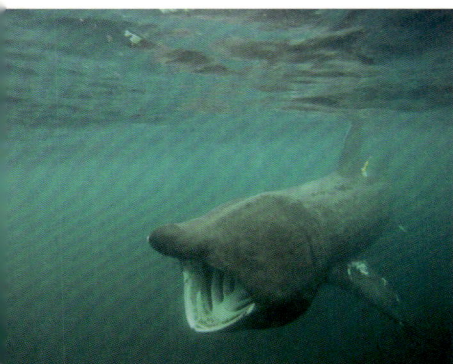

Whaling and Shark Fishing in Ireland

From 1908 until 1914 there was a Norwegian-owned whaling station on tiny Rusheen Island, off South Inishkea, and intermittently between 1909 and the early 1920's a second station operated from Ardelly Point in Blacksod Bay. Up to five steam whalecatchers were based at the two stations, and 130 fin, minke, blue, sei and sperm whales were caught and processed in the peak year of 1911. An early documentary film shows a catcher harpooning and bringing in a whale in 1909. Rusting relics of the old processing plant may still be found on Rusheen.

Between 1947 and 1975 basking sharks were fished commercially from Achill Island, with over 12,000 sharks caught. The fishery died out due to diminishing stocks but the last shark landing was as recently as 1984. They were often referred to as "sunfish", not to be confused with the true sunfish *Mola mola* (which is becoming more common around Ireland).

The anchorage at Inishkea South

Restored cottage on Inishkea South

Lichens thrive in the clean air of the islands

location and extreme exposure, they were first colonised in Neolithic times, and then were early Christian outposts around the 6th to 9th centuries. The ruins of St Colmcille's church and some beehive cells can be explored on Inishkea North. The islands were re-populated in the late 18th century, and fared relatively well during the 1845-49 potato famine, as the prevailing westerly winds did not spread the blight offshore, and fishing and salvage from wrecks could provide a living. A whaling enterprise in the early 20th century lasted only a few years. The two islands famously took opposing sides in the Civil War of 1922, with consequences which now appear comical. But the disaster of 1927 was a death-blow to the community, and the islands were evacuated in 1930. The derelict cottages still stand, with some being renovated as holiday houses, or as summer fishing bases. The islands are used for grazing and are a major breeding site for Atlantic Seals; and – appropriately, as *Inis Gé* means "Island of the Geese" – barnacle geese are resident in winter. In summer (apart from the commonplace seabirds) corncrakes, lapwings and peregrine falcons can be seen.

Inishglora is the largest island in the small archipelago a few miles north of the Inishkeas. Like so many Irish islands, it was a religious centre with a settlement

The Storm of October 1927

Late October of 1927 was marked by strong and persistent southwesterly winds over Ireland, but on the afternoon of the 28th it was calm enough for herring boats to put to sea from several ports, including Cleggan and Inishbofin, Inishkea and Lackan Bay. However an intense secondary depression of 976 hPa then swept through, producing strong southeasterlies quickly veering north-west and strengthening to severe gale force, and raising steep and confused seas. Many of the boats, which were under oars or sail, foundered or were swept helplessly ashore. Nine men were lost from Lackan, ten from the Inishkeas, nine from Inishbofin and sixteen from Cleggan. Fishing being a family business, many were related; the casualties included four Goldricks, three Kearneys, three Laceys, two Reillys and two Murrays. Two communities never recovered; the village of Rossadillisk near Cleggan was left deserted, while the Inishkeas were evacuated within a few years of the disaster. The last survivor, Pat Reilly, born on Inishkea South, died in 2008, five days short of his 101st birthday.

founded by St Brendan, patron saint of sailors. The island was inhabited from time to time, but was finally abandoned in favour of mainland life in 1936. The ruined buildings at the eastern end of the island are used by storm petrels as nesting sites. The island lacks a comfortable anchorage, the only possibility being just off its south-east end on a boulder bottom.

The pier at Inishkea South

Portnafrankagh (Frenchport), just north of Annagh Head, is the last safe anchorage south of Erris Head, and accessible in all but heavy onshore weather. Remotely situated 8km by road from Belmullet and devoid of facilities, it is nevertheless a convenient port-of-call for a yacht on passage as no significant deviation is required from the coastwise route, and for many it makes a useful point of departure for the crossing to west Donegal. This coast is a site for wave

Relics of whale processing on Rusheen, Inishkea

The Children of Lir

One of the most appealing of Celtic legends is the story of Fionnuala, Aodh, Fiachra and Conn, the daughter and three sons of Lir, a nobleman of the Tuatha De Danann. In a classic wicked-stepmother story with echoes of Snow White or the Sleeping Beauty, Lir's second wife Aoife, having failed to get a servant to kill them, turned the children into swans who had to spend 900 years that way before being restored to human form. Of course when that occurred, they instantly crumbled to dust. This happened on Inishglora, where such an event can easily be imagined. The name *Aoife* (approximately pronounced "Ee-fa") is today borne by one of the ships of the Irish Naval Service. If you should happen to be challenged at sea by this vessel, you are advised to be very circumspect. Great longevity can be a mixed blessing.

St Brendan's chapel, Inishglora

Eagle Island

Eagle Island

Eagle Island lighthouse was built between 1831 and 1836, as one of a pair. Despite its base being 60 metres above sea level, the west tower was almost destroyed by a wave while under construction. Severe weather damage was sustained in 1836, 1850, 1861, 1894, 1936, 1987 and 1988. In the 1861 storm the east tower was partly filled with seawater, and the keepers had to drill holes in the door to drain it so that they could get in. At this time the families of the keepers also lived on the rock, but after the storm of 1894 again wrecked the east tower, it was closed down and at the same time the families were moved to houses ashore. The lighthouse has been automatic since 1988.

energy testing, and well-chosen, for it is subject to some of the biggest seas around the Irish coast. The edge of the Continental Shelf is little more than twenty miles offshore here, and the sea is 40 metres deep right up to the cliffs of Eagle Island.

Less than a mile north of Frenchport is the tiny creek of **Scotchport**. This is a practicable anchorage in settled weather, and a favourite spot for divers. The creek was the base from which the lighthouse on Eagle Island was, until 1969, supplied by small boats; the boathouse provides a useful identifying landmark for the creek. The passage inside Eagle Island is wide and clear, as is the one inside the islet of Carrickhesk to the north-east, enabling – in reasonable weather – a closeup view of the cliffs and stacks. Erris Head itself, three miles further, is a different kettle of fish, consisting of a group of islands and rocks extending four cables from the mainland. The northward passage of Ireland's western flank is complete. Donegal's west coast lies to the north-east, whilst Donegal Bay lies open to the east. Hopefully the prevailing winds will prevail, and offer some downwind sailing!

Scotchport

Erris Head. The Stags of Broad Haven on the horizon, left.

Memorials at Scotchport

"Dear Lord,
Be Good To Me,
The Sea Is So Wide
And My Boat Is So Small."
In Memory Of The Crewmembers
Who Rowed The "Rose" And
The "St Mary" To And From
Scotchport And Eagle Island

JAMES DONOGHUE   HARRY WILLIAMS
MARTIN DONOGHUE   PETE WILLIAMS
ANTHONY GALLAGHER   PATSY KILKER
JOHN GALLAGHER   TOM KEANE
MARTIN GALLAGHER   JOHN KEANE
ANTHONY GALLAGHER   JOHNNY McANDREW
MICKEY DIXON   MARTIN McANDREW
JAMESEY DIXON   JOHN McANDREW
JOHN DIXON   PADDY TOM CAREY
ANTHONY DIXON   JOHN REILLY
MARTIN RUA DIXON   PAKE McINTYRE
ANTHONY RUA DIXON   MIKE GAUGHAN
SEAMUS MOR SHEVLIN   ANTHONY GALLAGHER

Ar dheis Dé go raibh siad agus
Solas síoraí da n-anamacha

In Loving Memory Of
CHARLIE WILLIAMS
and
MARTIN GALLAGHER
Who Left Here 6TH June 1911
And Perished On The Atlantic
May They Rest In Peace

4 The North-West Coast
Erris Head to Bloody Foreland

Bunbeg

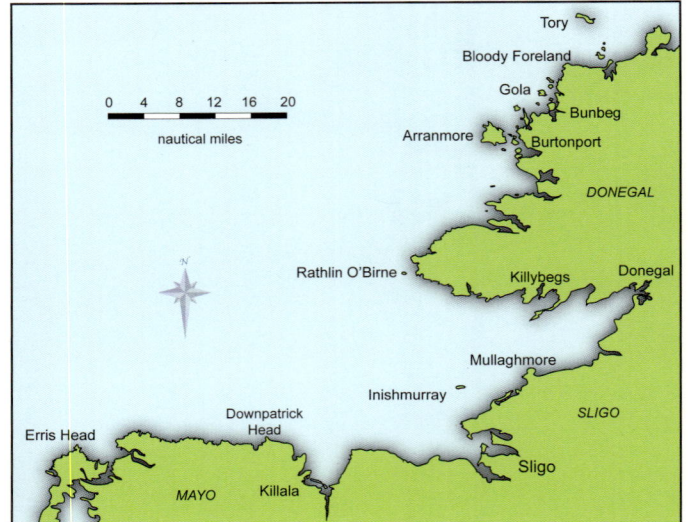

It is on the north-west coast that the ancient battle between the Land of Saints and Scholars and its oldest adversary is fought most intensely. Fifty miles west of Arranmore in December 2011, the M4 weather buoy recorded a wave of 20·4 metres, the highest ever measured off the Irish coast. On the beaches of County Sligo, surfers live in hope of encountering "prowlers" up to 15 metres high.

Fortunately for the cruising sailor, it is only very rarely like that. But the contest has created a battleground of stunning and varied beauty and scale. The bleak moorlands of Mayo drop hundreds of feet to the sea, with a succession of cliffs and caves, offlying skerries and stacks. The overhanging Downpatrick Head marks the end of the cliffs, and although just 35m (115 ft) high, it is no less distinctive and spectacular. West of Killybegs, the rugged jutting chin of Donegal climbs in rough hills to the peak of Slieve League and then falls abruptly two thousand feet to tiny pebble beaches inaccessible from the land. Between these

The Stags of Broadhaven

Clashymore harbour, Inishmurray

portals, Donegal Bay reaches eastwards past the wide Killala Bay and the surfers' beaches to the port of Sligo and the sheltered approaches to Donegal town. The distinctive table-mountains of Sligo, of which Benbulben (525m, 1725 ft) is the most famous and the most prominent, dominate the view to the east. The shores here are low, with many stretches of sandhills built by the wind and the remorseless energy of the Atlantic. Offshore is the deserted Inishmurray with its ancient monastery, while on the north side of the Bay the haven of Killybegs shelters a port which annually lands more fish than any other in Ireland or the UK.

North of Dawros Head and the anchorage at Church Pool are the Rosses, a pink granite coast of great beauty and variety, with many islands of which Arranmore is the largest, and the little harbours of Burtonport and Bunbeg nestling amongst the rocks. The low and bouldery point of Bloody Foreland, Ireland's north-western tip, was not the scene of some great slaughter but gained its name from the red glow imparted to its granite by the setting sun. This coast is overlooked by Errigal, a 749m (2,457ft) quartzite cone rising 500 metres from its adjacent valley floor. Its peak reflects the light in a unique way, and – visible for many miles out to sea to the west and north – it is often referred to as Ireland's most iconic mountain.

Teelin pier

Errigal, Donegal's highest peak and Ireland's most iconic mountain

Passage Planning

The choice facing the cruising sailor is often whether to explore Donegal Bay or aim straight across from Erris Head towards Rathlin O'Birne. The shortest crossing between safe anchorages in west Mayo and west Donegal is 68 miles from Frenchport to Church Pool, and neither place is safely navigable in the dark, but the fear of forfeiting distance made good to the west prevents many from taking easier and more rewarding options. As a glance at the chart will confirm, a

Rock arch at Portacloy (below)

Downpatrick Head (below right)

Suilven across Donegal Bay

By 18.30 we were off Eagle Island with an increasing wind – the anemometer was now reading force 7 – and a big but easy sea. *Suilven* was travelling very fast and the boomless trysail was a blessing giving us peace of mind from the dangers of gybing. Andrew cooked dinner and we ate below in turns as *Suilven* raced on into the growing dusk. At 22.00 it was blowing so hard that it seemed to make no difference to our speed when the trysail wrapped itself against the mast and rigging. With Andrew asleep below, I sailed on through the night on a course of E.N.E. for Aranmore, the wild loneliness of the passage more evident without his presence in the cockpit. I kept thinking how odd it was that a little racing yacht like *Suilven* should be out there on such a night in these desolate waters; it all seemed like a strange dream, and yet there ahead on the starboard bow was the loom of Rathlin O'Birne swinging over the horizon.

I waited until we had drawn the distant light abeam before I called Andrew, who was amazed that we should have travelled so far, for it was only 02.30, and we had sailed nearly 100 miles since leaving our anchorage in Achill Sound.

Iain W Rutherford, At the Tiller, 1946

point of departure further east along the Mayo coast shortens the crossing; from Broad Haven by nine miles, from Portacloy by 15 and from Killala Bay by 23. It is just 32 miles from Killala to Teelin, west of Killybegs. These courses also offer the opportunity to admire the cliffs of Mayo at close range, rewarding in itself. The key to a successful crossing, north- or southbound, is an early morning start, which keeps all options open in terms of ports of arrival.

As an objective from Mayo, the shallow and rock-strewn South Sound of Aran does not offer an all-weather or all-tide approach, so in that case an unwelcome detour west and north of Arranmore may be required to reach a safe haven after a long day's voyage.

An exploration of Donegal Bay is well worth the effort, and its coastwise circumnavigation is straightforward. There are no significant offlying dangers, and the harbours and anchorages are well described in the Sailing Directions.

A curious grey seal pup comes up for a look around

Leabgarrow on Arranmore Island

Pebble beach at the foot of Slieve League

Pebble beach at the foot of Slieve League

Cottage on Inishcoo, in the Rosses

Killala harbour has a shallow bar, and Donegal Town itself is barely accessible to a yacht, but there are delightful anchorages a short dinghy trip down-river. Sligo has a yacht pontoon in the centre of town, and the busy but spacious Killybegs welcomes yachts. When weather permits, a visit to Inishmurray will be an unforgettable experience.

A cruise around Donegal Bay, taking in Killala, Sligo, Inishmurray, Mullaghmore, Donegal, Killybegs and Teelin, could fairly be said to provide a snapshot view of Irish coastal scenery, history, culture, economics and recreation, all in the course of 75 miles.

The Rosses are in themselves a perfect cruising ground in miniature, and their ambience extends out to Tory Island and east along the coast to Sheep Haven, Mulroy Bay and Lough Swilly. But that is for another chapter.

Tidal streams are not a factor in passage planning on this coast, although tidal heights are a primary consideration at a few places like Killala and Arranmore.

Sea angling boats at Killala

Gubacashel Point lighthouse at the entrance to Broad Haven

Broad Haven to Killala

The fine open bay of **Broad Haven** makes a welcome break from the austere coast of north and west Mayo, and although its outer part is not particularly sheltered, the ever-present Atlantic swell will be felt less and less as Gubacashel lighthouse and Broad Haven itself are approached. The inner reaches lead to the town of **Belmullet**, a familiar name from the weather reports, but a harbour too silted to be of practical use. The popular option is to anchor or take a mooring at **Ballyglass**, the fishermen's pier and lifeboat station near the entrance. Apart from a water tap there are no shore amenities at Ballyglass, but Belmullet, eight kilometres by road, is the region's principal town, and is well supplied with shops, restaurants and pubs. It is also an Irish language centre with a fine theatre, and an arts festival each July.

Opening off a shallow sandy cove on the east side of Broad Haven Bay is the entrance to **Ross Port**, a remote place and normally a very quiet nook but a name now associated with controversy. The pipeline from the offshore Corrib gas field comes ashore here and has been the focus of a protracted environmental campaign, involving international and local activists. While the track of the pipe is invisible, the protest slogans are not, but the inlet has in any case a shallow bar and an uncomfortably fast tidal stream.

Ross Port

Ballyglass

Benwee Head and Parson's Rock, east of Broad Haven

The cliffs to the east of Broad Haven are awe-inspiring, but hidden among the craggy headlands are the small inlets of Portacloy and Porturlin. **Portacloy** is directly opposite the unmistakeable Stags of Broadhaven; another spectacular landmark is the Buddagh, just west of the entrance. This is the most northerly point in Mayo. The more sheltered but less spacious **Porturlin** is three miles further east, just beyond Pig Island. In quiet offshore weather Portacloy is a delightful overnight stop but Porturlin is now almost entirely taken up with fishing-boat moorings. Neither place offers facilities ashore.

The Stags of Broadhaven, 90m (300ft) high, dominate the view to seaward.

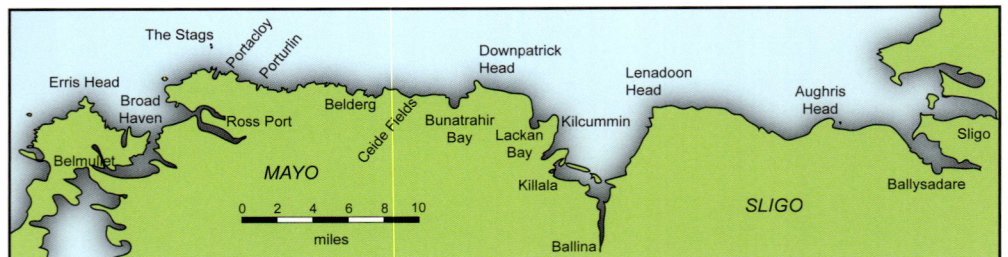

The Buddagh guards the entrance to Portacloy

Downpatrick Head

There is a tunnel right through the largest islet. These rocks are a mecca for kayakers, who can explore their caves and channels. Larger vessels should stay outside!

Belderg Harbour, properly Belderrig, is another bay that can be a welcome bolt-hole on an otherwise challenging coast. Again, there are no amenities other than the small pier used by local fishermen. However, a 2km walk inland brings you to the scattered village and its hostelry. Bunatrahir Bay and Lackan Bay, respectively west and east of the spectacular Downpatrick Head, are pretty, but not recommended as anchorages.

In complete contrast to the cliffbound coast to the west, the historic village-town of **Killala** lies behind dunes and the sandy Bartragh Island, with a harbour accessible over a shallow bar by a channel with good leading marks. The quay is busy with sea angling boats and has limited deep-water space, but an alongside berth is usually available. This may well be the first chance to step off the boat and walk to the pub since leaving Inishbofin!

The Céide Fields visitor centre atop the cliffs

The Céide Fields

Halfway between Belderg and Bunatrahir Bays on the cliffbound north coast of Mayo is a conspicuous pyramidal building. This is the Céide Fields visitor centre, set in the largest Stone Age site and the oldest known field system in the world. Covering several square miles, the Céide Fields are over five thousand years old, and lay buried beneath the peat until a generation ago. The schoolmaster of Belderg, cutting turf for fuel in the 1930's, had noticed that there were stones beneath the ground, laid in patterns that could only be manmade. His son became an archaeologist, and later led the investigation of the site. The evidence suggests a settled community of Neolithic farmers, with no need of strong defences against enemies, who kept cattle and cleared extensive forests for building materials and fuel. Something – possibly a change in climate to colder and wetter – led to encroachment by blanket bog, which obliterated the site for thousands of years. The name is approximately pronounced "Kayd-je".

The Céide Fields are well worth a visit but a little awkward of access for cruising sailors. The safest option is by taxi from Killala, 23 km, but if the weather is settled, Belderg Bay is a practicable anchorage within 6 km of the site.

Killala Round Tower overlooks the harbour, with its old training walls

Killala has been an ecclesiastical centre since St Patrick established a church in the fifth century. A fine 12th-century round tower dominates the village, and there are three ruined abbeys in the area. The River Moy, famous for its salmon fishing, meets the sea in the south-east corner of Killala Bay, and although the river channel is well-marked for small local craft, the bar at the river mouth is one of the most hazardous in Ireland.

Kilcummin, on the west shore of Killala Bay and surprisingly sheltered, has visitors' moorings and no tidal restrictions, and while it lacks Killala's supermarkets and restaurants, it does at least have the essential pub.

Sea holly grows in profusion on the west coast

The French invasion of 1798

After the débâcle of Bantry Bay in 1796, and despite continued lobbying by Irish Republicans, the French government was reluctant to stage any more Irish adventures. But they agreed to raids on a smaller scale, and after widespread armed rebellion had broken out in eastern Ireland in 1798, sent squadrons of warships to the north and west. In August, 1,100 men under General Humbert landed unopposed at Kilcummin on Killala Bay, and (reinforced by Irish volunteers) routed a much larger British force at Castlebar. The British regrouped, and two weeks later the Franco-Irish army was crushed by overwhelming force at Ballinamuck in County Longford.

A week after Ballinamuck, another small French force led by the Irish republican James Napper Tandy arrived at Arranmore in Donegal with arms and ammunition for the rebels. No sooner had he hoisted his standard on Rutland Island than Tandy heard of the disaster in Longford, and having gathered almost no local support to his cause, immediately weighed anchor and sailed for Norway.

A third raid in October, led by Commodore Bompart with nine ships, 3,000 French troops and Wolfe Tone, was followed from the Bay of Biscay by a steadily growing Royal Navy squadron, and brought to battle near Tory Island. The French fleet was comprehensively defeated and only three of its ships made it home. The battered and dismasted flagship *Hoche*, with Wolfe Tone aboard, was towed into Lough Swilly where Tone was arrested. He was tried and condemned but cheated the hangman by cutting his own throat in prison.

The invasions of 1798 were ill-timed: the main rebellion on land had been put down in June, two months before Kilcummin, and by late summer Ireland was heavily garrisoned on land and well-guarded by sea.

Napper Tandy was eventually extradited from Hamburg and was also sentenced to death, but was allowed to leave for France where he died in 1803. Jean-Joseph Humbert was repatriated in an exchange of prisoners, later fell out of favour with Napoleon, and went to America where he fought the British at the Battle of New Orleans in 1812. He ended his days there, as a schoolmaster, in 1823.

CG Stn (ru)

The coast of Ireland has many large and conspicuous buildings labelled "CG Stn" – often with an appended "(ru)" – on the charts. In the 19th and early 20th century the Coastguard's job was a very different one from that of his modern counterpart. The Coastguard was essentially a military (or perhaps more accurately naval) service under the Crown, with responsibilities including not only the safety of seafarers but the prevention of smuggling and the watch for seaborne invasion. Over 140 stations were built around the Irish coast, many in places where smuggling was believed to be rife or disaffection was suspected. The relationship between Coastguard personnel and the locals was often a little distant. The Troubles of the early 1920's saw the Coastguard, like the old Royal Irish Constabulary, regarded by the Republicans as an occupying force, and many stations were attacked and burnt. In 1920, the Royal Navy's Admiral Reginald Tupper commented:

'It is from my point of view essential to have officers and men in the coast watching service, principal ports and signal stations who understand the Navy and have been accustomed to work with it. And who also are in close touch with and understand the natives. Although the number of Coastguard Stations attacked since the present rebellion began has been considerable, the general feeling of the coastline population is not hostile to the Coastguard. In a few localities this statement must be modified, but it is believed that the attacks on the Stations generally speaking have been organized and ordered by the Central Committee of the Irish Republican Brotherhood and carried out by men the majority of whom have come from a distance and who have coerced a few of the local men into joining them in these raids. When the present rebellion has subsided, I submit that it would be a sound policy to increase the Coastguard Force in Ireland, establishing in the south-west, west and north-west of the country men, and their families, who have had more experience of civilized life than obtains in those localities normally. This would have the effect of civilizing the neighbourhood'.

The distinctly colonial and patronising tone speaks volumes. The Admiral's optimism was misplaced, and with the partition of Ireland in the following year the Coastguard service in the new Free State was disbanded. It would be another seventy years before the country again had a Coast Guard, now on modern lines with safety and environmental protection as its sole concerns (and with its name spelt as two words). Meanwhile in Northern Ireland the old service evolved rapidly into the modern one.

Old Coastguard Stations: the one at Bunatrahir in Co.Mayo (left) has been refurbished as an hotel, but the station at Cashla Bay remains roofless and derelict. The hundred or more surviving buildings display only two or three architectural styles, and those are quite distinctive

Sligo Bay

A low rocky coast stretches 20 miles eastwards, its sandy bays the favourite haunt of surfers. Three largely drying estuaries open into Sligo Bay, the middle one with a deep channel leading to Sligo itself, but south of it, **Ballysadare Bay** provides a charming remote anchorage tucked behind a sandy spit. Far upstream the river is a magnet for salmon anglers and white-water rafting enthusiasts.

Sligo, as an historic port, has a safe and well marked entrance, a deep channel up to its commercial quays, and a yacht pontoon close downstream of the bridge in the middle of town. This is four miles from the open sea, and although the tide

Surfers' paradise: a heavy swell breaks on Lenadoon Point, Killala Bay.

137

Benbulben overlooks the entrance to Ballysadare Bay and Sligo

runs strongly through the Yacht Club's anchorage at Rosses Point, it diminishes upstream. The delightful and atmospheric county town of Sligo has a modern persona that is woven around its literary heritage, and the central figure is the poet and Nobel laureate William Butler Yeats. Yeats is to Sligo what Shakespeare is to Stratford — forever associated with the place, and still a cultural and economic driver. Yeats' mother came from Sligo, he spent much time there as a child, and he regarded it as his ancestral home. The whole family had formidable talent: his brother, the accomplished painter Jack, had followed in his artist father's footsteps, whilst his two sisters were active in the Arts and Crafts movement founded by William Morris.

Sligo is an attractive and interesting place to visit, and its yacht pontoon is all the more welcome for being the only such facility for many miles. It is also only a few hundred metres from the regional fuel distributor's yard and a large shopping

William Butler Yeats

A Fair Day in Mayo, by Jack Butler Yeats, sold at auction in Dublin in 2011 for €1 million

W.B.Yeats

William Butler Yeats was born in Dublin in 1865 and published his first poems in 1885. Together with Augusta, Lady Gregory, he founded the famous Abbey Theatre in Dublin in 1904, and he wrote its opening play *Cathleen ní Houlihan.* The work may have sparked the Easter Rising of 1916, and Yeats would later write

> *"Did that play of mine send out Certain men the English shot?"*

His life and work were greatly influenced by the dramatic events of Irish politics at the time. Like his near-contemporaries Oscar Wilde and George Bernard Shaw, Yeats was of Anglo-Irish stock, and he came to support the cause of Irish nationalism only gradually. He had met the love of his life, the ardent nationalist Maud Gonne, in 1889, and although she inspired many of his works and influenced his views, she resolutely refused to marry him.

Yeats was a giant of 20th-century literature, and was awarded the Nobel Prize in 1923. In 1922 he became a Senator in the new Free State legislature, and argued with great vision and eloquence for a more pluralist and tolerant Irish society. He died in 1939 and is buried at Drumcliff near Sligo.

The Song of Wandering Aengus

I went out to the hazel wood,
Because a fire was in my head,
And cut and peeled a hazel wand,
And hooked a berry to a thread;

And when white moths were on the wing,
And moth-like stars were flickering out,
I dropped the berry in a stream
And caught a little silver trout.

When I had laid it on the floor
I went to blow the fire a-flame,
But something rustled on the floor,
And some one called me by my name:
It had become a glimmering girl
With apple blossom in her hair
Who called me by my name and ran
And faded through the brightening air.

Though I am old with wandering
Through hollow lands and hilly lands,
I will find out where she has gone,
And kiss her lips and take her hands;
And walk among long dappled grass,
And pluck till time and times are done
The silver apples of the moon,
The golden apples of the sun.

W.B.Yeats

The Metal Men

Two identical figures each known as the Metal Man act as navigational aids in Ireland – one on a tower on Great Newtown Head at Tramore, Co.Waterford and the other (left) on a beacon in Sligo Harbour. The statues are cast iron, four metres tall, and are dressed (and painted) in the uniform of a naval petty officer of Napoleonic times. It is believed that four of these figures were made from the same mould. The third is at Sorrento Point, Dalkey, but the fate of the fourth is unknown.

The Sligo beacon was established on Perch Rock in 1821, and has a light as well as the statue. The Metal Men each have an outstretched arm, which points up the channel to Sligo and out to sea at Tramore.

centre. As the largest town in the north-west, Sligo has excellent facilities and good road and rail communications.

Donegal Bay

In the sixth century St Molaise founded a monastery on **Inishmurray**; in 807 AD it was attacked by Viking raiders, who murdered the Abbot and brought the monastic settlement to an end, making the island a place of pilgrimage. The remarkably intact remains of the monastery are unforgettable, as too are the deserted houses. The island has also some evidence of earlier, prehistoric occupation.

In 1911, 74 people – an already diminishing population – lived in thirteen houses on Inishmurray. Although in the census of that year most of the islanders listed their occupation as 'fishing', Inishmurray had long been famous for its *poitín*. The real mainstay of the island's economy was illicit distilling, on a surprisingly large scale. It was facilitated by the difficulty of access, and no doubt also by the fact that it was almost impossible to take the islanders by surprise. Despite the best efforts of the authorities, it was not prosecutions but the shortage of sugar caused by the Second World War that killed the trade in whiskey, and was one of the factors leading to the evacuation in 1948. Anchoring at the rock-girt Clashymore Harbour is very weather-dependent and requires care, but the tranquillity and sense of history make the effort very worthwhile.

Sligo's pontoon

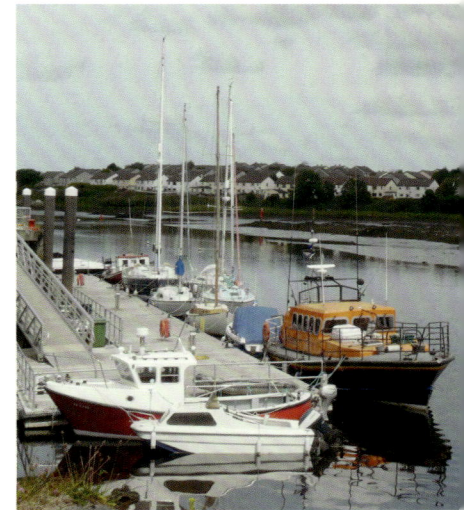

Mirror dinghies prepare to race at Sligo YC

Land of Saints and Scholars

This overworked and often misused expression owes its origin to the fact that the fall of the Roman Empire in the fifth century had little impact on Ireland. Over the next 500 years, the rest of Europe was intermittently in turmoil, with invasions, mass migrations and widespread destruction and loss, and in many places, survival took priority over scholarship. But in Ireland a relatively sophisticated Celtic society was unmolested, and endured, with lawgivers and poets highly revered. After the conversion of its leaders to Christianity around 450 AD, Ireland saw a remarkable flowering of monastic culture. The monasteries – some of them in almost absurdly remote places – were the intellectual powerhouses of their day, and from them Ireland sent a steady stream of scholar-missionaries, including men like Columba and Brendan, to Britain, Europe and beyond the known world. One source lists 165 Irish saints between the fifth and tenth centuries.

The period of world history that – from its lack of surviving records and remains – came to be called the Dark Ages, gave Ireland the monasteries of Inishmurray, Skellig Michael and dozens of others, and a wealth of written treasures that have survived to this day.

Sixth-century beehive hut and ancient monastery buildings on Inishmurray; the enclosing cashel wall may be two centuries older still

Opposite: *(top) The entirely natural quays of Clashymore Harbour, Inishmurray*

(bottom) The drying harbour at Mullaghmore

Not casual graffiti, but a loving memorial, still regularly refreshed, to the vanished inhabitants of Inishmurray, at the doorway of their now-roofless home

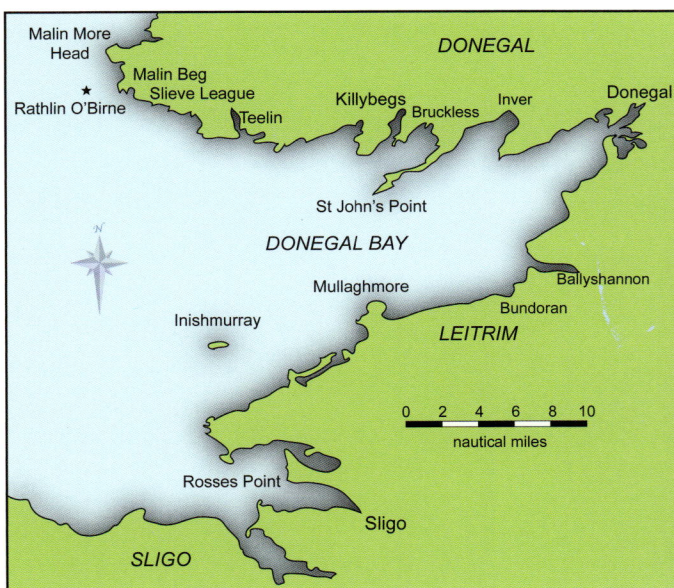

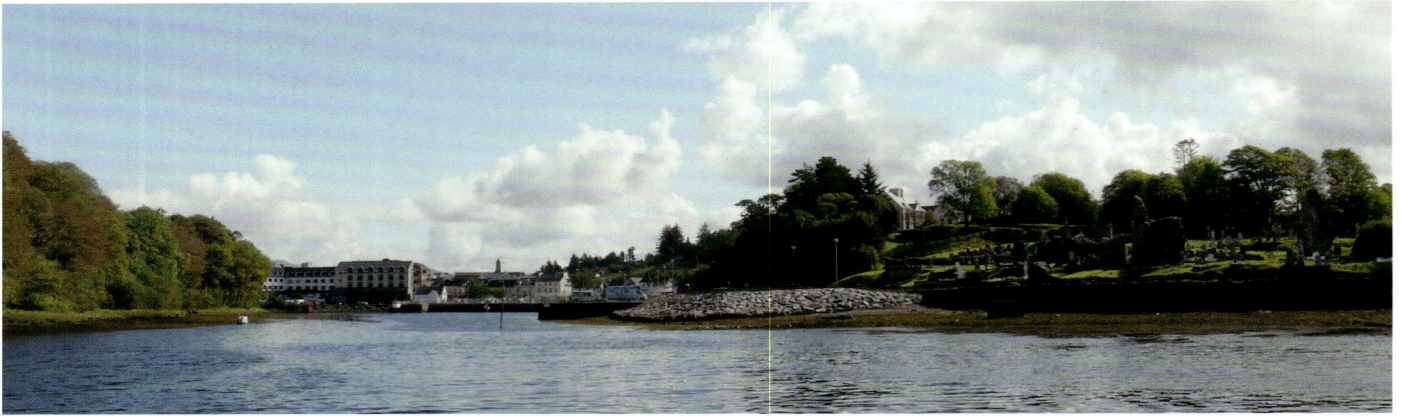

Donegal town from the river approach

Donegal Castle

(below) Inver Bay

(below and right) Killybegs by night and day

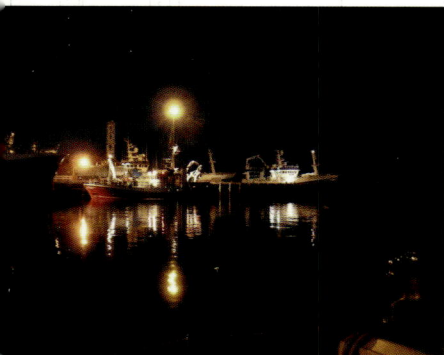

The holiday village of **Mullaghmore** has a drying harbour dating from the 1830s and a more recent breakwater extension and pontoon. The bay is a little subject to swell but the village is a lively place with hotels and pubs.

Despite its name, **Donegal** is not the county town (which is Lifford, further north and inland), but as a popular tourist destination and the business centre of the southern half of the county, it has good shops and supermarkets, restaurants and pubs. The excellent tourist office is near the town square, called the Diamond – and actually triangular! The town lies at the head of a sandy estuary whose channel has been well buoyed, but the last mile or two are best completed by dinghy. There are visitors' moorings.

Between Donegal and Killybegs, the bays of **Inver** and **Bruckless** offer anchorage in quiet and pretty surroundings.

Killybegs has the finest natural harbour on Ireland's west coast, so it is perhaps not surprising that it has become the country's premier fishing port, landing over 100,000 tonnes each year. Most of the fishery is for mackerel, herring and pilchards, and carried out in winter, so the summer cruising visitor will see the fleet (of very large vessels) preparing for the start of their season in September and October. There is also some cargo traffic at the deep water quays. Alongside berthing is available beside small fishing boats at the town pier, and there are visitors' moorings. Killybegs is a busy and semi-industrial spot, but in summer,

Teelin has a fine deep-water pier

when the fishing is quiet, the town turns its attention to tourism. The Maritime and Heritage Centre describes how Killybegs started as a monastic centre, and grew into a fishing and commercial port in the relatively recent past. It goes without saying that – with the possible exception of sails – Killybegs can repair anything marine. Its boatyard has, at the time of writing, the biggest travelhoist in Ireland.

The sheltered and strategically-situated haven of **Teelin** offers a complete contrast in terms of shoreside amenities, but its deep-water pier is secure in all weathers and there are visitors' moorings. The excellent Rusty Mackerel pub is just far enough away for the sailor on foot to work up a thirst.

The coast westwards from Teelin to Malin Beg Head is awesome and spectacular, overlooked as it is by **Slieve League**, whose precipitous cliffs tumble from its summit 597m (1,972ft) to the sea. In all but the calmest of weather the view is best admired from a safe distance, but on very special days, it is possible to get up close. The shore reportedly has some uncharted rocks, so the voyage of

(above and left) the cliffs of Slieve League from above and below

White Strand Bay; Rathlin O'Birne, beyond

Opposite: *The cliffs of Slieve League*

The (formerly) Nuclear Lighthouse

For twenty years the lighthouse on Rathlin O'Birne was the test-bed in Ireland for new and experimental power sources, and since 1900 has employed six different ways of producing light. Equipped from 1907 with a paraffin vapour lamp, it was electrified in 1974 using a 33-watt radio-isotope-powered generator with diesel backup. Rathlin O'Birne's nuclear age lasted until 1987, when wind power replaced the isotope source. But small wind generators need too much maintenance, and in 1993 they in turn were replaced by solar panels. These proved so successful that by 2012, 26 of Ireland's 72 lighthouses, and almost all of its 2,000-odd beacons and buoys, had been converted to solar power.

exploration must be made with care. The towering cliffs distort the perception of scale: what appear from seaward to be tiny sandy beaches in coves at the foot are actually of three-inch pebbles, and quite dangerously steep.

West of the highest cliffs are the wide and sandy horseshoe **White Strand Bay** and the tiny, rocky and steep-sided **Malin Beg Bay** with its extraordinary rock stacks. In quiet weather these bays make useful lunch-stop anchorages. The Sailing Directions give the only available guidance, since there is no large scale chart. The little rocky island of **Rathlin O'Birne**, with its lighthouse, lies a mile west of Malin Beg Head and is the westernmost point of Donegal; a landing is possible in quiet weather at the steps on the island's east side. In Rathlin O'Birne Sound the tide runs north for nine hours out of twelve, but it is not strong, and the bold promontory comprising Malin Beg and Malin More Heads, despite its position and exposure, is one of the less challenging of the western headlands.

Rathlin O'Birne

Tormore (143m, left) on the coast north-east of Glen Head

Opposite: *(top) Glen Bay*

(bottom) Church Pool

Malin Beg to the Rosses and Bloody Foreland

The stretch of coast northwards from Malin Beg Head presents another spectacular succession of cliffs and stacks. There are temporary anchorages in **Glen Bay** and **Dawros Bay** on the way north, but the sandy inlets of Loughros More and Beg have dangerous entrances, and the first good anchorage – with visitors' moorings – is **Church Pool**, in the lee of Inishkeel four miles east of Dawros Head. St Conal founded a monastery here in the sixth century, and the preserved ruins of two later churches overlook the anchorage. There is also a graveyard with some very fine Celtic carved stones and slabs.

In settled weather, anchoring in Portnoo Bay, on the other side of Inishkeel, is an alternative, closer to the small holiday village of Portnoo which boasts an hotel, a couple of pubs, a shop, a watersports club and a golf course. Both bays have splendid sandy beaches. It can be a busy place in the holiday season!

Whale-watching offshore

The commoner cetacean species are found right up to the coast. But those fortunate enough to venture well offshore, towards and beyond the edge of the Continental shelf, will find a very different species diversity, including white-sided, white-beaked and striped dolphins, and deep-diving specialists such as long-finned pilot whale, sperm whale and the elusive family of beaked whales. These are all species rarely seen inshore, unless stranding. Where possible make a note of date, time, position, species, group size, behaviour, with a full description of any diagnostic features. Digital photography has made recording so much easier, and photographs can be emailed to sightings@iwdg.ie.

The Irish Whale and Dolphin Group has developed a range of resources to encourage the public to report observations. Among these are a species profile section on www.iwdg.ie covering all 24 species; a *Guide to the Identification of the Whales and Dolphins of Ireland* and a companion DVD (2006); and a waterproof A4 *Boat User's Guide to Irish Whales and Dolphins*.

Padraig Whooley, IWDG

Chapel Bay, Arranmore

Ballagh Rocks guard the North Sound of Aran

The Arranmore ferry emerges from Burtonport

As the gannet flies it is barely 15 miles from Crohy Head to Bloody Foreland, but this distance encompasses a fascinating miniature cruising ground: the Rosses. The continuous onslaught of the Atlantic against an ancient and durable granite coast has resulted in a jumble of islands, sandy estuaries and bays, and offshore rocks, all overlooked by Arranmore Island with its high western cliffs and its lighthouse to seaward, and by Errigal, Donegal's signature mountain, inland.

The approach from the south is either via the shallow South Sound of Aran, or outside the island to enter the deeper North Sound from the north, the choice dependent on weather and rise of tide. Chapel Sound offers an alternative access to the bays on the south side of Arranmore. Pilotage of the shallow and tortuous channels among the islands and reefs requires the largest-scale charts, the Sailing Directions to hand and, above all, the stalwart old ally Spatial Awareness.

Arranmore is seven square miles of rough hill ground, more suited to walking

and wildlife than agriculture, and its people – 450 in number in 2011 – have traditionally looked to the sea, or across it, for their livelihood. This part of Donegal used to send hundreds of migrant farmworkers to Scotland every year, and many islanders have family connections with Glasgow. Appropriately, as this is part of the Donegal Gaeltacht, there is an Irish language college for young students. The island boasts five pubs and a nightclub, indicative of its popularity as a holiday destination in summer, when the population more than doubles.

The lighthouse on Rinrawros Point, dating from 1798, was the first to be built in Donegal. It is a three-kilometre walk from the principal village at Leabgarrow on the Sound, from where ferries sail regularly to Burtonport. There are visitors' moorings in the anchorage north of Leabgarrow where the Severn-class Arranmore lifeboat is stationed.

The summit of the island is Cluidaniller (*Cnoc an Iolair*, Eagle Hill) which at 225m (750ft) affords fine views of the whole west Donegal coast from Glen Head to Tory Island.

Aranmore lighthouse

Buildings old and new on Rutland Island overlook the channel to Burtonport

The narrow but deep channel between the islands and into **Burtonport** is well marked. Burtonport's pier offers a sheltered alongside berth and makes an ideal base for exploring the islands and bays of the Rosses. Once home to a sizeable fishing fleet, it now shelters the Arranmore ferries, shellfish boats, the RIBs of the summer residents on the inshore islands, and the diving boats. (In 2010 local divers found what is believed to be a Spanish Armada galleon south of Rutland Island.) Burtonport has good pub seafood and its pier has the only quayside diesel pump between Galway and Portrush. The week-long Burtonport Festival of music and fun is held every July.

Burtonport

Burtonport's fishing fleet has all but vanished since this picture was taken in the early 1990s

The West of Ireland

"The night was broken by nothing louder than the splash of a couple of seals sliding into the water, and we slept soundly until our eyes were prised open by the light streaming through the scuttles and under the curtains above us. I lay on dreaming for a few minutes, wondering where we would be tonight. We could make 80 miles comfortably in daylight if the wind was north west. If it was much south of that we would be lucky to make a quarter of the distance. From here in the sound you could not tell the true direction. Would we finish the day under the mountains of Achill, in a creek at Broadhaven, anchored among the fishing fleet at Killybegs, or no further than Church Pool, Portnoo? Half the appeal of sailing is its gypsy uncertainty. The motorist has his degree of freedom all the time; he can drive the length of Ireland any day. For sailors, freedom of movement is more valued because it is never certain; you may be stuck for a week in a harbour you are sick of the sight of, then suddenly be free to sail 100 miles with less effort than it took to make ten miles to get there."

Wallace Clark, Sailing Round Ireland, *1976*

Cruit Bay offers wonderful day-sailing for a small boat and a beautiful anchorage for a larger one.

As well as offering a beautiful cruising ground, the islands between Arranmore and Bloody Foreland provide fascinating social and historical insights. The southernmost, **Cruit**, is bridged to the shore and as a popular weekenders' retreat has its fine modern houses and golf course. The four true islands of **Owey, Gola, Inishmeane** and **Inishsirrer** have an entirely different ambience and culture from that, but much in common with each other. They lost their permanent populations in the 1960s and 70s, when support for offshore island communities was unheard of, but the people never lost touch with their island homes, and some went back year after year to fish or tend livestock. Despite that, by the 1990s, most of the houses had fallen into disrepair through the ravages of winters, and the islands had an air of dereliction. Wandering past the deserted cottages was a ghostly experience.

But since then much has happened, and the former islanders and their

Anchorage on the south-west side of Gola

Restoration work on Gola is progressing with care

Opposite: *(top) Owey*

(bottom) Bunbeg

descendants have found new heart, together with the Donegal Small Islands Co-operative promoting the islands as a cultural and holiday destination. On Owey (evacuated in 1977), after six zero returns in succession, the 2006 census recorded 27 people – not so much a permanent population, perhaps, as a determined statement of intent. Gola has had a power cable laid from the mainland, but no poles or overhead lines were permitted to deface the island, and the supply runs underground. A little memorial has been built on Gola to two of the victims of the 2001 Twin Towers attack, who were descendants of Gola islanders, and it has become something of a place of pilgrimage. There are no grandiose new houses – in stark contrast to the view of the mainland coast from these islands – but the old cottages have been faithfully and tastefully modernised. All four islands are (at the time of writing) still occupied only seasonally, and there are no scheduled ferry services.

The boat slip on Owey

Báidín Fheilimí

One of the best-known children's songs in the Irish language originated on Owey. The title, *Phelim's Little Boat*, is approximately pronounced *Bawjeen Eye-limay* and the tune is familiar far beyond the shores of Ireland. Like many another hero of children's folklore, poor Phelim comes to a sticky end.

Báidín Fheilimí d'imigh go Gabhla,
Báidín Fheilimí is Feilimí ann.
Báidín Fheilimí d'imigh go Gabhla,
Báidín Fheilimí is Feilimí ann.

(Curfá)
Báidín bídeach, báidín beosach,
Báidín bóidheach, báidín Fheilimí
Báidín díreach, báidín deontach
Báidín Fheilimí is Feilimí ann.

Báidín Fheilimí d'imigh go Toraigh
Báidín Fheilimí is Feilimí ann.
Báidín Fheilimí d'imigh go Toraigh,
Báidín Fheilimí is Feilimí ann.

Báidín Fheilimí briseadh i dToraigh
Iasc ar bhord is Feilimí ann.
Báidín Fheilimí briseadh i dToraigh
Iasc ar bhord is Feilimí ann.

Phelim's little boat went off to Gola,
Phelim's little boat and Phelim aboard,
Phelim's little boat went off to Gola,
Phelim's little boat and Phelim aboard

(Chorus)
A tiny little boat, a lively little boat,
A lovely little boat, Pheliim's little boat,
A straight little boat, a true little boat,
Phelim's little boat and Phelim aboard.

Phelim's little boat went off to Tory,
Phelim's little boat and Phelim aboard,
Phelim's little boat went off to Tory,
Phelim's little boat and Phelim aboard

Phelim's little boat was wrecked on Tory,
Laden with fish and Phelim aboard,
Phelim's little boat was wrecked on Tory,
Laden with fish and Phelim aboard.

Gweedore Harbour at low tide

Errigal dominates the skyline from the anchorage at Gola

Cruit Bay is a beautiful anchorage with bays of golden sand. Owey, across a narrow but easily navigable sound, has no good anchorage, but a boat slip in a narrow cove, usable in settled weather. The inside passage to Gola through Carnboy Channel offers some tricky pilotage challenges, but the approaches through Gola's South and North Sounds are clean and deep, and Gola has three lovely anchorages. A little rise of tide may be required for the passage inside Inishmeane, but the narrow Inishsirrer Strait is nearly four metres deep.

Nicholas Rock and its beacon, in Cruit Bay

The cliffs and caves of Gola are a paradise for kayakers

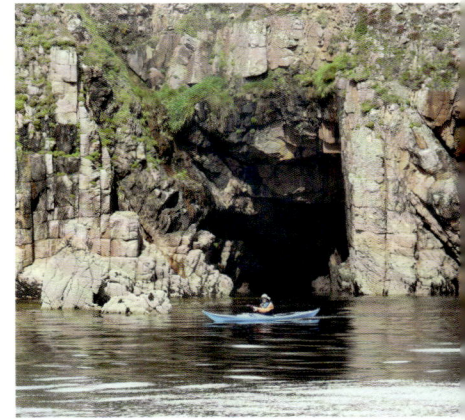

The area around Gweedore, on the mainland, is one of the country's more densely populated rural areas, and the view from the sea takes in an astounding number of houses scattered across otherwise bleak and windswept slopes. Many of these are recently built holiday homes, and the vista can scarcely be said to commend the planning process to the eye, particularly given the stark beauty of the surroundings.

A shallow and tortuous, but well-marked, channel leads through the sandy Gweedore Harbour between golden beaches to the snug harbour of **Bunbeg**. Once alongside, shelter is total and the pub is a pleasant half-mile stroll.

And now it is just three miles to Bloody Foreland and the north coast. But because we follow the sequence of the Sailing Directions, the continuation of this story on that coast is the subject of the last chapter of this book; for now, we return to Carnsore Point and set our course northwards.

Bloody Foreland

The East Coast
Carnsore Point to Carlingford Lough

(top) *Three Howth 17s, well into their second century, go out to race*

I f Ireland's south-west coast passages are like minor roads, and those of the west coast more like off-road tracks, then by comparison this stretch of the east coast might be likened to a maritime motorway.

The coastal passages between Carnsore and Carlingford are all too often regarded as the routeway to somewhere else. Cruising yachts rush by, heading to or from Ireland's south-west coast, Brittany, and England's south coast, or north to Scottish waters and beyond. They follow the precept "time and tide wait for no man", for south of Dublin the tide is the commanding factor, with the power to add effortless miles to the day's sail, or conversely to make progress frustratingly slow.

The salient features of the coast between Carnsore and Dublin Bay are the sandbanks which parallel the coast, between a mile and ten miles offshore.

Howth Yacht Club and Marina

These hazards have always been well buoyed, and marked also for many years by lightships, later replaced by the revolutionary telescopic Kish lighthouse and by two LANBYs which have now in turn been replaced by large high-intensity buoys. The shallow ridge of the long Arklow Bank is the site of seven wind turbines, each tower 73m (241ft) high, and 124m (407ft) to the top of the blade arc. This spectacular piece of engineering gives the Bank a daytime prominence that few Lighthouse Authorities could provide!

Looking landward, low ground backed by distant hills, behind Carnsore Point and around Wexford, gives way to higher and nearer hills overlooking the coast, with Tara Hill and Arklow Rock both prominent landmarks. The Wicklow Mountains, modest in height behind Arklow, reach over 900m (3,000ft) between Wicklow and Dublin Bay, and extend into sea cliffs at Wicklow and Bray Heads.

Dublin Bay is the sailing epicentre of this coast, with the city of Dublin not only the Republic's capital but – by a factor of ten – its largest city, and also its busiest commercial port. There are 1,600 marina berths in the Greater Dublin area.

Poolbeg Lighthouse and the entrance to the Liffey and the Port of Dublin

Baily lighthouse, Howth

Howth Head stands guard over Dublin Bay, its isolated 167m (550ft) summit a conspicuous landmark. To the north lie the islands of Ireland's Eye and Lambay, with a scatter of low islets off Skerries and the lighthouse on Rockabill offshore. North of Skerries a low and sandy coast stretches past the mouth of the Boyne to Clogher Head, where the fishing harbour of Port Oriel offers a handy stopover.

Dublin has of course connections by air to many parts of the world, and frequent ferries to Liverpool and Holyhead. Ferries sail from Rosslare to Fishguard, Pembroke, Roscoff and Cherbourg.

The Arklow Bank windfarm, pictured from Howth, 30 miles away. The bottom halves of the turbine towers are below the horizon. Wicklow Head is on the right

Passage Planning

Navigation in the southern Irish Sea and St George's Channel is dominated by tidal considerations. The Irish Sea and Liverpool Bay are fed from both north and south; at High Water at Cork and Malin Head it is Low Water at Dublin and Belfast, and *vice versa*. This creates tidal streams of up to four knots in both St George's Channel and the North Channel.

It goes without saying that the best strategy is to sail with a fair tide, for an adverse stream of such a strength makes for slow progress indeed. However, on the northern part of this coast between Rockabill and St John's Point the tidal atlas

*The magnificent **Hallowe'en** at the RIYC pontoon, Dun Laoghaire. She was built in 1926 to compete in the Fastnet race, and her overall length of 70 feet, right up to the handicap limit, was regarded as being not quite sporting*

(Above) Sunrise over the East Pier at Wicklow

(Below) Dalkey Island

shows "slack" for twelve hours out of twelve. But the rise and fall of tide here is large, and this means fast tides in the narrow entrance to Carlingford Lough. Given this tidal regime, passages south of Howth must be planned with the tidal stream in mind; and while further north the coastwise stream can be disregarded, the tide will still govern if Carlingford Lough is the destination. Sailing non-stop, a course outside all the banks will mean slightly weaker tide, with the option of slipping inside the banks when the tide is fair, and moving outside again when it is foul. A bit more work for the navigator, but worth it, perhaps.

A local exception to this is the coast between Wicklow and Greystones, which is clean enough to permit sailing – with care! – within a hundred yards of the beach, largely avoiding the tide. To a lesser extent the same tactic can be employed between Arklow and Cahore Point. Fortunately for those in less of a hurry, there are ports and anchorages each no more than twenty miles apart between Carnsore Point and Dublin Bay.

From Carnsore to Rosslare, tidal streams of around three knots combined with shallow water over a rough seabed can make for a bumpy ride, and wind-over-tide conditions anywhere will raise a short steep sea. But in the Irish Sea, when

Tuskar Rock

The Ha'penny Bridge, Dublin

Rosslare Harbour

Carnsore Point

Wexford Harbour

the wind doesn't blow the sea doesn't roll, and an offshore wind quickly flattens any residual swell.

Carnsore Point to Arklow

Rosslare is one of Ireland's main ferry ports, and its man-made harbour is mostly devoted to large Ro-Ro ships. The westernmost quay may be available as a berth, although this is very much a commercial port environment with all that that implies. There is anchorage in the bay, clear of the harbour area. The streets above the harbour have shops, pubs and restaurants. The holiday village of Rosslare itself is two miles further north, and has a renowned spa hotel.

Wexford was established in Viking times, and developed thereafter into an important medieval town. It retains much of this character, and is a rewarding place to explore, but its approaches from seaward are shallow and there is not much rise of tide. The well-buoyed channel across the Bar and the wide harbour is navigable by boats of limited draft, and Wexford Harbour Boat and Tennis Club is situated just above the bridge across the River Slaney. The excellent Wexford Festival Opera takes place in October each year.

Cahore Point is an important landmark, as it marks a change in the pattern of extensive banks and channels offshore. The Moneyweights and Rusk Banks to the south converge with the coast to a narrows here, and the gap at the Sluice has the fastest tide on the coast. Between Cahore Point and the southern end of the Arklow Bank is a nine-mile deep-water gap.

Pollduff

Rosslare Spit

In times gone by the sandspit forming the south side of Wexford harbour extended almost two miles further north. In 1642, a fort was built on its extremity, and this was followed by almost fifty houses; the precincts of the fort eventually extended to 750 acres, and it was beseiged by Cromwell's army. In later years it was used as a Custom House, and in the 19th century a lifeboat station, known as Rosslare Fort, was established there. Things began to go downhill in the latter part of the century as houses fell into disrepair and the school closed – this was really a pretty remote part of the world. Land reclamation in Wexford harbour was probably responsible for erosion of the spit by diverted currents, and in the winter of 1924/25 it was breached by a storm. The following winter it lost almost a mile of its length. Thirty years later the end of the spit had shifted westwards, and in 1965/66 it was breached again, near to where it now terminates protected by concrete armouring and groynes. By 1983 the second mile of the spit, north of that point, had been washed away. The present buoyed channel to Wexford follows the line of one of the breaches of 1925, and the only sign of the old fort is a quarter mile north of the channel, marked on the chart as "Ruins (awash at HW)".

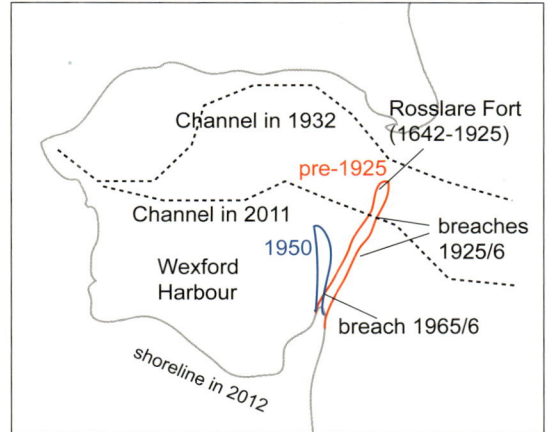

Pollduff is a convenient anchorage in a bay partly protected by a pier and overlooked by a pub, and is useful when awaiting a fair wind or tide, while **Courtown**, five miles to the north, has a shallow and very crowded harbour. These are popular weekenders' retreats.

Arklow lies at the mouth of the Avoca River, and like most Irish east coast towns was founded by the Vikings, although the estuary may have been known to the ancient Phoenicians, trading here for tin and copper. The harbour has a long and proud maritime history, and today has a small marina, and riverside pontoons for visiting yachts. Although Arklow no longer operates as a cargo port, the local company Arklow Shipping is Ireland's biggest shipowner and (at the time of writing) manages a fleet of 44 vessels. Their distinctive green hulls are a familiar sight in almost every European port. A century ago Arklow had

Wexford

Courtown harbour

A competitor passes Wicklow Head at the start of the Round Ireland Race

The Antifouling Avoca

The Avoca River is one of Ireland's most scenic, rising in the Wicklow Hills and passing through the renowned Meeting of the Waters before reaching the sea at Arklow. Until very recently, from the angler's and environmentalist's point of view it was not so pretty, because copper mining in the Vale of Avoca up to 1982 caused the river to have a high acidity and copper content. From the sailor's point of view, however, leaving your boat in Arklow for a week or two was as good as a haul out and scrub. However remediation measures have brought the salmon back to the river, and yachts in Arklow now need as much antifouling as they do anywhere else.

a notable fleet of schooners trading under sail; one of the last of them, the *De Wadden* of 1917, is preserved at Liverpool. Tyrrell's yard built fishing boats, lifeboats, Francis Chichester's *Gypsy Moth III* and the sail training vessel *Asgard II*. This and much more of Arklow's maritime history can be explored by visiting the Maritime Museum, near the marina.

The Sailing Club, close by the marina, welcomes visitors. The town itself is a 700m walk away, with a good selection of pubs and shops, and there is a new shopping centre at the bridge. The bridge, with its 19 stone arches, was built in 1759 and is the longest of its type in Ireland. Arklow Maritime Festival is held each year on the first Monday of August.

Wicklow to Dublin Bay

The port of **Wicklow** is home to an enthusiastic sailing club, perhaps best known as the organising body of the Round Ireland Race, which takes place in June of alternate (even) years, and is the central event in the town's Round Ireland Fest. The race starts and finishes at Wicklow. The Sailing Club is renowned for its hospitality, and it is open most summer evenings. Yachts berth on the East Pier, adjacent to the club and the lifeboat slip.

This county town is an attractive place, with busy quaysides and main street in

Opposite: (top and bottom) Arklow

Robert Halpin of Wicklow and the *Great Eastern*

The first transatlantic telegraph cable was laid in 1858 but broke down the following year. In 1865, with the 29-year-old Robert Halpin from Wicklow as first officer, Brunel's *Great Eastern* attempted to lay a replacement cable from Valentia, but it snapped 600 miles short of Newfoundland. A diarist on board the ship, with charming Victorian understatement, records that "Mr Halpin" – as he watched the broken end of the cable disappear into 2000 fathoms of water – "uttered more than his usual allowance of oaths." With heroic effort they dragged for the cable and grappled it several times, but each time the grappling wire snapped before they could bring the cable aboard. The following year, they started again from Valentia, and not only did they succeed, but they went back out and recovered the broken end from the previous year, so ending up with not one but a pair of cables coming ashore at the appropriately named village of Heart's Ease, Newfoundland. Triply appropriate for Halpin, evidently, as his future wife was a Newfoundlander.

Promoted to master of the *Great Eastern*, Captain Halpin went on to lay the first French cable, from Brest to St Pierre, and in his career at sea – which ended before he was 40 – he laid cable in every ocean, a total of 26,000 miles of it. His death in 1896 at the early age of 59 was due to a bizarre accident – he nicked himself while cutting his toenails and died of gangrene. His monument stands today in the main street of his native town, and the old Town Gaol in Wicklow incorporates a Halpin Museum devoted to his achievements.

Halpin was not the only Irishman to lay Atlantic cables. Captain Henry Moriarty RN, as navigator of HMS *Agamemnon*, had laid the 1858 cable, and was in the same role on board the *Great Eastern* in 1865/66. It was thanks to his quick thinking and accurate navigation that the broken end was found. Moriarty was born in 1815 in the signal tower on Dursey Island, County Cork.

Wicklow

Wicklow's Gaol and Halpin Museum

close proximity. Like Arklow, it has rail connections to Dublin and Rosslare.

For those who like to intersperse their sailing with a round of golf, there are two courses close to the town. There are many other tourism opportunities in the area, including coastal and hill walking, and the views from the hill above Wicklow Head are spectacular. On a clear day, the mountains of the Lleyn Peninsula in Wales, sixty miles away, may be visible. The octagonal tower behind the headland

ILV **Granuaile** *off the Black Castle, Wicklow*

The Ships of the Irish Lighthouse Service

Eighteen ships have served the Irish Lights, the most celebrated of these being *Isolda*, built by Vickers in Dublin in 1928. On 19 December 1940, while servicing the Barrels and Coningbeg lightships off the Wexford coast, she was attacked and sunk by a German aircraft. Five of the crew were killed. The present *Granuaile*, third of the name, was built in 2000. Her design, which has many of the features of oil-rig supply ships, has become a model for similar vessels all over the world. Her 360° diesel-electric drives and satellite positioning enable her to hold station automatically to within a metre, without the use of anchors. This means that she can snuggle up and pass a hose ashore to refuel a lighthouse like the Fastnet directly – compare the time and labour involved in ferrying diesel and water ashore in drums. But *Granuaile* also has a double-skinned hull – just in case! She carries a helicopter, but her boats are traditionally clinker-built in wood. They take such punishment in the course of their work that they must always be capable of repair on board, and a ship's carpenter with a stack of larch planks is easier to provide at sea than an environmentally-controlled GRP workshop. Servicing the Irish Lights used to require two ships, whereas *Granuaile's* versatility means that not only can she cope alone, but she has some spare time, and has been chartered for work as varied as surveying, salvage, and television productions.

The mountains of Wales seen from Wicklow Head

FV Bridget Carmel

The Harbour Wall Paintings of Wicklow

The parapet wall of the East Pier at Wicklow is renowned for the paintings of many ships which have called at the port. They are the work of local artist, photographer and postman Pat Davis, and are remarkable not only for their artistic merit but also their outstanding technical accuracy, painted on what, it must be said, is a very challenging substrate.

PS Waverley

is the surviving one of a pair of lighthouses built in 1781, and now managed as holiday accommodation by the Irish Landmark Trust.

Wicklow's Tourist Information Centre is on Fitzwilliam Square, near the inland end of South Quay.

Eleven miles up the coast from Wicklow, the harbour at the pleasant commuter town of **Greystones** has had a chequered history. Until 2008, its pier head was a wide circular concrete caisson which had been intended as the base for the new Kish Bank lighthouse in 1965: but it had a fatal flaw, and so was demoted to serve for forty years as a breakwater for the little drying harbour. A new and much larger harbour project was then undertaken, but it fell foul of economic circumstances and by 2011 had stalled, with fine new harbour walls complete but the proposed marina basin sealed off, and the project's residential development (essential to repay the investment) still on the drawing board. If and when the harbour develops, the details will be in the Sailing Directions; at the time of writing, the outer harbour basin might provide a refuge in a storm, but there are as yet no accessible quaysides.

The huge man-made harbour of **Dun Laoghaire** has been a major yachting centre since the early 19th century. The harbour was built between 1817 and 1842 as an alternative to the (then) shallow and difficult port of Dublin, and its completion led to the transfer of the Holyhead packet service from Howth in 1826, and the construction of Ireland's first railway to the new port – from 1821 until 1921 called Kingstown – in 1834.

The first two of Dun Laoghaire's famous yacht clubs – the Royal Irish YC and the Royal St. George YC – were founded in 1831 and 1838 respectively, followed

The view northwards from Wicklow Head

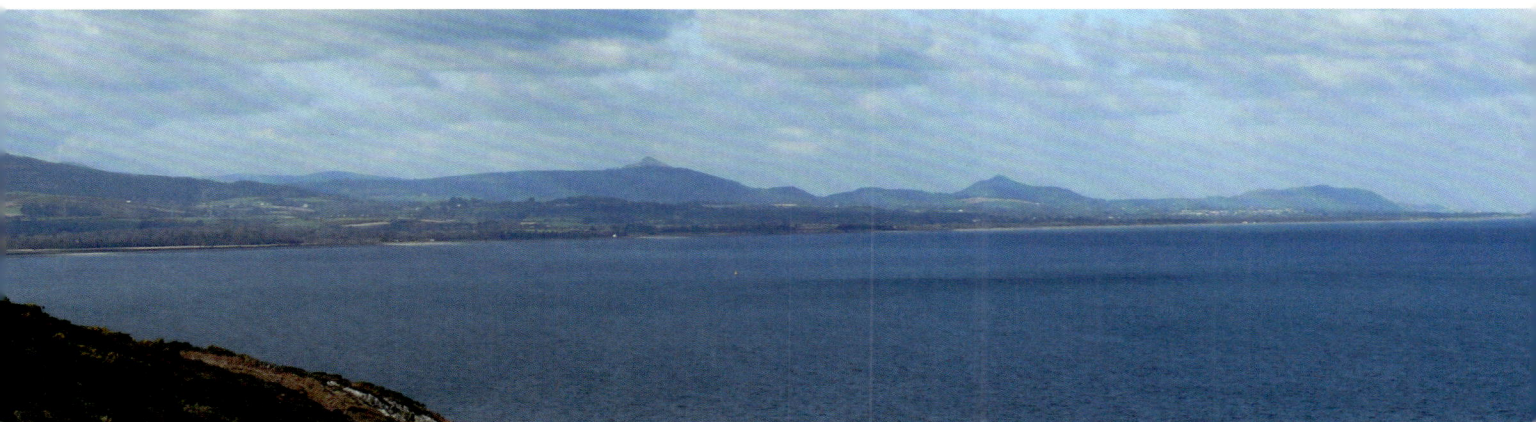

Killiney Bay and Bray Head

(Below) Optimists are dwarfed by a LANBY under repair at the Irish Lights' yard beside Dun Laoghaire harbour

Opposite: *(top) Dun Laoghaire Harbour and Marina*

(bottom) Dun Laoghaire Marina and the Royal Irish YC clubhouse

Dublin Bay: Dun Laoghaire (foreground) and the unmistakable chimneys of Poolbeg power station.

by what is now the National Yacht Club in 1870. Their three magnificent Victorian clubhouses are home to thriving and most hospitable sailing communities, and are a pleasure for cruising sailors to visit. These developments followed the yachting boom of that time, the first Dublin Regatta having been held in 1828. Dun Laoghaire Motor Yacht Club was formed much more recently – in 1965 – and is situated at the western end of the waterfront, overlooking the historic Coal Harbour, which lacks deep water berths.

The biggest change in recent years has been the development of Dun Laoghaire's 820-berth marina, protected by new breakwaters, a first-class facility that has vastly increased the capacity of the harbour for leisure craft. The port of Dublin has meantime taken over the lion's share of the cross-channel ferry traffic, and Dun Laoghaire harbour's recent commercial use has been limited to accommodating one high-speed ship, which (at the time of writing) provides a service to Holyhead only in summer. The harbour is also the base of the lighthouse service, with the Irish Lights' engineering depôt and offices adjacent.

Dun Laoghaire is a convenient port of call for a visit to Dublin. The railway station is close by the harbour, and the town itself has two shopping centres with all types of retail outlets, as well as a chandlery, banks, pubs, restaurants and a multi-screen cinema all within walking distance of the marina.

Ireland's capital city of **Dublin** straddles the mouth of the River Liffey, and was originally a Viking settlement, but developed continuously through

The **Jeanie Johnston** *replica at the Dublin City Moorings*

Raft-up in Dublin's Grand Canal basin, with the new Theatre behind

Cill Airne

MV *Cill Airne* was built in 1961 as a passenger tender for liners calling at Cork Harbour and was one of the last examples of riveted shipbuilding in Europe. After serving for many years as a training ship for marine engineers she was beautifully refurbished in 2008 and is now a floating restaurant in the Liffey.

Norman, Tudor and (most lastingly, in architectural terms) Georgian eras to be the administrative centre of the island. The city was the scene of violent and dramatic events in 1920-22, when it became the capital of the new independent Ireland, but its built heritage was spared much of the less desirable redevelopment affecting British cities in the 1950s and 60s.

Dublin has been an organised port since 1707, and today handles over 7,500 vessel movements per year, 28 million tonnes of cargo and 1·8 million passengers. This level of traffic makes it essential that the Port Authority's excellent Leisure Craft Guidelines are studied before approaching the river channel; the document is available at www.dublinport.ie and the key elements of it are reproduced in the Sailing Directions.

The fully serviced mooring facility in the city is at **Poolbeg** Yacht & Boat Club, 3km from the city centre and downstream of the opening bridges, and convenient of access from seaward. Poolbeg's new clubhouse and 100-berth marina, completed in 2005, is an excellent facility as good as any other European city can offer. The club is sociable and welcoming, and a regular city bus route connects its location with the city centre.

Dublin City Moorings, upstream of both the opening East Link and Samuel Beckett Bridges, comprise a pontoon on the north bank close to the city centre. At the time of writing the facility is – sadly – not available to cruising yachts and its current occupant is the *Jeanie Johnston* Tall Ship & Famine Museum, well worth a visit. The city is perhaps most famous for the literary output of its citizens and natives – James Joyce, Oscar Wilde, Jonathan Swift, Bram Stoker and Samuel Beckett, to name but a few – and was, in 2010, the fifth in the world to

Poolbeg Marina

The River Liffey, Dublin Port docks and Poolbeg Marina

be awarded the accolade of UNESCO City of Literature. Dublin is, of course, highly geared for tourists, and there is a lot to see, whether your interest is literary, historical, social, cultural, or just enjoying a busy city. Needless to say copious information about Dublin is readily available on the Internet.

Jeanie Johnston

Jeanie Johnston was a three masted barque built in Quebec in 1847. In the following year, owned by a Tralee shipowner, she made the first of 16 emigrant voyages across the Atlantic, returning with cargoes of timber. In seven years she carried 2,500 emigrants, and (uniquely) not one life was lost aboard, thanks in large measure to the skill of Captain James Attridge of Castletownsend, who never overloaded her, and the ship's doctor Richard Blennerhasset.

In 1993 construction of a replica was begun in a purpose-built yard at Blennerville near Tralee in Kerry, from where the orginal ship had made her first outward voyage. The project was a cross-community and international one, and was dogged by legal, financial and practical difficulties. The cost ran four times over budget. The replica is 30% smaller than the original ship, and for stability reasons has proportionately wider beam and shorter masts. Her 4·6-metre draft posed problems in getting her afloat – there is not quite 3·6m in the river channel to Blennerville at HW springs. (Edye's survey of 1855, still the basis of the current chart there, shows much the same) and the Blennerville Cut to Tralee can never have been deep enough to take an ocean-going ship. While the original vessel was advertised to sail from Blennerville in 1848, she must surely have employed a tender.

Nevertheless the *Jeanie* represented a triumph of replica shipbuilding, fundraising and teamwork. It was only on her completion in 2002 that the question arose of what the finished vessel was actually *for*. She made a successful transatlantic voyage in 2003, and took part in the 2005 Tall Ships Race. She was then privately operated and subsidised as a sail training and passenger vessel until 2008, but was rejected as a national Sail Training ship to replace *Asgard II* in 2009 because of her slow speed, limiting draft for her size and large minimum crew requirement.

The original *Jeanie* was sold in 1855, and sank in the Atlantic three years later while eastbound with a cargo of timber. All the crew were saved, maintaining the ship's impeccable record to the end.

The Baily, Howth

A trawler heads out of Howth past Ireland's Eye

Opposite: *Howth Harbour and Marina, and Ireland's Eye*

Howth to Carlingford Lough

Although a great deal smaller than its counterpart at Dun Laoghaire, **Howth** harbour has a lot in common with its southern neighbour and rival, not least in that early in the 19th century, it was the landing port for the Holyhead packet-boats.

From around 800AD Howth was occupied by Norsemen, who were finally ousted by King Brian Boru following the Battle of Clontarf in 1014. The Normans arrived in 1177 to establish what was to become a permanent presence, not only here but throughout the east of Ireland.

Today, Howth is a prosperous residential suburb of Dublin, and its harbour has a large fishing fleet and a 350-berth marina that was one of the first in Ireland. When the harbour was dredged and redeveloped in the 1980s, separate facilities were set up for fishing and leisure craft, a form of marine management that works very well and is common elsewhere but still rare in Ireland.

Howth Marina is owned and managed by Howth Yacht Club, whose fine modern clubhouse offers a full range of facilities to visiting sailors. Howth has an excellent rail link in the form of the DART (Dublin Area Rapid Transit) which links it with the city and continues south as far as Greystones.

There are excellent restaurants – the legendary Abbey Tavern is a few hundred metres from the marina – and for the more energetic there are fine walks around Howth Head and out to the Baily. This was the last of the Irish Lights to be automated, in 1997; there has been a light on this tip of Howth Head since 1668, and the present structure was built in 1814 by George Halpin Senior.

Sheltering Howth from the north is the small rocky island of **Ireland's Eye**, which – like many others around the Irish coast – became the site of an early Christian monastery in the 6th century. The remains of St Nessan's Church date from around 700 AD and there is a 19th-century Martello Tower. History does not record how the monks got along with their Viking neighbours in Howth – most monasteries came off second best!

Ireland's Eye is a bird sanctuary and home to a dozen species including gannets, as well as grey seals. There is an anchorage off Carrigeen Bay on the west side, which is ideal for an exploratory visit. A circumnavigation by dinghy in early summer will give a superb view of the resident birdlife.

Erskine Childers and the 1914 Howth Gun-running

The author of *The Riddle of the Sands* is one of the most enigmatic of Irishmen, not least because of the dramatically split loyalties which his career reveals. Born into an Anglo-Irish family, he was orphaned at the age of twelve and brought up by his grandparents at Glendalough House, Co.Wicklow. He served in the Boer War and worked as a parliamentary clerk at Westminster, drafting legislation for debate in the House.

He wrote *The Riddle of the Sands* in 1903. It is almost certainly autobiographical although whether Childers was "Davies" or "Carruthers" is never likely to be known for sure. In any case, it was acknowledged by Winston Churchill as opening his eyes to the possibility of a seaborne assault on an open beach, and Childers may be considered to be one of the earliest architects of D-Day. With such an impeccable record of loyalty to the Crown, it was perhaps surprising to find him in July 1914 using his yacht *Asgard* (under the burgee of the Royal Cruising Club) to smuggle 900 Mauser rifles from Germany into Howth to arm the Republican Volunteers. But the influence of his American wife Molly, his experiences in the Boer War, and the contentious Home Rule debate, had turned him into an ardent Irish nationalist. The shipment of 14,000 rifles into Larne aboard the steamer *Clyde Valley*, for the loyalist Ulster Volunteers, and the failure of the government to act against the retired army officers who had organised this treasonable act, must have deeply offended his sense of integrity and fair play. Despite that, he volunteered in the same year for war service in the Royal Navy and served with great distinction, winning the Distinguished Service Cross as an early naval aviator.

After the war he turned again dramatically to Ireland, was introduced to Collins and de Valera, joined Sinn Féin and in due course became Director of Publicity for the first Dáil. He was Secretary to the Irish delegation at the peace treaty talks in 1921, and opposed the retention of the oath of loyalty to the Crown. He sided with the anti-treaty party in the ensuing Civil War, and in November 1922 was arrested by Free State forces, tried by a military court, and executed for possession of a pistol originally given to him by Michael Collins.

His son Erskine Hamilton Childers was President of Ireland in 1973-4, and his granddaughter Nessa Childers is, at the time of writing, MEP for Ireland East. *Asgard* served for many years as the national sail training vessel, and is (at the time of writing) being reconstructed at the national museum site at Collins Barracks in Dublin, sadly with no forecast date for completion.

Malahide Marina

Malahide was until a few years ago just a charming little town which was rather inaccessible to yachts. Building a 350 berth marina and dredging and buoying the channel changed all that, and it is now one of the main sailing centres in the Dublin area; meanwhile the town has also become a fashionable suburb.

Malahide Yacht Club is the main organisation for competitive sailing here, and there is a long tradition of dinghy racing on Broadmeadows, the semi-tidal lagoon west of the railway bridge, and keelboat sailing in the lower estuary. Today, the marina and its buoyed channel have changed the emphasis, with power craft in the majority at the marina. Malahide has excellent facilities and a good rail connection with Dublin, and is the closest yacht harbour to Dublin Airport, just eight kilometres away.

Rogerstown Inlet, close to the north, offers a quieter alternative, and in its

Martello Towers

There are approximately fifty of these distinctive squat circular forts dotted around the coast of Ireland. They were built in Napoleonic times, and there are examples also in England and all over the former British Empire. Ireland, with its loyalty to the Crown always viewed askance, was a particular focus of this defensive infrastructure programme. A Martello tower mounted a single large-calibre gun, set on a central pivot point and with a carriage running on circular rails round the parapet, to provide a 360-degree arc of fire. In 1794, the Royal Navy had laid seige to the fort at Punta Mortella (Myrtle Point) near Calvi in Corsica, but their cannons made little impression on its thick walls, and Admiral Hood's report gave the Admiralty's engineers food for thought and inspiration for the design. However "Mortella" was miscopied as "Martello" and so the name – albeit accidentally more martial, being Italian for a hammer – derives from a misprint. The Corsican tower was later captured (like many another coastal fortress) from the landward side, and was blown up – with some difficulty – by the British in 1803. The ruins are still standing, apparently uncared for and uncelebrated. In Ireland, the Martello towers' guns were never fired in anger, but the only Martello tower ever captured anywhere was the one at Fota Island, Cork Harbour, attacked by Captain William Mackey and his men during the Fenian uprising of 1867.

Almost all the Irish Martello towers survive in some shape or form, and many are private dwellings; James Joyce and Oliver St John Gogarty lived in the one at Sandycove in Dublin, which is now a Joyce museum. The Killiney fort, privately owned, has been substantially restored to its original condition, complete with its gun.

The Martello Tower on Ireland's Eye

Loughshinny

appearance and approaches from seaward is not unlike the estuary at Malahide, but without the marina, or the dredging! There is just enough depth to lie afloat, but due to the density of moorings it might be better to borrow one than try to anchor. Rush Sailing Club is based at the pier. The approach is over drying sands, so timing is of the essence.

A little further to the north again, **Loughshinny** stands on a small bay which has anchoring depth south of the pier. It is sheltered from westerly weather, but open to the east. There are a shop and a pub ashore.

Lambay lies a couple of miles east of Rogerstown Inlet. The largest island off the east coast, it was the site of a stone axe factory in Neolithic times, and was

Rockabill, six miles north of Lambay

Lambay

The fallow deer herd on Lambay

The Wreck of the *Tayleur*

Tayleur was a 1,750-ton full-rigged iron ship built on the Mersey in 1853. She was chartered by the White Star Line for the Australian cargo and passenger trade, then booming after the discovery of gold. On her maiden voyage in January 1854, she ran aground on Lambay Island in thick weather and a gale; her compasses had not been properly calibrated, her rigging was slack and her rudder was undersized. Between 297 and 380 people died, the uncertainty being because nobody knew how many were on board. But one confident and dreadful statistic is quoted; of the one hundred women aboard, only three survived. This was to a large extent because the voluminous garments of the time prevented any possibility of climbing or swimming to safety.

The wreck lies in 18 metres of water, close to the south end of Lambay.

Opposite top: *Drogheda*

Skerries

mentioned by Pliny and Ptolemy. St Columba may have founded a monastery there in the sixth century, and during the Williamite wars of the 17th century it was used as an internment camp. In 1904 Lambay was bought by Cecil Baring, later Lord Revelstoke, who commissioned Sir Edwin Lutyens to rebuild its 16th-century castle and lay out grounds, cottages and farm buildings in Arts and Crafts style. The estate on Lambay represents Lutyens' finest work in Ireland, and Lambay has Ireland's only outdoor real-tennis court. Unfortunately for the passing sailor, the owners do not welcome casual visitors, and landing may be regarded as out of the question. The island is today an organic farm, and home to some unusual fauna including a herd of fallow deer, a mob of wallabies and a colony of grey seals. Temporary anchorage is available in four places around the island, and its cliffs are home to thousands of guillemots, kittiwakes, puffins, shearwaters, and – most recently – a new colony of gannets.

Six miles north-west, the bay at **Skerries** provides a good anchorage, and the pier might give a berth at neaps for a cruising yacht. As the name implies, the coast here is studded with rocks and islets. The village ashore is a former fishing community, but is now firmly in the commuter residential category, with the added bonus of many pubs, restaurants, and some heritage features such as the restored water mill, and two windmills that are currently being renovated. The very active Skerries Sailing Club welcomes visitors.

The River Boyne at Tom Roe's Point, below Drogheda

Newgrange

North from Skerries, the old drying harbour of **Balbriggan** is awkward of approach and offers no convenient berth. From here a ten-mile sweep of sandy shore is interrupted by the projecting breakwaters where the historic River Boyne meets the sea. The river channel is regularly dredged, for the town of **Drogheda,** four miles up, is an important cargo port, and an anchorage can be found to one side within the river-mouth; but although the river is peaceful and pretty, finding an alongside berth that is both convenient and secure, in the town, might be difficult.

Which is a great pity, for just 10 km away is one of Europe's finest Neolithic monuments. Newgrange passage tomb is a large and complex structure that had astronomical, spiritual, religious and ceremonial importance, as well as being a place of burial. There is an excellent visitor centre, which explains that Newgrange was built before the Great Pyramids and Stonehenge, and that its passage has a calendar function, for sunlight penetrates to the chamber only on the shortest day. The opportunity for an invitation to see this in person is subject to a ballot!

The Historic River Boyne

On more than one occasion the banks of the Boyne have been the scene of events which shaped the course of history. In 1649, following the execution of King Charles I, the Marquis of Ormond was confirmed by the new king-in-exile, Charles II, as Lord-Lieutenant of Ireland. Although himself a Protestant, Ormond had achieved enlightened compromise agreements with Catholic landowners in the troubled years following the rebellion of 1641. After the king's execution, Ireland became a stronghold of Royalist support, and Oliver Cromwell, as Parliament's appointee as Lord-Lieutenant, personally led an expedition to secure its loyalty for the new Commonwealth. In September 1649 Cromwell led 14,000 men in an assault on Drogheda, then one of the most heavily-fortified towns in Ireland and under Ormond's orders to stand fast. The town fell after a day of heavy bombardment, and the Parliamentary troops, with orders of "no quarter" and fired by religious zeal, behaved with savagery; 2,000 of the defenders were killed, many in cold blood, in an atrocity that put the name of Cromwell at the top of the Irish list of historical hate figures from that day to this.

Forty-one years later and three miles upstream, the Franco-Irish army of Catholic James II and the Anglo-Dutch troops of Protestant William III met, with an outcome that was to be pivotal in the future of both England and Ireland and carve the name of the river and the date of 1690 indelibly in the folklore of Ireland's Protestant tradition. However the Battle of the Boyne – which actually took place on 11th July, new style, not the 12th – was pushed off the next day's front pages by the almost simultaneous defeat of an Anglo-Dutch fleet by the French navy at the Battle of Beachy Head. It is usually also forgotten that the Boyne was the first victory for the forces of the League of Augsburg, a grand alliance of nations against the territorial aspirations of James's strongest ally Louis XIV. The League had the support of the Pope.

Irish history is seldom as straightforward as it seems.

The old drying harbour at Port Oriel

Drogheda has all the facilities of a town of 30,000 people, and a large shopping centre a short walk from its quays.

On the north side of Clogher Head, the tiny harbour and pier at **Port Oriel**, dating from 1885, was greatly improved in 2007 by the addition of a substantial quay and breakwater, making it a thoroughly useful harbour and a convenient stopover close to the rhumb line course along the coast. It is also the base of a substantial fishing fleet, so can be crowded at times! Clogherhead village is a kilometre inland, and the general area is a popular seaside destination with fine beaches, golf courses and many caravan parks, so the local infrastructure is better than might be expected for an apparently remote stretch of coast.

The shallow and sandy bay of **Dundalk** has a winding and almost drying channel between old training walls to the town's quay, which still receives small cargo vessels. The north side of the bay is overlooked by the scenic Cooley Mountains, and beyond them by the higher and more massive Mountains of Mourne to the north-east of Carlingford Lough. The approaches to the Lough

Port Oriel, with the Cooley and Mourne Mountains in the distance

Clogher Head and Port Oriel

View north from Clogher Head towards Dunany Point

Albert Cashier

Albert Cashier, a native of Clogherhead, fought with General Ulysses Grant's army in the American Civil War, was taken prisoner but escaped, and after the war worked as a farmhand in Illinois. He spent his declining years in a Soldiers' and Sailors' Home, died in 1915 and was buried in his army uniform.

None of which would make an exceptional story for an Irish emigrant were it not for the fact that Albert was actually a woman, born Jennie Irene Hodgers. Several people discovered the truth during her life, but they all kept her secret safe.

should be negotiated with care, for as well as the Imogene Rock off Cooley Point, and the long and shallow Ballagan Spit, the southern approach via the Hoskyn Channel to the main channel is a dog-leg around a series of reefs and shallows; something of a pilotage exercise. The main ship channel to the ports of Greenore and Warrenpoint runs from the Hellyhunter buoy offshore and passes north of the extensive mid-channel Haulbowline rock, with its tall lighthouse. The tides run at up to five knots in the narrows, and its channel buoys have little dory-shaped hulls to cope with the current. The attractions of the lovely Carlingford Lough are decribed in the next chapter.

Carlingford Lough and Haulbowline lighthouse

The *Táin Bó Cúailnge*

The ancient story of the Cattle Raid of Cooley is a classic of Celtic mythology, and the plot has its roots in the perennial issue of female equality. Queen Medb (Maeve) of Connacht is not content because her prize bull, unhappy with being owned by a woman, has deserted to join the herd of her husband Ailill. Determined not to be outdone, Medb attempts to rent the only other bull of equal potency in Ireland, the famed *Donn Cúailnge*. When her agents admit that if they hadn't been able to lease the animal, they'd have stolen it anyway, the game is on.

The armies of Connacht and Ulster eventually fight a great battle over it, but in the early stages of the conflict the sole guardian of the Bull of Cooley is the young hero Cú Chulainn, who (with alternating help and hindrance from supernatural agencies) overcomes all odds until reinforcements arrive. Medb's army is forced to retreat, but manages nevertheless to capture the bull and take it back to Connacht. However the two bulls then fight, and the victorious but mortally wounded Bull of Cooley wanders home to die.

This classic story has many elements found in the mythology of other cultures (for example, the Labours of Hercules), and it can be traced back to the 8th century. Its name in Irish is approximately pronounced "Tawn Bo Coolinya".

Thatched houses at Clogherhead

The North-East Coast
Carlingford Lough to Fair Head

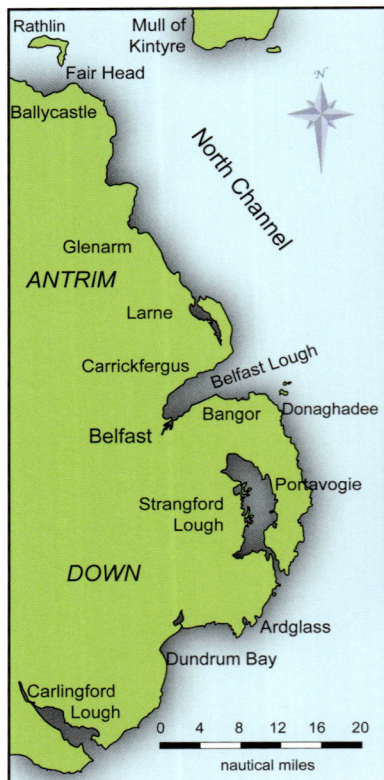

Effectively the eastern shore of Northern Ireland, this stretch of the Irish coast has four large and very different inlets, and great variety of scenery. Seen from a yacht cruising northward from the Dublin area, the impressive bulk of the Cooley and Mourne Mountains climbs out of the sea to dominate the view to the north and west, and makes a complete contrast to the low and largely featureless coast between Howth and Dundalk. The Cooleys rise to 590m (1,936ft) at Slieve Foy, and the Mournes to 852m (2,796ft) at Slieve Donard. After the dearth of natural harbours to the south, Carlingford Lough provides a welcome haven, though with a challenging entrance if tide and wind are opposed. The lough forms the boundary between the Republic and Northern Ireland, and is the only fjord on this coast; Strangford Lough is a submerged drumlin basin, and Belfast Lough is more like a ria, a drowned river valley. In different ways, the Ice Ages shaped them all.

Close north-east up the coast from Carlingford Lough is the crowded harbour of Kilkeel, with Northern Ireland's largest fishing fleet. The smaller fishing port of Ardglass, across Dundrum Bay, has a handy marina close to the rhumb line course.

Strangford Lough is a unique and delightful stretch of water, an inland sea studded with islands, and a Marine Nature Reserve treasured by all who take their recreation there. The fastest tidal streams in Ireland, at up to eight knots, are encountered in its entrance channel, and these streams have been harnessed for power generation.

The waters off the rocky coast of the Ards peninsula, between there and Belfast Lough, are a well-trodden path for leisure sailors and commercial shipping alike.

Puffins on the Isle of Muck, off Larne

The harbour at Portavogie is dominated by its fishing fleet, but Donaghadee has a good visitors' berth in its harbour. Belfast Lough is a fine stretch of open water, and a very busy sea-route. There are excellent marinas on either shore at Bangor and Carrickfergus, and there are now pontoon berths on the Lagan in the heart of Belfast itself. From here north to Fair Head, the coast of Antrim is cliffbound, with the busy ferry port of Larne at the entrance to its shallow lough. The beautiful Glens of Antrim, where the valleys cut into basalt escarpments, reach the sea in wide bays. The headlands become more dominant and the tides stronger until the corner is reached at Fair Head, a bold and unmistakable 190m (623ft) promontory looking across to the Mull of Kintyre and Rathlin Island.

The Bar Pladdy buoy, at the entrance to Strangford Lough

Passage Planning

In principle Ireland's east coast is sheltered from the prevailing westerlies, although the direct course from Howth to the South Rock buoy passes more than 20 miles from the coast at Dundalk Bay. Just like the coast to the south of Dublin, the main consideration when planning a passage through the North Channel is the tide, which becomes progressively stronger as one sails north, in contrast to the very weak streams between Howth and St John's Point. The transition to markedly strong tides takes place around South Rock, where the flow can exceed two knots; apart from a spurt at the Copelands, it remains much the same until north of Larne, when the rates progressively increase to over four knots at Torr Head, and up to six knots around Rathlin, where the sea can be

Bangor Harbour and Marina

Carlingford Marina

(Right and below) Carlingford Lough

turbulent. Strangford Narrows constitutes a tidal gate for all but fast power craft: catching a whole tide when going north out of Strangford Lough is a particular conundrum, for leaving on the first of the ebb means missing the first couple of hours of north-going tide outside. Leaving on the last of the ebb means plugging about three hours of foul tide, but this may be deemed worthwhile in order to get the full six hours through the North Channel. In any case, the key to a swift and successful passage around this corner of Ireland is to work the tides, particularly on the 35 mile stretch from the Maidens to Bengore Head, 12 miles west of Fair Head.

Carlingford Lough to Strangford Lough

Carlingford Lough has commanding scenery. It has been a commercial port for centuries, with first Carlingford village, then Newry at the head of its ship canal,

Carlingford Marina

Greencastle, Carlingford Lough

and now Warrenpoint and Greenore as the centres of operations, and the deep-water ship channel is buoyed and marked all the way to the head of the lough. The shallows on either side are used to grow shellfish, including the oysters for which the lough is famous.

A scatter of islets and reefs near the entrance shelters a useful passage anchorage at **Greencastle**. The charming medieval town of **Carlingford**, established before 1200 by the Norman invaders of Ireland, was an important fishing port and trading town until the war-torn 17th century, and the remains of its castles, mint, town gate, and friary may be seen. The old harbour and its approaches dry out, but there is a marina just north of the town. Carlingford Sailing Club, at the old harbour, is a hospitable place, and the town has excellent restaurants. The annual Carlingford Oyster Festival takes place over an August weekend.

At the head of the lough **Warrenpoint** nestles below the Mountains of Mourne. It developed as a port for the ancient town of **Newry** before the canal was built, and is now again the lough's chief port, handling RoRo ferries, container traffic, grain and general cargo, as well as being a holiday and residential town. Berthing

Carlingford harbour and castle

The Mountains of Mourne

is available for visiting yachts in summer in the Town Dock, a short step from the town's amenities. The Maiden of the Mournes festival takes place here during the second week in August. Two miles up-river from Warrenpoint, amid lovely wooded surroundings, the refurbished **Newry Canal** is entered at the Victoria Lock and continues a further four miles to the Albert Basin, where yachts can moor in the middle of town. Originally, the Canal reached Lough Neagh, 18 miles to the north, and was built to transport coal from the Tyrone coalfields to the port of Newry.

The coast to the north-east and the crossing of Dundrum Bay are dominated by the Mountains of Mourne, which really do, in the words of Percy French's famous song, "*sweep* down to the sea". The Mournes are visible in good conditions from Howth to Belfast Lough – a stretch of 80 miles and a fair day's sailing in anyone's book. The fishing port of **Kilkeel** offers an alternative landfall if the tide is ebbing hard out of Carlingford Lough, while the little harbour of **Annalong** is an intriguing stopover in settled weather. St John's Point is low but well marked by its distinctive yellow and black lighthouse.

Ardglass makes a very convenient port of call when on passage, as it is only a mile and a half from the Rockabill to South Rock rhumb line. Phennick Cove

The compact harbour of Annalong

Opposite: *(top) Warrenpoint*

(bottom) St John's Point and Slieve Donard, Northern Ireland's highest mountain

SS *Great Britain*

Brunel's revolutionary *Great Britain,* completed in 1845, was at the time the biggest ship ever built. As the first iron screw steamer, she was massively over-engineered, a feature which was to be the saving of her when she was only a year old. She left Liverpool for New York on 23rd September 1846, and her captain apparently mistook the then-new light on St John's Point, County Down, for the Calf of Man, and left it to starboard. Fortunate not to run on to the Cow and Calf rocks, the ship drove hard up on the beach in Dundrum Bay. Brunel later wrote to a friend:

I have returned from Dundrum with very mixed feelings of satisfaction and pain, almost amounting to anger, with whom I don't know. I was delighted to find our fine ship almost as sound as the day she was launched, and ten times stronger in character. I was grieved to see her lying unprotected, deserted, and abandoned by all those who ought to know her value and ought to have protected her. The result, whoever is to blame, is that the finest ship in the world, in excellent condition such that £4,000 or £5,000 would repair all the damage done, has been left lying like a useless saucepan, kicking about on the most exposed shore you can imagine, with no more effort or skill applied to protect the property than the said saucepan would have received on the beach at Brighton.

It took a year, and the combined ingenuity of Brunel and another great engineer, James Bremner, to refloat her, but she stayed afloat for another 90 years, and is now preserved as a museum ship in the drydock in Bristol where she was built.

Phennick Cove Marina, Ardglass

Marina, behind its own breakwater within the fishery harbour, has good facilities, and the attractive little town has supermarket, shops, and a good choice of restaurants and pubs. Like Carlingford, this was a Norman port established in the 12th century, and there are the remains of seven castles which may once have formed a defensive perimeter wall. The whole area, called Lecale, was a Norman stronghold, with its power base in Downpatrick.

Strangford Lough

Strangford Lough is a Marine Nature Reserve, and one of those places just made for messing about in boats – although without the crowds, the pressure on space, and the petty rules and regulations. Set amongst the gentle rolling hills of east Down, this is the boating nursery of Ulster, where sailors of all ages

St Patrick's Rock, between Ardglass and Strangford Lough

Ainmara of 1912 alongside the 99-years-younger pontoon at Strangford

enjoy cruising under power and sail, and where dinghy and one-design sailboat racing flourishes. The task of maintaining this idyllic environment is overseen by the Strangford Lough Management Committee, a voluntary body which represents all who use the lough and its immediate surroundings, and it takes an interest in the development of facilities, as well as the conservation of the local environment and habitat. This is not a highly developed waterway – for there no large marinas, few pontoons or boatyards, and no chandleries or yachtbrokers. It is in fact reminiscent of the boating environment of a generation or more ago. The modest marina facilities at Ardglass and **Portaferry** provide well-placed points of departure at either end of the lough's challenging entrance channel. Portaferry has an excellent small marina, and **Strangford** village, on the western

Strangford

Islands and Pladdies

The scenery of eastern County Down is characterised by *drumlins*, a word which (along with *whiskey*) is one of the few that English has derived from Gaelic; in this case 'little ridges'. Strangford Lough is the underwater part of this landscape, where only the tops of these low hills of boulder clay, the detritus of the last Ice Age, remain above sea level. They form about 60 islands, many of baffling similarity. Those which do not rise above the high water mark are known as *pladdies*, in this case a Norse word: 'flat islands'. The pladdies of Strangford Lough are boulder shoals, rising – usually gradually and ringed by weed – from deep water. There are at least 40 of these; the pladdies and other dangers are marked by 41 pole beacons which are maintained with great dedication by the lough's eleven sailing clubs. Many of the pladdies provide haul-outs for the lough's population of seals; the lough's voluntary Code of Conduct imposes a five-knot speed limit when close to shores and pladdies.

As in Clew Bay, it is often claimed, invariably by a man on a bar stool who has never taken the trouble to count them, that there are 365 islands in Strangford Lough.

Strangford Narrows

The Vikings named it *Strang-fjord*, strong inlet, surely for its sluicing tide, and the older Gaelic name of *Cuan* points to the apt comparison with its namesake in Argyll. On a spring tide, 400 million tonnes of water pass through the channel – locally known as The River – in six hours, reaching a speed of eight knots and creating the Routen Wheel, one of Ireland's only two named whirlpools. Entry during the flood is seldom a problem, but an unaccustomed 13 or 14 knots over the ground may call for sharp pilotage.

The ebb is a different matter, for standing waves where the mass of moving water meets the Irish Sea are no joke, and in a fresh onshore wind may be dangerous. Departure timing is important! The entrance is well marked and lit, and by day – and with care – there are minor channels which avoid the worst of the tide.

Since 2008 the channel has been the site of a one-megawatt tidal generator, with two rotors well underwater mounted on a concrete pillar conspicuously painted red and black as an Isolated Danger. Concerns that it might be more of a danger to the seal population have been addressed by tagging large numbers of them, and not only has the exercise been reassuring but it has also revealed that – rather like the lough's sailors – they spend long weekends away in Dublin Bay and the Isle of Man.

The constriction imposed by the Narrows also has the result of delaying high and low water in the body of the lough to two hours later than on the coast outside.

Angus Rock beacon, in the entrance to Strangford Lough

shore opposite, offers a visitors' pontoon berth for half a dozen yachts. Both villages have pubs, restaurants including the acclaimed Cuan at Strangford, and food stores. North of Strangford is the popular anchorage of **Audley's Roads,** now somewhat taken up with moorings. The main channels in the body of the lough are straightforward in daylight, and eleven new beacons and buoys were installed in 2011, allowing safe passage by day or night to Killyleagh, Whiterock and Kirkcubbin. The minor channels of the Quoile River and Ringhaddy Sound remain unlit, but are daymarked.

The **Quoile** was once navigable almost to the county town of Downpatrick, but the construction of a flood-control barrage in 1957 imposed a new head of navigation at Castle Island, where the headquarters of Quoile Yacht Club now stand. It is a pretty and sheltered corner of the lough. The club welcomes visitors,

Opposite: (top) the ferry leaves Portaferry for Strangford across the Narrows

(bottom) the Quoile, contender for the world's slowest pace of life

The SeaGen tidal generator at Strangford

The classic Nicholson 32 **Courante** *in Strangford Narrows*

Audley's Tower and Audley's Roads

Houses and Castles

Strangford Lough is ringed by fine houses and antiquities. The 18th-century Castleward with its gardens and the 15th-century Audley's Tower, both overlooking Audley's Roads, are run by the National Trust, which also manages Mount Stewart, north of Greyabbey and accessible by bus from Portaferry or Kirkcubbin. The garden of its 98-acre estate is described by the Trust as "one of the most inspiring and unusual" in its care. Delamont Country Park is a short walk from Mullagh Quay in the Quoile. The remains of Nendrum Abbey, sacked by the Vikings in 974 AD, stand on Mahee Island, which also has ruins of buildings dating from 450AD, and the remains of a tide mill, an interesting rarity. Mahee, Sketrick, Castle and Don O'Neill Islands have fortified remains.

has all-tide short-stay pontoon berths for a few boats, and visitors' moorings.

Killyleagh was once a commercial port, shipping the produce of the farmland that surrounds the lough. Its Yacht Club and anchorage are close south of its now-silted harbour, and the town has shops, restaurants and pubs. East Down YC has a landing pontoon a mile to the north inside **Island Taggart.** The sheltered channel of **Ringhaddy Sound** is one of the most popular mooring spots in the lough, and for many years has been a popular base for cruising yachts. Strangford Lough Yacht Club is in **Whiterock Bay**, with pontoon landing facilities. A mooring is normally available and the clubhouse has food and drink on offer most days in summer. Down Cruising Club, in the next inlet to the north, is best known for its ex-lightship clubhouse – the *Petrel* of 1917 – permanently moored in **Ballydorn** since 1968. Alongside her is the club's pontoon, with shore power, diesel (for members and visitors to the lough only) and water. Between Whiterock and Ballydorn and bridged to the shore is **Sketrick Island**, on which is Sketrick Marine Centre – chandlery, sail loft, and sailing school – and the acclaimed Daft Eddy's pub and restaurant. The eponymous Eddy was a smuggler of two centuries ago who met his end in a gun battle with the Revenue men.

Kirkcubbin is the only anchorage on the east side of the lough north of the narrows. There is an active sailing club, and the bay, although exposed to the west, has been made safely accessible by new buoyage. Further north is **Newtownards** Sailing Club, at the northern limit of navigation. It has some visitor moorings

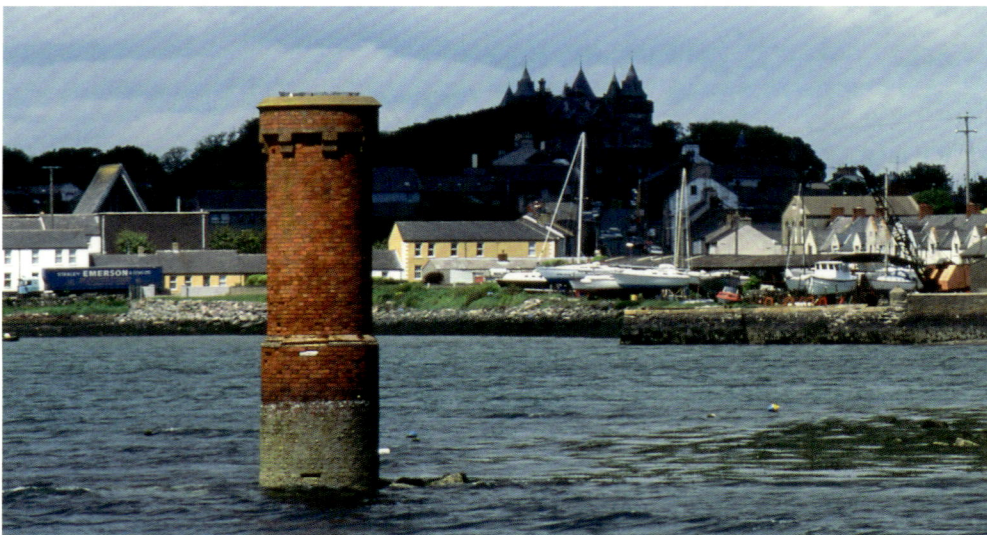

The beautiful Mount Stewart was the home of Castlereagh, possibly the most hated politician in British history. In 1845, while spending £150,000 on its renovations, its owners the Londonderrys gave £30 to famine relief. But its gorgeous gardens date only from the 1920s

Opposite: *Strangford Lough YC at Whiterock Bay. A new clubhouse replaced this 1930s building a few years ago*

The Town Rock beacon at Killyleagh now has a directional light atop

Ringhaddy Sound

useful for a visit to Mount Stewart.

Strangford Lough appeals to more than leisure sailors – birds and fish abound, and the whole area is a wildlife reserve, and an important sanctuary for migratory birds. There are around 130 species on record, and half the world's population of Brent geese winter here. Castle Espie Wildfowl and Wetlands Centre, not far north of Whiterock, is worth a visit by road. Underwater are some species unique to these parts, including soft corals, sponges, starfish and horse mussels – but unless you dive, the best way to see them is to visit Exploris, the superb aquarium at Portaferry.

The Ards Coast and Belfast Lough

The 32-mile coastal passage from Ardglass to Bangor can be broken by anchoring in **Knockinelder Bay,** three and a half miles north of Strangford Bar, or **Ballywalter Bay**, eleven miles north; or alongside in Donaghadee Harbour, just six miles short of Bangor. **Portavogie**, almost at the halfway point on this passage, is a secure harbour, but can be a busy one because of its fishing fleet.

South Rock Lighthouse

South Rock lighthouse, designed and built by Thomas Rogers at the behest of Lord Kilwarlin to help reduce the number of wrecks on this treacherous coast, was completed in 1797, and operated for eighty years. The idea was sound and the construction of the lighthouse was superb; indeed it was so well built that it is thought now to be the oldest wave-washed lighthouse tower in the world.

The tower is sixty feet high, with the bottom twenty of solid masonry. The entrance door is thus twenty feet up from the rock, and there are two further floors above that. Until 1820, when cottages were built on the coast nearby, the lighthousekeepers' families lived here too, with all water and supplies brought by boat from the shore. In the lighthouse the kitchen cupboards still exist, as does the indentation in the seaward-facing window sill that served as a sink.

It was quite soon realised that the lighthouse was in the wrong place, as ships continued to run on to the North Rock and The Ridge which runs about three-quarters of a mile to seaward from the tower. Eventually, in 1877, it was replaced by a lightship stationed nearly two miles farther out to sea. Although some ships were still lost in foggy weather, the lightship proved to be so successful that the station lasted for 132 years.

The cost of maintaining a light vessel is high, and in 2009 the last one, the old red *Gannet,* was replaced by a buoy with nine-mile range. This displays the same Fl (3) R as did the lightship, but is powered by solar panels and two wave generators rather than *Gannet's* diesels.

In 1972 the copper and glass lantern was stolen from the South Rock tower, but the stone work, so cleverly set flush into the rock, is essentially perfect. Since the lantern was removed, cormorants have taken over, and the floors are covered with a deep layer of foul-smelling guano.

John Clementson

The South Rock – Ireland's first rock lighthouse, and Ireland's last lightship

The Lightships of Ireland

Ireland's first lightship was stationed off the mouth of the Liffey in 1735. By 1900 there were eleven lightship stations: the Daunt, near Cork; Coningbeg and the Barrels, at Carnsore Point; the Lucifer, Blackwater, South and North Arklow, Codling and Kish, on the banks off the east coast; and South Rock and Skulmartin, off County Down. By 1976 only the Coningbeg and South Rock remained, and now they are all gone, replaced by buoys and the Kish lighthouse. The South Rock was the last, in 2009.

Over the years one lightvessel foundered in heavy weather, another was run down by a cross-channel steamer and sunk, and a third was torpedoed. On 7 February 1936 the Daunt Rock lightvessel *Comet* dragged her anchors in a storm; in appalling conditions, Ballycotton lifeboat carried out a 79-hour mission and succeeded in rescuing all seven of the crew. One gold, three silver and four bronze medals were awarded to the lifeboatmen, and a painting of the rescue was chosen for the postage stamp issued to mark the 150th anniversary of the RNLI in 1974. The *Comet*, remarkably, survived; she was eventually sold in 1965 and became a 'pirate' radio station. Other rôles filled by former Irish lightships are as sail training vessel and now floating museum at Inveraray in Scotland, museum ship at Kilmore Quay, clubhouse for Down Cruising Club at Ballydorn, and floating restaurant on the Seine in Paris. It has not escaped the notice of astute purchasers that lightships have unusually thick hull plating, and tend to last a very long time.

The rescue of the crew of the Daunt Rock lightship in 1936

There are no facilities for leisure craft, but the harbour offers a welcome to those prepared to take it as they find it. **Donaghadee** has a picturesque harbour, originally built for the packet service to Portpatrick, 20 miles away on the Galloway coast, traffic that came to an end when the ships outgrew the harbours. Space for visitors is limited, but there is a dedicated berth just inside the south breakwater, below the lighthouse. The seaside town is a charming and busy place.

Portavogie

Cruising Ireland

Donaghadee Harbour

Opposite: *(top) Sunset over Belfast Lough*

(bottom) Carrickfergus Marina

The compact **Copelands Marina** occupies a flooded former quarry, snug and secure but with a tricky entrance, close south of Donaghadee harbour, Offshore, the **Copeland Islands** are an attractive place to explore in fair weather. **Chapel Bay** on Copeland itself is open to the south, but protected from moderate seas and swell by the rapid tide, the Magic Rocks and the Deputy Reefs. **Port Dandy** is a pretty cove on the west side. Donaghadee Sound is well marked, the islands are a Site of Special Scientific Interest (SSSI), and there is a bird observatory on Lighthouse Island. The islands' first lighthouse, marking the southern side of the entrance to Belfast Lough, was built here in the early 18th century and rebuilt in 1815, but replaced in 1884 by the present tower on Mew Island, further to seaward.

The important and busy seaway of **Belfast Lough** has been a yachting centre for a very long time. The Royal Northern YC was founded in 1824 with fleets here and in the Clyde, the Royal North of Ireland YC at **Cultra** dates from 1899, the Royal Ulster YC, famous as the club from which Sir Thomas Lipton issued his *America*'s Cup challenges, began life at Bangor in 1866, and Carrickfergus Sailing Club can trace its roots to the Rowing Club founded in the same year. The excellent marinas at Bangor and Carrickfergus provide or host a complete range of marine services, and with the city of Belfast a short distance away by train or bus, either harbour makes an ideal touring base or rendezvous for crew changes.

Carrickfergus Castle

BEWARE
Slippery surfaces
especially in wet or
frosty weather

Belfast Port

As a town of 50,000 people, **Bangor** has an excellent range of supermarkets, shops, restaurants and pubs. Across the lough, the historic town and castle of **Carrickfergus** were the seat of Norman power in Ulster in the 13th century. The castle, open to the public, is well worth a visit.

The industrial revolution gave 19th-century **Belfast** rapid growth and increasing prosperity, and it became a classic Victorian success story and Ireland's only real centre of heavy industry. Today the capital city of Northern Ireland lives by a more modern mix of activities, but is still Ireland's second busiest port with 5,500 vessel movements each year. Tourism is becoming vital to the city's economy, and the Harbour extends a welcome to yachts at pontoon berths in the Abercorn Basin, in the heart of what has been dubbed the city's Titanic Quarter. Belfast has two airports, and ferry connections to Cairnryan and Liverpool.

Belfast and its Shipyard

Starting as a marshy river mouth, Belfast's port experienced rapid development from 1785, and by the middle of the 19th century began to bear a close resemblance in plan to what is seen today. The first sizeable ship, *Comet*, was built in 1812, followed eight years later by the first steamboat, the 200-ton *Belfast*. By 1841 Belfast was a major port, and work began to create a new deep, straight channel. The spoil from the Victoria Channel became Queen's Island, to where the shipbuilding industry relocated. Edward Harland came to manage Hickson's shipyard in 1854; he was joined in 1857 by Gustav Wolff, and he bought the yard the following year. Harland & Wolff Ltd was incorporated in 1861, and would dominate the shipbuilding industry for the next century, becoming one of the main economic drivers of the city and the province. The yard employed 36,000 workers during World War II. Its iconic gantry cranes Samson and Goliath, built in 1969 and 1974, dominate the skyline of Belfast Harbour.

Today Harland & Wolff repair ships, build wind and tidal turbines, and continue to accept challenges in heavy engineering.

Opposite: *Bangor Marina*

The passenger tender **Nomadic**, *now preserved in Belfast, was built by Harland & Wolff in 1911 to service the* **Titanic** *and her sisters at Cherbourg*

Black Head

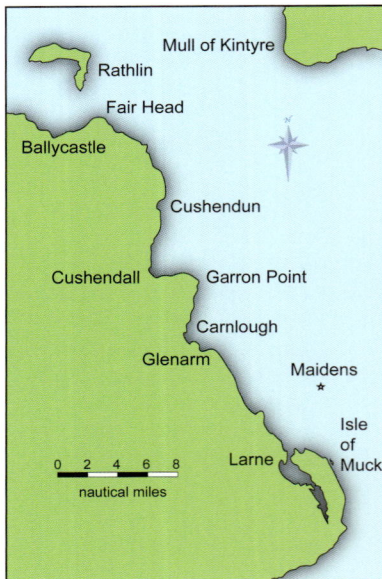

The Antrim Coast

From Black Head to Fair Head and beyond, the coast is dominated by the lovely hills, cliffs and glens of Antrim. The characteristic escarpments begin with Cave Hill, overlooking Belfast Lough, and continue almost unbroken for 55 miles to the Causeway Coast. On this coast, thanks to powerful tides, a speed over the ground of seven to ten knots is possible under sail. This makes a leg from, say, Bangor to Rathlin or Ballycastle, or to Sanda or Campbeltown, achievable in one tide, but there are six or seven places, including a marina at Glenarm, to break the journey.

Black Head marks the northern side of Belfast Lough. Near here the Gobbins cliffs were exploited in 1902 by railway developer Dean Berkeley Wise who created the Gobbins Cliff Path; three miles of dizzying paths, tunnels and bridges which gave Victorian and later tourists a good reason to take the train to nearby Whitehead. Closed at the time of writing, it is to be hoped that the path will reopen.

Island Magee is not in fact an island but the peninsula enclosing Larne Lough. On its north-eastern corner is the tiny and cliffbound **Isle of Muck**, joined to the shore by a drying spit of sand and boulders. This provides shelter from wind and swell — from north or south as required, both bays are usable — and convenient anchoring depths on a sandy bottom. The island is a nature reserve with one of the largest colonies of cliff-nesting seabirds in Northern Ireland. Kittiwakes, guillemots, fulmars and razorbills all breed here. You may also see a

The Islandmagee "massacre"

Many sources report that in 1642 the Scottish troops based at Carrickfergus threw the entire population of Islandmagee off the Gobbins cliffs. The death toll is variously reported at anything up to 3000, although 300 is a more often-quoted figure. However an "Inquisition" into the matter soon afterwards revealed that very few were killed, and only one person – a local girlfriend of a Scottish soldier – threw herself off the cliffs. The original depositions are in the Library of Trinity College Dublin. There had been "an incident" but it was relatively minor compared to the often-suggested allegation that the whole or even most of the native Irish "had been driven over the cliffs". The Magee clan did survive, but many moved away because there had been animosity, culminating in a number of murders, between some Scottish settlers and the native Irish. Of the few people found guilty of murder and – as we would now call it – terrorism, some were flogged, some were sent to "Barbadoes", and a very few were executed.

- Hugh P. Kennedy QC, direct descendant of the Magees of Islandmagee.

The Gobbins

Landing on the Isle of Muck

peregrine falcon, puffins, otters, and seals. Access is restricted to members of the Ulster Wildlife Trust, who manage the island. However, landing is a hazardous business, as the intruder is immediately attacked by the gulls, and the best and safest way to see the birdlife is to tour the cliffs by dinghy.

The busy port of **Larne** was one of the first in the world to commercialise roll-on, roll-off transport when in 1948 a pioneering service to Preston was set up with a war-surplus tank landing ship. The port has no facilities for yachts but the hospitable East Antrim Boat Club can usually find a mooring for a visitor at

East Antrim Boat Club's anchorage at Larne

The Antrim Coast

the yacht anchorage south of the RoRo berths, and the ambience of the shallow Lough, beyond the industrial environment of the Port, is pleasantly rural. What Larne does of course offer is excellent transport connections, by train or bus to Belfast, and by sea to Troon, Cairnryan and Fleetwood.

Brown's Bay is a sheltered north-facing bay just east of the port entrance, a handier spot for a short stop whilst on passage, and **Ballygalley Bay** is an open bay and occasional anchorage four miles north of Larne.

The very convenient marina at **Glenarm** is almost exactly halfway between Belfast Lough and Ballycastle or Campbeltown. The picturesque village has shops, cafés and pubs. Its castle has been the seat of the McDonnell Earls of Antrim for 400 years; the estate runs an organic farm, and the castle is also used for functions. The walled garden and tearoom are open daily in summer, but the castle itself is open to the public only occasionally.

(Below) **Princess Victoria** *was one of the earliest RoRo car ferries* *(Bottom)* **RNLB** Sir Samuel Kelly*, preserved at Donaghadee*

Princess Victoria

On the morning of 31 January 1953, in a storm force northerly wind, the ferry *Princess Victoria* left the Scottish port of Stranraer. North of Loch Ryan, as she turned south-west for Larne, the low, simple, manually-operated gates at the after end of her vehicle deck were forced open by breaking seas. Free-surface water on board had inevitable consequences; listing and Not Under Command, she first requested the assistance of tugs and then signalled distress.

Rescue operations were hampered by poor visibility, communication difficulties and errors in reporting the ship's position as she crabbed westwards, her radar disabled by the list but her engines still running to hold her bows northwards into the wind, sea and slackening tide – 'not under command' had been fatally misconstrued by the rescuers as meaning 'without power'. The spring tide turned against the wind about 1230, worsening her plight; her engines failed and by 1358 she was on her beam ends, five miles north-north-east of the Copelands. She sank at 1400. Donaghadee lifeboat rescued 31 people, but 133, including Captain James Ferguson, died.

The storm was one of the worst natural disasters to strike Europe during the 20th century. 91 more people were lost at sea around the UK, and the following day a huge storm surge flooded the southern shores of the North Sea, killing 1,835 people in Holland and 307 in England.

The design of the *Princess Victoria* was held to blame for her fate, but in her favour it must be said that – in much worse weather – she stayed afloat four hours longer than the likewise ill-fated *Estonia* or *Herald of Free Enterprise* in the 1980s. The same lifeboat *Sir Samuel Kelly* was based briefly at Courtmacsherry in County Cork 26 years later, and from there she rescued ten survivors of the disastrous Fastnet Race of 1979.

Glenarm Marina

Before Glenarm Marina was developed, the old harbour at **Carnlough** was the usual staging post; a charming place, if a little prone to silting. The village has good pubs and shops. **Red Bay**, at Cushendall, and **Cushendun Bay** to the north, offer anchorage in offshore weather, and Red Bay has visitors' moorings. Glenariff Forest Park and its Waterfall Walkway are gloriously scenic, but at three miles away up the glen from Cushendall, planning and a taxi ride are needed.

Carnlough Harbour

Carnlough Harbour

Fair Head, Torr Head in the distance

The last few miles to Fair Head are the most spectacular on this coast, and at Torr Head the tide can reach four and a half knots. The conspicuous former coastguard lookout and Lloyds Signal Station stands atop the cliffs of this small promontory, and was well sited to observe all the North Channel traffic, as the Kintyre coast is just 12 miles away. The Station was established in 1822 and abandoned in the 1920s. A close look at the chart will reveal **Murlough Bay**, midway between Torr and Fair Heads where the cliffs reach 220 metres in height. This is a spectacular temporary anchorage in settled weather or gentle offshore winds, and just out of the tide.

Working the Tides...

Under the circumstances we cried "halt" and edging into the shore, south of the narrows, dropped the hook in an eddy pool and took life easy. It was agreed to remain here quietly till the water underneath us was going horizontally in our direction, and the water above had ceased to come down vertically. Eddy pools are fascinating places and are only found with care and are to be treated with respect. With a tide running through a narrow channel and indented coast line there are places where the current will spring off the point of a small bay and run for a hundred yards with the main stretch, then turn and flow slowly in a circle back to the point. Inside this area is a place of calm and rest where a good ship may spend six hours of that tide in peace, and see the roaring current rushing past some few yards out. But when the tide turns this same spot will very likely be the centre of some most disturbed water where no one would think of anchoring.

Brendan Maguire, "Maid of York", ICC Annual 1952

The profile of Fair Head, with its fluted dolerite cliffs at the top and its jumbled scree at the foot, is unmistakable. There is deep water right up to the shore, so a close approach is possible – even at the risk of vertigo or at least a crick in the neck. This is the 190m (623ft) north-eastern cornerstone of Ireland.

...and Watching the Sky

The sailor lives under an inverted bowl of which the floor is the sea; seven-eighths of what he looks at is sky. Even on days of settled weather it is constantly changing. We had set out that morning under a blue sky with a few fair weather cumulus. A white wall of cloud, a hand high on the western horizon, slowly approached and grew higher, a little front coming through. As it grew overcast, shafts of light played on the islands. The sun was setting up his backstays, and the water alongside looked like black Guinness. It rained for long enough to make Henry on the helm reach for his cap, then the sun came out again to glint on every wave on scarps, ridges and valleys, scalloped and chased, which constantly formed and disappeared. The wind was no more than a gentle zephyr, the swell beginning to die.

Wallace Clark, Sailing Round Ireland, 1976

The North Coast
Fair Head to Bloody Foreland

Racing on Lough Swilly, the north coast's most active sailing centre

Eider ducks breed along this coast

The rhumb-line course from Fair Head round Malin Head to Bloody Foreland is just eighty miles, yet this is a coast of great variety, stunning scenery and many superlatives. It has Ireland's most famous rock feature, the Giant's Causeway, and her most remote island community, Tory. It is a world hot spot for basking sharks, and with its many wrecks, a magnet for divers. A coast of two halves: the tideswept Sea of Moyle, between this coast and the southernmost Hebrides, is often placid but can also be turbulent, while offshore to the west of Malin Head the ocean swell prevails. In the east, the cliffs and sandy bays are broken by just one large inlet, the wide and shallow Lough Foyle; in the west, the coast is deeply indented by the splendid Lough Swilly, Mulroy Bay and Sheep Haven, and sprinkled with many more offshore rocks and islands. The coast calls for careful passage planning, particularly in the rounding of Malin Head. Fast passages can be achieved, but the slow ones, taking in the many

Portrush

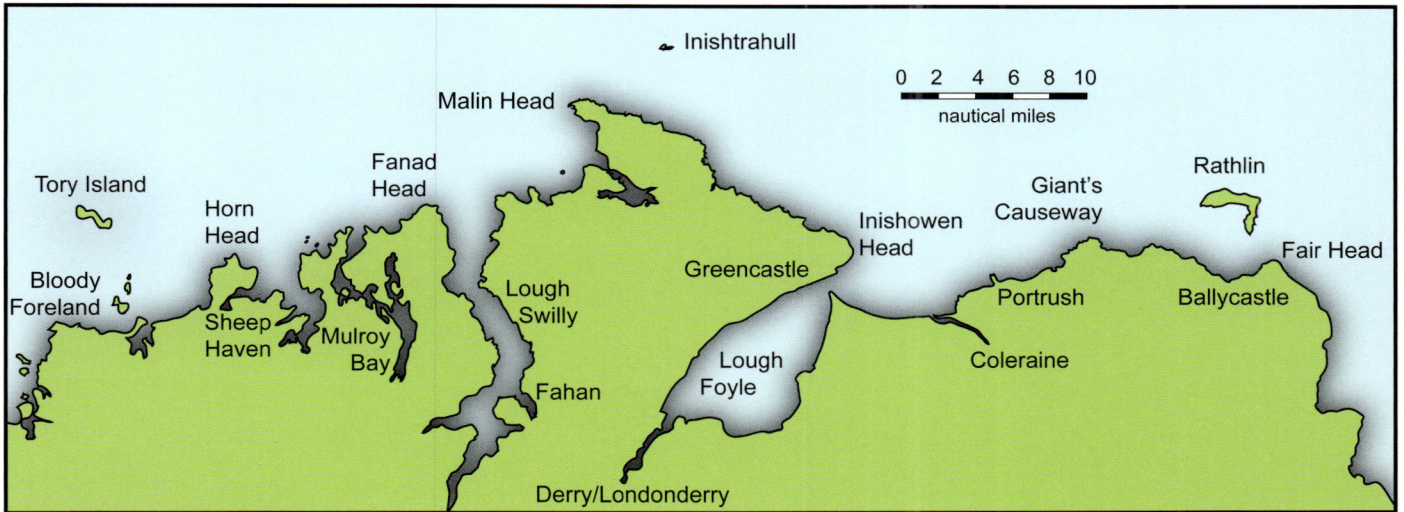

and varied havens of the coast, are usually more rewarding. There are marinas at Ballycastle, Coleraine and Fahan, and excellent pontoon facilities at Rathlin Island, Portrush, Derry, and Rathmullan in Lough Swilly. Derry, Coleraine and Portrush have good rail and road transport connections with Belfast, and bus services link Derry with the Donegal coast. City of Derry Airport has flights to destinations in Ireland and Great Britain.

The coast has many classic tourist attractions: apart from the Causeway, north Antrim has the birdlife of Rathlin, the famous Rope Bridge at Carrickarede and the celebrated Bushmills Distillery. The historic city of Derry, or Londonderry, has much within its ancient Walls to fascinate the visitor, and there are several renowned championship golf courses within easy reach of this coast.

Passage Planning

The crossings from Scotland are short: Rathlin is just twenty miles from Port Ellen in Islay or the anchorage at Sanda off Kintyre. From Crinan in Argyll's cruising heartland to Inishtrahull is 70 miles, either through the Strait of Corryvreckan

The Mull of Kintyre (above) and Altacarry Head on Rathlin (below) are only twelve miles apart.

The snug anchorage of Portmore, Inishtrahull

Rathlin Harbour

The north coast is a habitat of basking sharks

Opposite: (top) The Giant's Causeway

(bottom) Malin Head and the Garvan Isles at sunset

Tory Island

and west of Islay, or via the Sound of Jura. The latter passage is an interesting tidal exercise, for the first six hours of the passage to Ireland will be with a south-going tide from Crinan, followed by six hours of west-going tide from Islay to Inishtrahull. Getting on that conveyor can make for a very fast crossing!

Given the choice, it will pay to have favourable tides even for the shorter coastal passages, particularly from Fair Head to Bengore Head, and between Lough Foyle and Malin Head. Rathlin Sound has a six-knot tide at springs. To the west the tidal regime is more benign, mostly a knot or less when coasting; slightly faster further offshore. The ship channel and narrows of Lough Foyle are best taken with the tide, and the successive sets of narrows of Mulroy Bay are a tidal study in themselves.

Ballycastle Marina

Dulse and Yellow Man

Ballycastle's Lammas Fair is renowned for two specialities: dulse – elsewhere in Ireland known as *dillisk* – is the dried form of the edible red seaweed *Palmaria palmata*, and Yellow Man is a crunchy honeycomb sweet made from butter, golden syrup, brown sugar and vinegar, with baking soda skilfully added at a critical stage to produce the bubbles. The two delicacies have been immortalised in song:

Did you treat your Mary Ann to some dulse and Yellow Man,
At the Ould Lammas Fair in Ballycastle-O?

Dulse (left) and Yellow Man

Opposite: *(top) The Manor House overlooks Rathlin Harbour*

(bottom) Seabirds crowd the cliffs of Rathlin. The colonies of puffins, guillemots and razorbills draw thousands of visitors to the island

Fair Head to Portrush

From the east, the cliffs of Fair Head form a dominant foreground to a vista that includes Bengore Head twelve miles away, and the distant outline of the hills of Inishowen and the cliffs of Glengad Head. To the north is the characteristic profile of Rathlin Island, and on the horizon Islay and Jura; astern the peaks of Arran tower beyond Kintyre.

Ballycastle is a busy market town and the largest in this corner of Ulster. The names of Colliery Bay and Pan Rock on the chart give a clue to its surprising industrial history; in the 17th and 18th centuries, this was the centre of Ireland's coal and salt production. Mines were dug into the cliffs below Fair Head, a tramway was built to haul the coal, and also a harbour, now long vanished but commemorated in the name of Boyd's Wall, the eastern marina breakwater. Ballycastle later developed as a seaside resort, and today is best known for its traditional Lammas Fair, held on the last Monday and Tuesday of August. The marina is a good base for exploring the surrounding countryside, including Bushmills and the Causeway. The walk to the summit of Fair Head, about three miles, demands fitness and a head for heights, culminating as it does in the descent and ascent of the Grey Man's Path, a canyon slicing through the cliff face.

Rathlin is Northern Ireland's only inhabited offshore island and has a population of around a hundred. Six miles long and a mile wide, the island is home to the RSPB Seabird Centre, at its western end. The harbour, once just a

Bruce and the Spider

Legend has it that about 1305, having suffered many setbacks in his guerilla war against the English, the Scottish leader Robert Bruce was in hiding in a cave on Rathlin Island. There he was inspired by a doggedly persistent web-building spider to have one more attempt, a course that was to be crowned with success when, as King Robert of Scotland, he led his armies to victory at Bannockburn in 1314.

Sadly, the story is probably a myth. It didn't appear in print until 500 years later, and different versions put the cave in various parts of Scotland, or don't involve a cave at all. Similar stories have been told of other leaders including the biblical King David. What is not in doubt is that the Bruce empire spanned the North Channel – Robert's brother Edward had himself crowned King of Ireland at Carrickfergus in 1315, and remained powerful until his defeat and death three years later. Nor can anyone dispute the fact that Bannockburn copper-fastened Scottish independence for the next 300 years.

Bull Point, Rathlin Island (above) has an unusual 'upside-down' lighthouse, with the light (below) at the bottom of the tower

Rathlin's Prehistoric Axe Factory

Rathlin has some unique geology. The capping of basalt lava lies on top of chalk, which is exposed on the south shore. At Brockley, near the centre of the western limb of the island, there is a cave where Neolithic porcellanite stone axes were made. Porcellanite is an extremely hard rock capable of sustaining a sharp edge and taking a high polish. Axes made from it were highly desirable and there appear to have been only two localities where it was found – the other is at Tievebulliagh near Cushendun. The axes from Cushendun and Rathlin were exported across the whole of Ireland and Britain at some time between 4,000 and 2,500 BC.

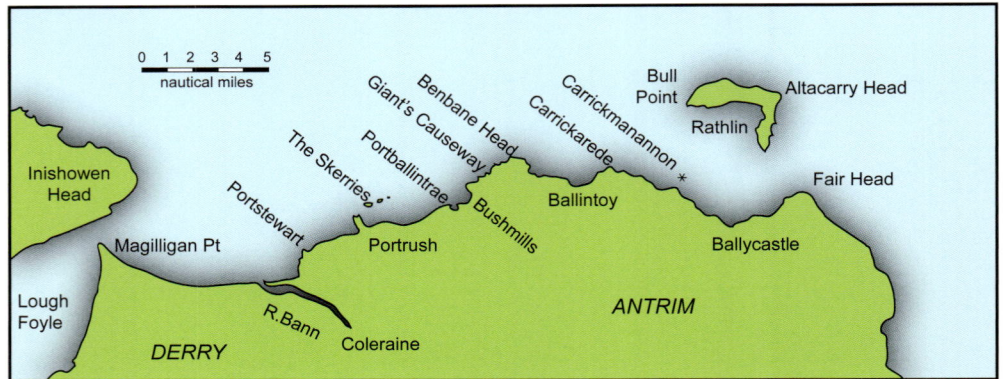

jetty in an open bay, is now well protected by rubble breakwaters, and the pontoon is a popular port of call for cruising yachts. Rathlin has a pub, a restaurant and a small shop and tourist information centre, and bikes are available for hire. A ferry service connects the island with Ballycastle.

The first essential in heading north-west from Ballycastle is to avoid the only-just-drying Carrickmanannon Rock. Named for the Celtic god of the sea, its most recent victim – in 2010 – was the Ocean Youth Trust ketch *Lord Rank*, which struck the rock and sank, fortunately without loss of life. The coast here is scenic and dramatic, but for the full experience the land tour is also required – particularly at Carrickarede!

Rounding Sheep Island – not too closely – opens up the entrance to **Ballintoy Harbour.** This is a pretty and photogenic place, and seethes with tourists on a fine summer day. The little shallow harbour, built for the export of coal and stone, is home to small leisure and fishing craft, and the anchorage in the bay can be subject to a sudden tide-engendered swell.

The anchorage off Ballintoy with Sheep Island beyond, and the white cliffs of Rathlin Island on the horizon

Ballintoy Harbour

The coast once had many salmon-fishing stations – tiny creeks and coves from where open boats went out to lay drift nets to trap the fish as they migrated along the coast to their spawning rivers. Port Moon, Carrickarede and Dunseverick were among these stations, and the name *Portbradden* itself means "salmon port".

The 111m-high Benbane Head marks the start of the spectacular cliffs and extraordinary rock formations surrounding the Giant's Causeway, a UNESCO World Heritage Site. The low-lying Causeway itself is hard to discern from seaward, although the dramatic rock features above – the Chimney Stacks, the Harp, the Organ and the Giant's Chair – are clear to see. This section of coast is mostly in the care of the National Trust, who maintain the coastal path which extends for 12 miles from the Giant's Causeway to Carrickarede.

The Causeway Coast

In the brave days of Celtic legend, the giant Finn MacCool built a causeway to Scotland to fight his rival Benandonner. But Benandonner used the causeway to cross to Ireland first. Caught unawares, Finn was hidden in a cradle by his wife Oonagh. When Benandonner saw the size of the 'baby' and tried a few of Oonagh's (literal) rock cakes, he thought better of his exploit and – terrified lest he meet the undoubtedly gigantic father – fled back to Scotland, tearing up the causeway as he went.

Alternatively, if you prefer a less romantic but equally remarkable version; almost all of County Antrim is a volcanic landscape composed of basalt lava flow upon lava flow, that erupted over 60 million years ago. Rising from the plains are occasional small hills that are volcanic plugs – the roots of volcanoes that fed the lava flows. Millions of years of erosion by rain, ice and wind have removed the upper parts of the volcanoes and much of the thickness of lavas, revealing the deeper levels. East of Portrush, the cliffs of Benbane Head display the internationally famous Giant's Causeway. It is identical in age and formation to the spectacular Fingal's Cave on the Hebridean Isle of Staffa. The black, vertically fluted cliffs are formed of several basalt lava flows which, on cooling, shrank and cracked to produce upright polygonal columns, similar to mud cracks produced by shrinkage in a drying-out lake bed. And this gives a clue as to the way these lava cracks were formed. When the thick lavas were cooling they were flooded by water which formed temporary lakes. This cooled the surface of the lava and the shrinkage cracks formed then worked their way down through the cooling lava. The actual Causeway columns are superbly exposed just above the tide line where they have been climbed over, painted and photographed by countless visitors. The columns are cut across by 'ball and socket' joints, regular horizontal saucer-shaped divisions created by shrinkage along the length of the column. The cooling proceeded from both top and bottom of the flow, as beautifully shown in the formation known as the Organ, and as can be seen in the cliff, the regularity is broken in the centre of the flow, where the upward and downward cooling cracks met. Easy to see, about half way up the cliff, is a break between two flows marked by a bright red two- or three-metre thick layer of soil, created by weathering of the flow beneath over a few thousand years before the next flow erupted. In quarries a few miles inland, the remains of plants and trees which grew in this soil can be seen.

Geological notes by Chris Stillman

Dunluce Castle. Many sources describe how in 1639 the castle's kitchens fell into the sea, taking seven people with them and leaving one person (variously described as a kitchen boy or an itinerant cobbler) sitting – presumably somewhat traumatised by the experience – in the surviving landward corner of the room

Opposite: *(top) Carrickarede, with its Rope Bridge*

(bottom) Benbane Head and the rock formations of the Giant's Causeway

The broad expanse of Bushmills Bay is followed to the west by **Portballintrae**, which looks – on the chart – like a cosy haven, but is subject to swell. Ashore, apart from a long-established hotel, there is little else except holiday homes. It is just over a mile inland to Bushmills village. A mile to the west and directly inshore of the Storks beacon, the clifftop Dunluce Castle is one of the most imposing historic structures on the Irish coast. It dates from the 12th-century Anglo-Norman period, but was based on an earlier fort. It was a constant focus of the disputes between feuding Irish and Scots clans, and amongst the Irish as well, a scene of bloody conflicts and sieges. It was abandoned in the late 17th century, but the ruins are maintained by the NI Department of the Environment, and the castle is open to the public all year.

The **Skerries** are a delightful group of little islands, a haunt of seals and seabirds, and although a port-hand buoy marks the safe channel offshore, Skerries Roads makes a lovely anchorage for a short stay, and Skerries Sound is deep, and wide

Basking Sharks

The north and west coasts of Ireland are world hot-spots for basking sharks. This is the second biggest fish in the sea, and typically reaches six to nine metres in length and five tonnes in weight. Formerly hunted for their liver oil, the sharks are now a protected species and have shown a recovery in recent years. They are not aggressive, but graze on plankton and other tiny organisms, cruising at about two knots just below the surface with their huge jaws gaping to filter their food. You will see them most easily in calm water – the blunt dorsal fin flopping from side to side, the tip of the tail breaking the surface as it swishes to and fro, and perhaps the snout creating a little bow-wave. They occur in groups, and one or two visible may indicate more underwater. Don't chase them or harass them – they are easily alarmed, but you may collide with one, which can be dangerous for both the shark and the boat. Take photographs and report sightings – for more information see www.baskingshark.ie. Basking sharks occasionally breach, leaping clear of the water – a rare and awesome sight.

Emmett Johnston, Irish Basking Shark project

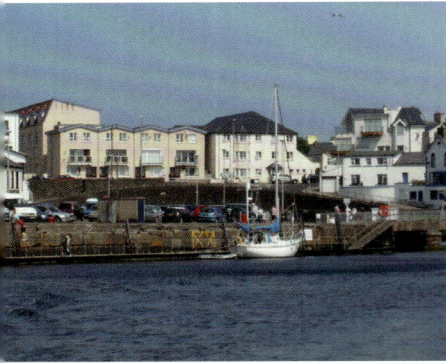

(above, right and below) Portrush. During a rescue operation in 2010 the Severn-class lifeboat **Katie Hannon**, pictured here, was swept on to the breakwater at Rathlin Island, and became a total loss. There were no casualties

The Spanish Armada

Among the many Armada wrecks around the Irish coast, the greatest loss of life was in the case of the *Girona*, which put in for repairs at Killybegs (then as now, an independent-minded place), collected the crews of two other wrecked Spanish ships and then headed north. Off the coast of what is now County Antrim her steering failed and she went ashore near Dunluce Castle with the loss of all but nine of the 1,300 aboard. The wreck of the *Girona* is a favourite site for divers, as is that of *La Trinidad Valencera*, which sank (slowly) in Kinnego Bay on the Inishowen peninsula of Donegal. Almost all of the 500-odd on board got ashore, where they were soon afterwards arrested and sorted into noblemen, officers and common seamen and soldiers. Most of the commoners were then immediately slaughtered, and 30 of the nobles and officers were ransomed.

Relics of the Armada may be seen in museums all around Ireland.

enough. **Portrush** is a cheery and busy town, its ambience a lasting legacy of the coming of the railway in 1855. At that time Belfast was a booming industrial city, and the little fishing village of Portrush developed into its seaside resort. The harbour, no longer used by commercial ships, is an excellent and convenient passage stop for cruising yachts, although the entrance can be exciting in strong west to north-west winds. There is a handy berthing pontoon, and diesel is available by hose. It is but a few steps into town, where there are the usual seaside delights. Royal Portrush Golf Club has two challenging links courses which can be used by visitors. Portrush Yacht Club, founded in 1894, is on the quay beside the harbourmaster's office, and there is a large restaurant complex nearby as well. PYC welcomes visitors, who can use the club facilities. You can pay your dues, have a shower, a drink, and a meal, all without leaving the harbour area.

Railway history was made when in 1883 the Giant's Causeway, Portrush

The Barmouth, where the Bann meets the sea. In this picture the river-water can be seen being swept eastwards by the flood tide. On the horizon is the Scottish island of Islay, 30 miles distant

and Bush Valley Tramway Company opened the world's first hydro-electric tramway. Running initially from Portrush to Bushmills, it was later extended to the Causeway. It derived its power from water turbines at the Walkmill Falls at Bushmills. The tramway closed in 1949. A heritage narrow-gauge steam railway still runs on the trackbed from Bushmills to the Causeway, but it is not as green as our Victorian forebears' invention!

Portrush to Lough Foyle

Two miles west of Portrush along a coast of low cliffs is the resort town of **Portstewart**, with a tiny harbour, and then a fabulous sweep of golden strand extends eight miles to Magilligan Point at the entrance to Lough Foyle. Two miles from Portstewart the Bann, Ulster's longest river, meets the sea. The river entrance is between stone breakwaters, simple to negotiate except in strong onshore winds. The well-marked channel leads to the port of **Coleraine**, five miles upstream. Just under a mile below the town, Coleraine Marina has 76 pontoon berths, with good shore facilities including fuel and a travelhoist; while Seaton's marina, a mile nearer the sea, has more rural surroundings. An opening railway bridge gives access to the commercial quay at the town, and repairs and chandlery are available. The comprehensive facilities of this busy university town make Coleraine a very useful port of call, and a snug berth in the river makes a good place to sit out adverse weather. Transport links are excellent.

West of the Bann the bold escarpment of Binevenagh overlooks the farmland and sand dunes of Magilligan, and Lough Foyle. An unmarked channel runs along

The Mussenden Temple

This conspicuous and iconic building on the clifftop between Castlerock and Magilligan, a copy of the Temple of Vesta in Rome, dates from 1785. It was built by Frederick Hervey, Earl of Bristol and Bishop of Derry, a fabulously wealthy, energetic and far-sighted man who also provided the district with many structures of a more functional nature, including the first bridge across the Foyle. The Temple, in the grounds of Hervey's mansion at Downhill, was a memorial to his young cousin Frideswide Mussenden (married, 31 years his junior, and with whom he was suspected of having a more-than-cousinly relationship). Mrs Mussenden died, aged 22, in 1783. Carved on its stonework, the building bears a rather heartless Latin quotation from Lucretius, which translates as:

"Lovely it is, when the winds churn the waves on the wide sea, to gaze out from the land on the great efforts of someone else."

The Temple, the Downhill demesne and the ruins of the once-grand house are cared for by the National Trust and are open to the public. The easiest access is from Coleraine.

Greencastle Harbour

the beach and inside the triangular Tuns Bank, while a more cautious course leads three miles offshore and round the Tuns buoy. Lough Foyle marks the boundary between the two jurisdictions, and its west shore is formed by the Inishowen peninsula of County Donegal. Across the narrows from Magilligan Point is the fishing and ferry harbour of **Greencastle**, the handiest stop-over on the coast here. The village is home to the National Fisheries College and the Inishowen Maritime Museum, and a car ferry crosses to Magilligan Point. There are shops, pubs and good restaurants, and the long-established McDonald's boatyard.

Lough Foyle is a wide expanse of very shallow water with a deep, dredged ship channel close to the west shore leading to the port of Londonderry. The commercial docks at Lisahally are 14 miles from the open sea, and the city centre is four miles further, with the last stretch wooded and scenic. The high-level Foyle Bridge spans the river at the city's northern outskirts.

Derry/Londonderry has seen much sectarian and political strife, and for many years was often in the headlines for the wrong reasons. But the city has an irrepressible energy, and has set about rebuilding a well-deserved reputation as an historic and cultural centre and a prime tourist destination. Its 17th-century city walls are the oldest intact example of such defences in Europe; walls that withstood the celebrated siege and survived to become a potent symbol of the divisions in its society. To paraphrase the writer H.H.Munro, Derry makes more history than it can consume locally. At the time of writing the city is scheduled as

Opposite: (top) Coleraine Marina, in the River Bann

(bottom) Greencastle Harbour and the coast reaching out towards Inishowen Head; Islay, Jura and Kintyre just visible on the horizon

Derry and/or Londonderry?

In 1613 the ancient Irish settlement of Derry – *Doire*, the oak-wood – as the site of a colony or "plantation" sponsored by the City and Guilds of London, was renamed *Londonderry*, and so it has remained to this day. The post office, the charts, the maps and road signs (at least in Northern Ireland), the Port and Harbour Commissioners and many other bodies all call it, officially, Londonderry. But in recent troubled times the "London" prefix became something of a flag, and it was often unofficially obliterated on road signs. The city has a substantial Nationalist majority, and so Londonderry is run by Derry City Council; the airport is officially City of Derry (but abbreviated to LDY); Ulsterbus services Londonderry and Bus Éireann runs to Derry, although their vehicles end up parked side by side in the same bus station; while a Unionist politician, in public, will be careful always to call it Londonderry.

But when politics are set aside, everybody just calls it Derry. The fact that the siege of the city in 1689, successfully defended for Protestant William III against the forces of Catholic James II, was a turning point in the political history of Ireland, gives the place a dilemma; a substantially Catholic and Nationalist city is iconic in a Protestant and Unionist tradition. But there are both Catholic and Protestant Bishops of *Derry*, and the anniversary of the siege is celebrated by Orangemen singing about guarding old Derry's walls.

Derry has developed a considerable talent for compromise, and this intractable conundrum of political semantics has been addressed by the adoption of the clumsy, but politically correct and non-controversial, expedient of labelling it as Derry/Londonderry.

Yachts from Lough Swilly, Lough Foyle and Coleraine race on the Foyle

__Opposite:__ The river winds from the Foyle Bridge up through the historic city of Derry/Londonderry

the finish of the 2012 Clipper Round the World Race, and has been nominated 2013 European City of Culture.

Its visitor berths are on a secure 200m pontoon at Queen's Quay, right by the rejuvenated riverside quarter, and close to the city centre, where there is much to see and do. Needless to say there is a wide choice of excellent shops, restaurants, pubs, museums and tourist attractions.

The Foyle pontoon at Queen's Quay in the city centre

Inishowen Head marks the entrance to Lough Foyle

Opposite: *(top) Inishtrahull*

(bottom) The anchorage at Portmore, Inishtrahull, with the old quay and sheerlegs crane built to service the lighthouse

Basking sharks, denizens of this coast, as they are typically observed

Inishowen and Lough Swilly

The rounding of Malin Head is usually the most demanding passage on the north coast, and Inishtrahull Sound is capable of generating its heaviest seas. This is also the breeziest corner of Ireland, with summer winds, on average, 25% stronger than those of Kerry. Good passage planning is the key, to take account of tides of up to three knots or more, and for a westward passage any moderate or fresh wind south of west will serve. In a modern, weatherly yacht, six or seven hours will suffice to complete the 50-mile passage from Portrush or Coleraine to Rathmullan, Fahan or Mulroy Bay.

The north-east-facing portion of the Inishowen coast is fronted by a line of rugged cliffs, rising to 260m (850ft) west of Glengad Head and broken by three sandy bays.

There are three available stopping places en route. The wide **Culdaff Bay** is bounded by rocky promontories, and these, together with the tide, help diminish the swell which tends to run in here. The anchorage is off the river mouth and the little pier at Bunagee, and the attractive village is a two-kilometre walk away. The area is popular for its beach, canoeing and surfing, but most of all as a diving and sea angling centre. Further north-west, the uninhabited **Inishtrahull** exerts a fascination for cruising sailors. Although just four miles offshore, it has

Greencastle

Racing drontheims alongside at Moville pier

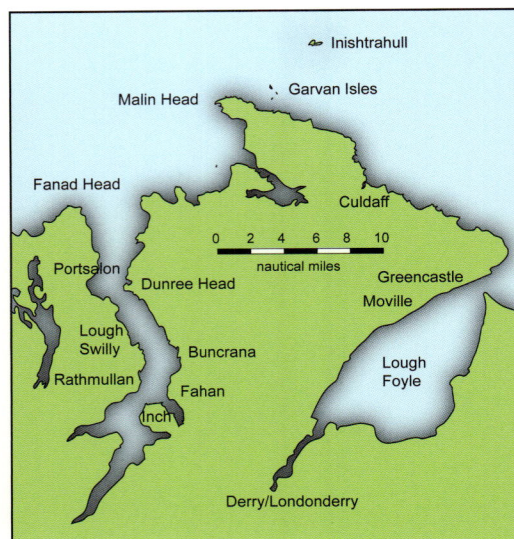

The Drontheim

With the exception of Tory Island which has its own unique style of currach, the traditional boats of Donegal and the north coast are clinker-built in wood, and double-ended. Many are still in use for inshore fishing, and small versions, traditionally yawl-rigged, are still being built and used for classic racing.

Most of these boats have come from the long-established yard of James McDonald and Sons of Moville and Greencastle. Like the McDonald family, the design of these craft can be traced to Scotland, but there are also close links to the style of Norwegian boats, hence the local name for them: "drontheim" or "dronthon" – a corruption of "Trondheim". Norwegian timber was often used for boatbuilding in Ireland, and boats were also imported from Norway in kit form.

an ineffable air of remoteness. The last of its people left the island in 1928, and the ruins of their houses and the school – with its poignantly misspelt nameplate "INISHTRHULL NATIONAL SCHOOL 1901" – still stand. Marking the northernmost point of Ireland, the island's lighthouse has always been important. The light of 1812, on the eastern summit, was replaced in 1958 by the slim concrete tower on the western one.

The rocks of the island are Lewisian gneiss, 1,800 million years old, the oldest in Ireland and the same as those of the Outer Hebrides and southern Greenland. Inishtrahull is a breeding ground of grey seals, seabirds and eider ducks, and has four red deer. **Portmore**, the small creek on its north side, provides an anchorage exposed only to the north-east – a relatively rare wind direction – and penetration by the Atlantic swell is mitigated by the tidal stream that rushes by.

Between the islets and reefs of the Garvans and the mainland shore, **Garvan Sound** is often the easiest and quickest route to Malin Head. **Malin Harbour** in Slievebane Bay is a good anchorage in offshore wind conditions, but is often subject to swell. Pubs, restaurant, supermarket and filling station are within walking distance. Malin Head weather station overlooks the pier, and Malin Head Marine Rescue Sub-Centre is a kilometre or so inland.

Ireland's North Point, with its conspicuous old signal tower, is two miles from here and a mile short of the shattered cliffs and stacks of the west-facing Malin Head itself. Here the view changes as the glorious vista of the coast to the west opens up: Dunaff Head, Fanad Head and Horn Head, and the distant summits

The red deer on Inishtrahull. The herd, which is not indigenous, was once larger but was culled because the deer were eating seabirds' eggs. This unusual diet was occasioned by the lack of any other source of calcium on the island

Grey seals on Inishtrahull

of Muckish and Errigal. The tide slackens, and the turbulence of the Sounds gives way to the long easy rhythm of the ocean swell. From here to Dawros Head, twenty miles beyond Bloody Foreland, stretches a wonderful and thrilling cruising ground of bold headlands, sheltered anchorages, intricate passages and islands large and small, peopled and deserted.

Close south of Malin Head the long inlet of Trawbreaga Lough offers no easy and safe shelter; it largely dries, and its west-facing entrance and shallow bar make it a dangerous place. The bold promontory of Dunaff Head seven miles to the south-west, and the lighthouse on Fanad Head opposite, mark the entrance to **Lough Swilly**. This deep, spacious and safe fjord was a strategic harbour for centuries, and it is surrounded by fortifications, from the prehistoric Grianan of Aileach on the hilltop south of Fahan Creek to six Napoleonic-era Martello towers, and gun emplacements dating from the First World War. Lough Swilly was one of the Treaty Ports, and the last one to be relinquished by the Royal Navy in 1938.

The navigable section of the lough extends from the open sea to just south of Inch Island, beyond which a channel meanders between wide drying mudbanks to Donegal's largest town of Letterkenny. The hazards in the lower lough are, by and large, close to shore and well marked, and the lough is the principal sailing centre on the north coast.

The holiday village of **Portsalon** is three miles within the Heads, and has

The Flight of the Earls

Following the Battle of Kinsale in 1601, the Ulster chief Hugh O'Neill, Earl of Tyrone, was briefly exiled before being pardoned by James I, on the King's accession in 1603. This attempt at reconciliation didn't work out, especially after the Gunpowder Plot of 1605 cast official suspicion on all powerful Catholics. O'Neill and his ally Rory O'Donnell, Earl of Tyrconnell, found their new terms of landholding under the Crown irksome, and in 1607, with about 90 followers, they sailed from Rathmullan in Lough Swilly for Spain. They hoped to return with a Spanish invasion fleet, but it was not to be. Tyrconnell died the following year and Tyrone in 1616. The "Flight of the Earls" was a watershed in Irish history, since it marked the final collapse of the old Gaelic aristocracy.

The Martello tower at Macamish Point on Lough Swilly

Malin Harbour, on Slievebane Bay

Cruising Ireland

The magnificent beach of Ballymastocker Bay, south of Portsalon in Lough Swilly

Rathmullan beach

Opposite: (top) Ireland's North Point and Malin Head

(bottom) Beneath the massive bulk of the Urris Hills, **Colleen Bawn** makes her way north past Dunree Head in Lough Swilly

visitors' moorings and a friendly pub and restaurant, but its bay is exposed to the swell which is broken further south by the jutting Dunree Head. **Macamish Bay**, on the west side, is a lovely spot with a beautiful little beach. The pier at **Rathmullan**, further south, has a 60-metre pontoon for yachts; the village buzzes with activity in summer and has good pubs and restaurants. On the east side Inishowen's largest town of **Buncrana** is trickier of access, but **Fahan**, where Lough Swilly YC is based, is only eight kilometres by road from Derry. Fahan Creek and the 140-berth marina are slightly restricted by tidal height, but secure in all weathers. The Yacht Club offers a warm welcome to visitors, and there are good restaurants and pubs in Fahan. Lough Swilly is a beautiful and relaxing place to explore, and the Knockalla Mountains and Urris Hills on either side offer splendid hillwalking.

Minke whales average 7 or 8m in length and are common around Ireland

Fahan Marina

224

The pontoon at Rathmullan

Macamish Bay

Lough Swilly to Bloody Foreland

After the rigours of Malin Head, the coast from Fanad Head to Horn Head is more benign, though still exposed to the north and west with many offshore rocks, few navigational aids, and an incessant swell. But it has two beautiful inlets, very different from each other and from Lough Swilly to the east.

Mulroy Bay is not really a 'bay' at all, but rather an inland sea like a miniature Strangford Lough – but without the yachts – and its beauty, tranquillity and its doubtless unusual ecosystem deserve to be more widely studied, appreciated and cherished. The entrance has a swift tide, and the sheltered water inside is scattered with islands and rocks. In contrast to the deep open water and plain sailing of Lough Swilly, this is a place for painstaking and satisfying pilotage, and has a dozen or more idyllic spots to drop an anchor in perfect peace. For many decades the entrance was inaccurately charted, based on very old information, and the visiting sailor had to rely solely on the ICC Directions: but following a new survey in 2006, the charts now show things as they are, and the channel has also been better marked, for the benefit of the ships serving the bay's fish farms.

For the sailor in a hurry, there are reasonable passage anchorages in the entrance bight. For those with time to explore, one, two or all three sets of Narrows may be negotiated. Beyond the First Narrows is the classic anchorage of **Fanny's Bay**, just a short walk over the hill from the holiday village of Downings on Sheep Haven. Beyond the Second with its new bridge – the clearance is nineteen metres – are **Bullogfeme**, **Carrick** and **Devlin Bays.** And beyond the Third is

Bullogfeme Bay, between the Second and Third Narrows of Mulroy Bay

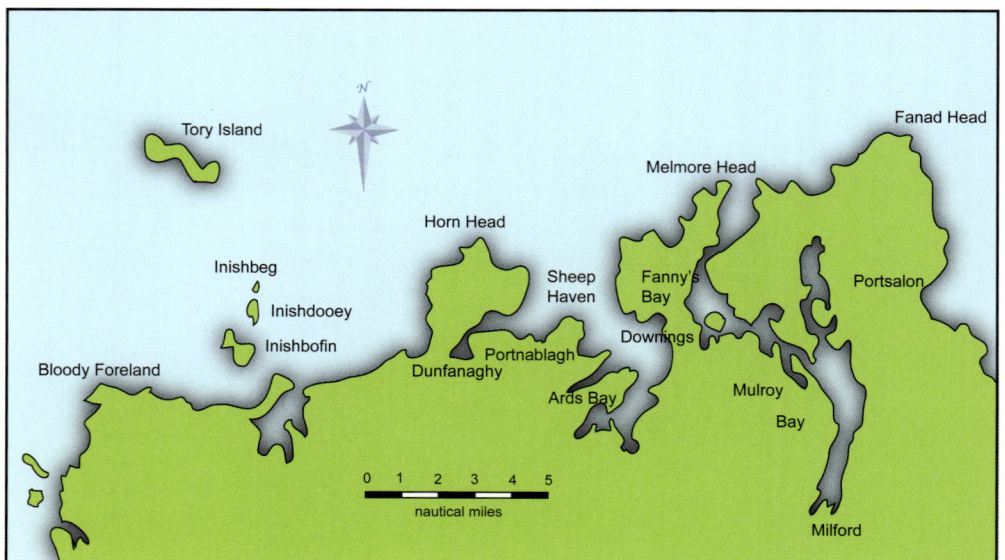

The Broad Water of Mulroy Bay is a very special place, deserving of better stewardship

the lovely **Broad Water.** It is hard to believe that the tortuous route amongst the ancient stone cairns marking the rocks was, until relatively recent times, followed by coasters serving the (now defunct) flour mill at Milford Quay at the very head of the waterway; and it is to be regretted that access to the North Water branch is barred for masted yachts by a low power cable.

Mulroy Bay is surrounded by a pastoral landscape, with not so much as a village on its shores, but for the small holiday complex of Carrowkeel on the Broad Water and the village of Milford two kilometres from its head. Milford has supermarkets, shops, pubs and a hotel. Much of the Bay is given over to fish farming, and both finfish cages and mussel lines will be encountered.

The Tides of Mulroy Bay

Mulroy Bay has an intriguing tidal regime. Imagine four open containers joined in series by three narrow pipes. Now half-fill the whole system with water, and lift the first container above the others. Water will flow reasonably quickly into the second container, and the rise in its level will cause a flow into the third container – but the further constriction will delay and limit the rise in level. Nevertheless, any rise in level in the third container will result in a flow into the fourth. But shortly after this begins, lower the first container below the level of the second. Now the flow is reversed from the second to the first; but water is still flowing from the third to the fourth. It takes quite some time before the flow at the third constriction is reversed.

Confused? Well might you be. But this is exactly what happens in Mulroy Bay every twelve and a half hours. The three sets of Narrows attenuate the tide – that is to say that they are not capacious enough, despite their best efforts, to allow the water levels in the Atlantic and in the Broad Water to equalise in the available time of six and a quarter hours. Their best efforts involve considerable tidal streams, up to six knots or more in the Narrows. But the rise and fall in the Broad Water, especially at neaps, is next to nothing. Of equal interest to sailors is the fact that – because of the progressive delay in the turn of the tide – it is possible to make one's way right up through the whole system on a slack tide.

There being no such thing as a free lunch, there is of course a catch. It is not so easy on the way out. A boat leaving the Broad Water and negotiating the Third Narrows on the second half of the ebb will find the tide already in full flood against her at the First. It is therefore necessary to compromise by leaving the Broad Water while the tide is still flooding quite rapidly through the Third Narrows, approaching slack at the Second Narrows, and ebbing at the First Narrows, to get out to sea with ample depth over the Bar. It all adds to the fascination of cruising on this coast, and Mulroy Bay is a beautiful place, not to be missed.

Muckish Mountain overlooks the anchorage at Downings in Sheep Haven

Opposite: *Horn Head, with Tory Island eight miles beyond*

From Mulroy's entrance at Melmore Head to **Sheep Haven** is a mere five rock-strewn miles, but keeping three-quarters of a mile offshore will ensure safe passage outside Frenchman's Rocks and Carrickguill's dangerous reefs. Sheep Haven is easy of access, ringed by beautiful beaches and overlooked – and partially sheltered – by the mighty Horn Head to the west, hence its popularity as a holiday area. It offers several anchorages, most of which are comfortable in south to south-west winds (and of course anything from the east), but as the wind veers to north-west, they become increasingly exposed. The possible exception is **Ards Bay,** tucked into the south-east corner beneath its Franciscan monastery and sheltered from all but the heaviest of weather, when even the swell from the south-west tends to be refracted to the innermost recesses of Sheep Haven.

Downings is a popular weekend resort, with restaurants and pubs, on a lovely sandy bay; there are visitors' moorings. **Binnagorm** and **Marble Hill Bays** are beautiful. **Portnablagh** is just a mile from Dunfanaghy, the attractive village-centre of the locality.

Downings Bay and pier

Horn Head

Opposite: (top) The harbour in Camusmore Bay, Tory Island

(bottom) Inishbofin, Inishdooey and Inishbeg

West Town is Tory's main settlement

Horn Head is the dominant feature of this part of the coast. Rising to 200m (650ft), it juts defiantly into the Atlantic, demanding respect from passing mariners. As it does not, however, jut north of the east-west rhumb line, and does not have fierce tides, it may be admired at leisure and seldom presents a challenge. But west of it are few havens; if the sailor is caught out and cannot make the little harbour at Tory or weather Bloody Foreland, he has little choice but to seek its shelter and run back to Sheep Haven.

But in more forgiving conditions, the choice is to visit Tory Island, or explore Inishbeg, Inishdooey and Inishbofin, a lovely group of small islands with a good anchorage, or head on west and south past Bloody Foreland.

Tory is a remarkable place, a bleak and windswept slab of an island. Almost as if Nature had played a bitter joke on it, its high cliffs face north-east away from the prevailing weather, and at its western end it becomes progressively more barren and scalped as it slopes steadily towards the Atlantic. Its reserves of peat have long since been exhausted, it offers no shelter from wind and weather and it has no natural harbours; indeed, until the late 1990s it had no harbour at all, merely a jetty in its south-facing bay. At that time the Sailing Directions said "Mailboat three times a fortnight". Tory was regularly cut off in winter,

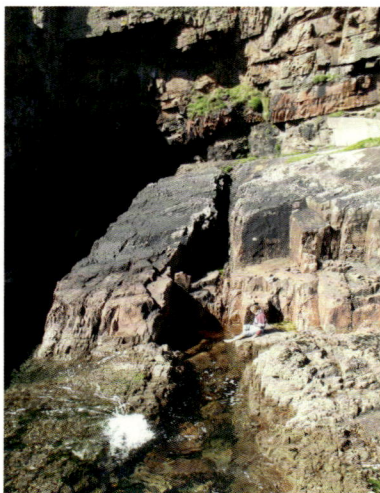

Port Doon, Tory Island

The Primitive Painters of Tory

Derek Hill, CBE, was an accomplished English artist who painted portraits of many public figures including Charles, Prince of Wales and the Taoiseach Dr Garret FitzGerald. In the mid 1960s he discovered Tory Island, and leased the old radiobeacon hut at the lighthouse as a painting retreat. Jimmy Dixon, one of the islanders, told Hill that he could paint better than that, and Hill took up the challenge and mentored Dixon, who insisted on using brushes of his own, home-made from donkeys' hair. Jimmy Dixon and several other Tory islanders including Jimmy Rodgers and Ruairidh Sarah MacRuairidh were true "primitive" painters; that is to say that they expressed their vision of their natural surroundings without training or artifice. Their paintings have a simplicity and innocence which has lent them considerable value. Their tradition has been carried on by the present King of Tory, Patsai Dan MacRuairidh, and by Antóin Ó Mionáin, who was professionally trained as an artist.

Jimmy Dixon died in 1970. Derek Hill came to live at Church Hill near Letterkenny and subsequently gave his house there, and his art collection, to the nation. He died, aged 83, in 2000.

Maritime transport old and new: the Tory currach is smaller than its cousins on the west coast, and of an entirely different shape. It is all but extinct.

(right) The modern ferry in Tory harbour

Opposite: *The stacks of the east end of Tory; Bloody Foreland, the islands of the Rosses, and Arranmore in the distance.*

sometimes for weeks at a time. Yet it was, and is, home to a hundred people. Now it has a fine little harbour and a dependable ferry, but the inhabitants of *Oileán Thoraigh* are still Ireland's most remote community, and have a way of life all their own. With the ferry service has come tourist income, and netting this has – to an extent – taken the place of netting salmon, which used to be a mainstay of the island economy and is now forbidden throughout the EU. The island elects a King, normally a lifetime appointment with no formal powers, but the present incumbent acts as a spokesman for the island and welcomes visitors in person. A meeting with Patsy Dan will not be forgotten.

Ornithologists value Tory as one of the few breeding grounds for the rare corncrake.

Inishbofin, the innermost island of the trio in Tory Sound, is connected to the shore by a drying sandspit, and is seasonally inhabited. Of the outer two, **Inishdooey** no longer is inhabited, and **Inishbeg** never was. The sandy Toberglassan Bay, off the sand isthmus that joins the two halves of Inishbofin, provides an anchorage, as also, in suitably quiet weather, does Inishbofin

Tory and the Tories

It is often said – indeed it was said in the 2008 edition of the ICC Sailing Directions – that the nickname of the British Conservative Party derives, by circuitous means, from Tory Island. A tempting thought, but not so. The island's name (*Oileán Thoraigh* in Irish) derives from *tor*, a clump or (in this case) rock stack – a word that has itself been adopted into English. The original Tories were 18th-century outlaws, and while the term is also Irish in origin, it derives from an entirely different word, *tóraí*, meaning a pursuer or robber. It was applied to the landowning party by their political opponents as a term of abuse, and was happily adopted by them as a useful shorthand.

Tory Island

roadstead to the south of the island. Inishdooey's monastic and church ruins, typical of those on so many Irish islands, can be explored from the landing place at its north-east end, but there is little in the way of an anchorage there. Inishbeg is even more awkward of access, and the rock-strewn Keelasbeg Sound between it and Inishdooey is suitable only for a small boat navigated with caution. Thanks to these islands' undisturbed remoteness, bird life is abundant: terns breed here, barnacle geese overwinter and there are about 20 breeding pairs of corncrakes.

The mainland coast is low and rocky, and the ferry pier at Magheraroarty provides a convenient anchorage and landing. Bloody Foreland, where our outward track is crossed, is just four miles to the west.

It is a curiously satisfying thing to demonstrate for oneself that the charts are correct, and that Ireland is, indeed, entirely surrounded by water.

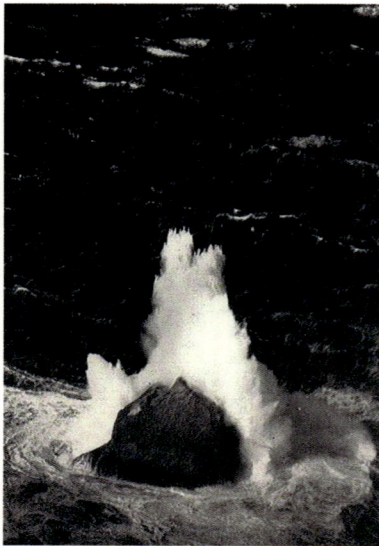

This spectacular picture of the sea breaking on Rockall dates from 1943

Rockall

The two jurisdictions in Ireland have argued over one more tiny piece of territory. This tooth of granite, a mere 21 metres of it above sea level, lies 239 miles north-west of Bloody Foreland and was for many years the subject of a courteous (but by no means trivial) territorial dispute between the UK and the Republic of Ireland. The colourful Irish politician Sean Loftus personified this by changing his name to Sean Dublin Bay Rockall Loftus in honour of two of his favourite causes, and the ex-paratrooper Tom McClean camped on the rock for 40 days in 1985 to underpin the British claim, a risky exploit given that waves estimated at 29 metres have been observed there. Most of the landings from yachts, including that of the Dangerous Sports Club, who held a dinner party (in formal evening wear) on Rockall before jumping off it, have been made under Irish Cruising Club skippers, including Mike Villiers-Stuart and Michael d'Alton. Without prejudice, it must be pointed out that Rockall is 164 miles from St Kilda, 199 miles from North Uist and 250 miles from Ardnamurchan Point, the nearest part of the Scottish mainland; and the UN-recognised boundary between the British and Irish territorial seas passes 40 miles to the south of it, making it British. The nearest Irish land is Tory Island at 233 miles, but the Irish claim rests on the fact that the nearest *mainland* territory, by a margin of eleven miles, is Ireland. However the 1996 Law of the Sea Convention, ratified by Ireland that year and by Britain in 1997, made the argument largely academic, since the existence and ownership of an uninhabitable islet like Rockall have now been agreed to have no bearing on seabed and fishery rights beyond a radius of twelve miles, an area already well inside the undisputed 200-mile limit from St Kilda. The ratification cost the UK 60,000 square miles of seabed.

Sailing Round Ireland

Gascanane Sound, between Cape Clear Island (foreground) and Sherkin Island

At the end of his delightful book of this title, published in 1976, Wallace Clark provided two pages of down-to-earth advice on planning a circumnavigation. Wallace himself had sailed round Ireland at least eleven times, and his book was not, of course, an account of a single voyage. Much of his advice is still valid, but since he wrote his Appendix the average cruising yacht has grown larger, faster and more comfortable, with a more powerful and reliable engine, and devices for communication and navigation which were undreamed of forty years ago. At home, she is probably kept in a marina; without that facility, she might never have been bought. Ireland's own infrastructure has developed greatly, there are now many places where a boat can be left in perfect safety and security, and transport and communication networks are vastly improved. However, the climate remains much the same, long stretches of the coast have no marinas, and the same challenging headlands are still there. The minimum time

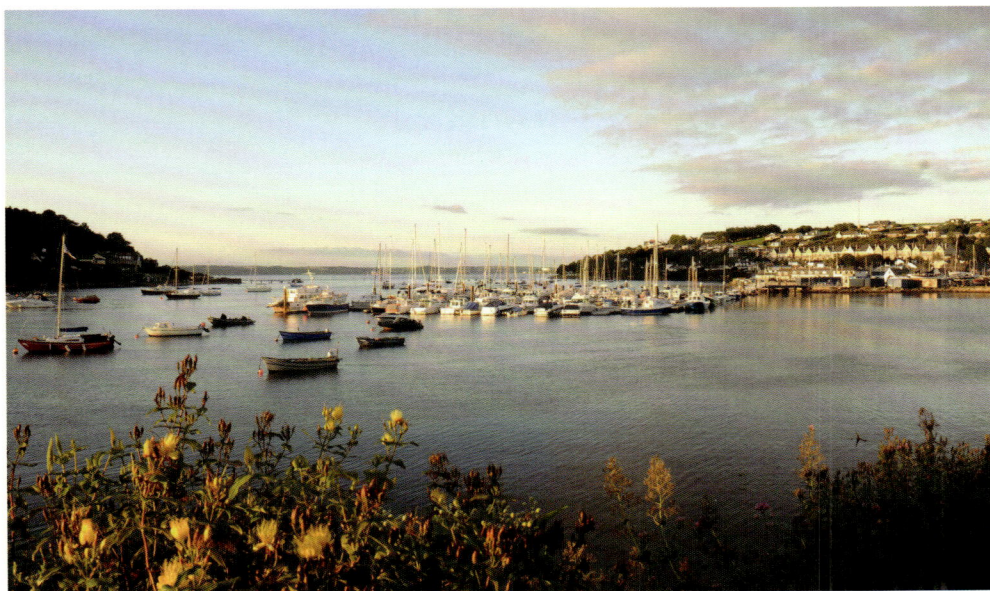

Crosshaven and the Royal Cork YC Marina

Cross-slab on Inishmurray

for a comfortable circumnavigation is still about three weeks from an Irish port, more from elsewhere: recent reports show an average of about four weeks for a continuous cruise logging between 850 and 1050 miles.

Clockwise or anticlockwise? A study of logs from the journals of various clubs suggests that few cruisers made their decision based on others' past experience, and few reported being glad – or sorry – about their choice of direction. There is no right or wrong way to go. The weather is notoriously unpredictable, but the following case can be made for the choice of anticlockwise, other things being equal.

A persistent west to south-west wind – not unusual – may make hard work of the westward passage of the long south coast; while in summer, east winds tend not to be so frequent, strong or enduring. As a depression passes, the southerlies blow on gloomy days of rain, whereas the west to north-west winds accompany sunshine and fluffy clouds. Much better, on the west coast, to sit out the rain in some convivial bolthole, and continue southwards on a brisk reach in the sun; while payback time going north on the east coast has at least the mitigating factor of being in the lee of the land.

Since other things are seldom equal, the starting point is an important factor, and it is useful to consider the following questions:

Currach at Inishbofin

- Do you plan to break the cruise, leave the boat and resume later, or are you prepared to do this if weather and circumstances are unfavourable?
- What are your crew arrangements? Are you planning to change crews at some stage?
- Is there any particular place you want to see or spend time in? Describing the attractions and challenges of the different parts of the coast is the whole purpose of this book!

Bear in mind that it is not unusual for circumnavigations to be curtailed and for the yacht to turn back and retrace her wake home. This does not count as 'failure'. But if you are starting in Wales and you want to spend time in west Cork, don't bank on getting there via Malin Head. The information on the two following pages may help further with cruise planning.

Logistics
Navigable Distances, Infrastructure and Transport

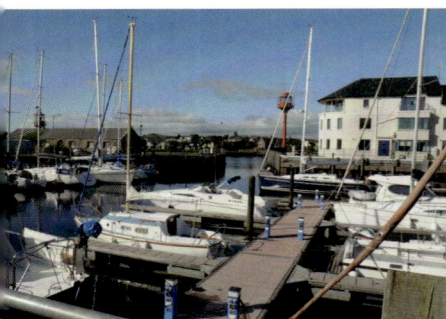

Arklow Marina

The following facilities offer safe and secure pontoon berthing, with deep water at all states of the tide. A yacht might safely be left for an extended period at any of them although this depends on berth availability and some have a limit on length of stay for a visiting yacht. Services vary from fresh water only, right up to full five-gold-anchor standard. Consult the *Sailing Directions* for more details.

South and West Coasts:
Kilmore Quay Marina
Waterford City Marina
Three Sisters Marina, New Ross
Crosshaven Boatyard Marina
Salve Marina, Crosshaven
Royal Cork YC Marina, Crosshaven
East Ferry Marina
Cork Harbour Marina, Monkstown
Cork City Marina
Kinsale YC Marina
Trident Marina, Kinsale
Castlepark Marina, Kinsale
Lawrence Cove Marina, Bere Island
Cahersiveen Marina
Dingle Marina
Fenit Harbour Marina
Kilrush Marina
Galway Harbour Marina
Sligo Harbour Pontoon

East and North Coasts:
Arklow Marina
Dun Laoghaire Marina
Poolbeg Y&BC Marina
(at the time of writing the Dublin City Moorings are closed to yachts)
Howth YC Marina
Malahide Marina
Carlingford Marina
Town Dock, Warrenpoint
Phennick Cove Marina, Ardglass
Strangford Pontoon
Portaferry Marina
Copelands Marina, Donaghadee
Bangor Marina
Abercorn Basin, Belfast
Carrickfergus Marina
Glenarm Marina
Ballycastle Marina
Seaton's Marina, Coleraine
Coleraine Marina
Foyle Pontoon, Derry/Londonderry
Lough Swilly Marina, Fahan

Cahersiveen Marina

Many of these places have hardstanding, or associated or nearby boatyards, where a yacht might haul out for the winter. The boatyards at Oldcourt and Rossbrin, Co. Cork, Askeaton (Co. Limerick), Killybegs (Co. Donegal) and Whiterock (Co. Down) do not provide secure alongside berthing but do offer haul-out and wintering on the hard.

Castlepark Marina, Kinsale

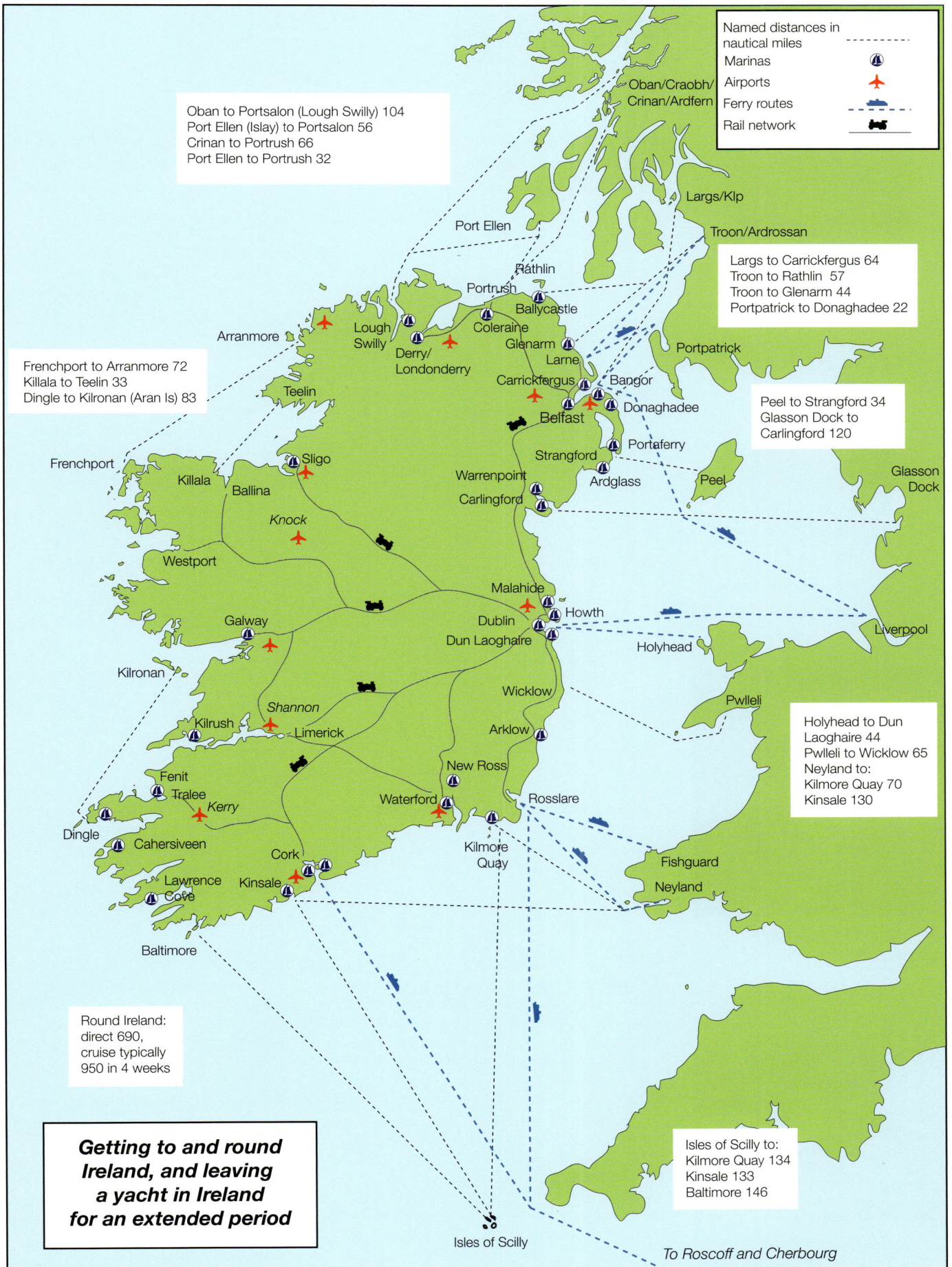

Named distances in nautical miles

Marinas

Airports

Ferry routes

Rail network

Oban to Portsalon (Lough Swilly) 104
Port Ellen (Islay) to Portsalon 56
Crinan to Portrush 66
Port Ellen to Portrush 32

Oban/Craobh/
Crinan/Ardfern

Largs/Klp

Troon/Ardrossan

Largs to Carrickfergus 64
Troon to Rathlin 57
Troon to Glenarm 44
Portpatrick to Donaghadee 22

Port Ellen

Rathlin

Portrush

Ballycastle

Coleraine

Glenarm

Portpatrick

Arranmore

Lough
Swilly

Derry/
Londonderry

Larne

Bangor

Carrickfergus

Donaghadee

Teelin

Belfast

Portaferry

Peel to Strangford 34
Glasson Dock to
Carlingford 120

Frenchport to Arranmore 72
Killala to Teelin 33
Dingle to Kilronan (Aran Is) 83

Strangford

Peel

Glasson
Dock

Frenchport

Sligo

Warrenpoint

Ardglass

Killala

Ballina

Carlingford

Knock

Westport

Malahide

Howth

Galway

Dublin

Dun Laoghaire

Holyhead

Liverpool

Kilronan

Wicklow

Pwlleli

Shannon

Arklow

Kilrush

Limerick

Holyhead to Dun
Laoghaire 44
Pwlleli to Wicklow 65
Neyland to:
Kilmore Quay 70
Kinsale 130

Fenit

New Ross

Tralee

Kerry

Waterford

Rosslare

Dingle

Cahersiveen

Cork

Kilmore
Quay

Fishguard

Lawrence
Cove

Kinsale

Neyland

Baltimore

Round Ireland:
direct 690,
cruise typically
950 in 4 weeks

Isles of Scilly to:
Kilmore Quay 134
Kinsale 133
Baltimore 146

**Getting to and round
Ireland, and leaving
a yacht in Ireland
for an extended period**

Isles of Scilly

To Roscoff and Cherbourg

Ireland
A potted history for cruising sailors

Richard de Clare, Earl of Pembroke, the first Anglo-Norman invader

Oliver Cromwell, perhaps Ireland's least-admired man

William III, victor of the Battle of the Boyne in 1690

Michael Collins, voted by historians in 2012 as Britain's toughest enemy

Irish history is a closed book to many outside the island, and Irish political allegiances often seem either medieval or inexplicable. Many visitors are uncertain about which flags – if any – they should fly, and some even wonder if history will get in the way of a welcome (it won't). The following is an attempt to help.

The old joke goes that when God made Ireland, the Archangel Gabriel asked him if he were not being a touch over-generous in the allocation of natural beauty and talented, friendly people. To which God replied "Ah, but wait till you meet the neighbours."

England first took a serious interest in Ireland in 1169 when the King of Leinster invited the Norman Earl of Pembroke over to give him a hand against his local rivals. The Earl, known as Strongbow, soon established a power base of his own.

Henry II of England decided to sort it out once and for all. He dropped by, with an army, in 1171, and from then on Irish allegiance to the English crown was officially demanded. But most Irish chieftains continued to rule their fiefdoms, and the Anglo-Norman settlers integrated and became "more Irish than the Irish themselves". Many surnames now regarded as characteristically Irish, such as Burke, Tobin, Dillon, Lynch, Barry and all those beginning with Fitz-, are actually Anglo-Norman.

Henry VIII, and then Elizabeth I, decided to *sort it out once and for all*, and set about asserting English sovereignty more strongly. Bloody warfare culminated in the defeat of the Irish, decisively at the Battle of Kinsale in 1601. Complicating things was the fact that Ireland had not been touched by the Protestant Reformation, and so looked to France and Spain, England's old enemies, as co-religionist friends. Religion was, from then on, a handy label to be applied to almost every Irish conflict, and a basis for rallying support to the cause of either side.

Elizabeth's successor James I, determined to ensure an Ireland loyal to the Crown, decided to *sort it out once and for all*. He attempted a comprehensive colonisation by Protestant English and Scots, in a process that might nowadays be considered ethnic cleansing. It got no further than Ulster, and even there it was patchy, but it was ultimately to define Northern Ireland as we know it today. Ireland ran its own version of the English Civil War of the 1640's, with Catholic (and often pro-Royalist) rebellion being followed by reprisals.

Oliver Cromwell decided to *sort it out once and for all*, and many Irish landowners were dispossessed and had their estates granted to officers of the Parliamentary army. After a brief replay in 1688-1690, including such memorable events as the Seige of Derry and the Battle of the Boyne, Ireland settled down to a hundred years of unchallenged English rule, essentially as a colony. There was an Irish Parliament in Dublin; it may have been little more than a talking shop, but some of the talk was of independence. There emerged the United Irishmen, an association largely of Catholics and Dissenters (members of Protestant churches other than the established Anglican Church), who were barred from public office. Given the opportunity offered by war between Britain and France, the movement grew into open rebellion, with abortive French invasions in support in 1796 and 1798 and another failed revolt in 1800.

Following these events, the British Prime Minister Pitt decided to *sort it out once and for all*. Direct rule was imposed, Ireland was integrated into the UK and the cross of St Patrick was added to the Union Flag to produce the design that we know today. But the events of 1796 – 1800 awakened Catholic solidarity and led to the formation of sectarian organisations of both faiths, of which the most enduring is the Protestant Orange Order. The last restrictions on Catholics and Protestant Dissenters were lifted in 1829, but the Famine of the 1840's and the inadequacy of response to it threw the cat amongst the pigeons once again, and the issue of land ownership became paramount, with the Fenian rebellion of 1867. Ireland then became the subject of sweeping land reforms, ultimately involving the forced sale of estates by the Anglo-Irish landowners and the division of those estates into smaller landholdings, in the late 19th and early 20th centuries. As a direct result, the landscape of rural Ireland today is shaped by family-owned small farms, and over 80% of Irish householders are owner-occupiers – the highest percentage in Europe.

In 1911, after fifty years of debate and two Home Rule Bills struck down by the House of Lords, Prime Minister Asquith decided to *sort it out once and for all*. His government passed an Act limiting the powers of the upper house and thus essentially guaranteeing that Home

Rule for Ireland, under the Crown, would soon be inevitable. By this time the more zealous Nationalists had redefined "Irish" as requiring the practice of the Gaelic language, Gaelic games to the exclusion of "English" ones, and – most importantly – the Catholic religion. Despite that, many Nationalist heroes were Protestants. But the Protestants of Ulster wanted nothing to do with Home Rule, and in 1912 Ulster declared a determination to resist it by all means. The scene was set for civil war, but the First World War supervened and Irishmen of all backgrounds flocked to the colours. At Easter in 1916, a splinter group of Nationalists staged a dramatic, doomed and initially derided coup by taking over by force the General Post Office and other key buildings in Dublin. The authorities over-reacted, and by summarily executing the ringleaders, assured the future of the Irish Republic. Public opinion abruptly reversed in favour of the martyred rebels. Yeats said "All is changed, changed utterly; a terrible beauty is born."

The terrible beauty went on to fight the British from 1918 to 1921, the British responding by deploying the hated "Black and Tans", a militia of ex-servicemen dressed in a mixture of police and army uniforms. The resulting stalemate led to the Treaty of 1921, when Prime Minister Lloyd George decided to *sort it out once and for all*. Ireland was granted self-rule with the proviso that six predominantly Unionist counties in the north-east of the island might opt out of the secession and remain part of the UK. These duly became Northern Ireland, while Michael Collins, leader of the Irish delegation at the Treaty negotiations and arguably the greatest Irishman who ever lived, fulfilled his own gloomy prediction by being assassinated within a few months.

Those opposed to the partition of Ireland, led by Éamon de Valera, declared a civil war on the new Free State. The memorial in Bantry records the names of twelve men who died between December 1920 and April 1923 "in defence of the republic". Only three of them were killed by the British; the other nine died as Irishman fought Irishman in the Civil War. Meanwhile the people of the new entity of Northern Ireland looked on. Each jurisdiction had its minority, who on the whole would have preferred if the sovereignty were otherwise.

The Free State in due course became the Republic of Ireland as de Valera embraced constitutional politics, and Northern Ireland was allowed to set its own course as a semi-detached part of the UK. As de Valera skilfully maintained its neutrality, Ireland was confirmed by the Second World War as a sovereign nation. But both parts of the island were dogged by sectarianism and introversion. The Republic's government was in thrall to the Catholic hierarchy, while the North had avowedly "a Protestant Parliament for a Protestant people". This had dramatic effects on both sides of the border. In the Republic, the Protestant population fell from 20% to 5% as partners in mixed marriages were required by the Catholic Church to bring up their children in the Catholic faith. In the North, there was wholesale discrimination against Catholics in electoral boundaries, job opportunities and the allocation of public housing. In 1969 that erupted in civil unrest, which was badly handled, and quickly exploited by republican extremists with a view to making Northern Ireland ungovernable. A durable compromise was reached only in 1998, by which time the Republic had grown in prosperity and become a more pluralist society and a respected member of the European Union, and institutionalised discrimination in the North had been eliminated. At the time of writing (2012) a mature relationship has developed among the governments of the three jurisdictions, although the two communities sharing Northern Ireland, long divided by folk memories, churches and schools, have much bridge building still to do. National allegiance, not economics or social philosophy, is still the basis of the province's politics, and looks set to remain so. For a century, the children of Ireland and the UK have been taught little – sometimes even nothing – about the history of their nearest neighbours, and that has left a legacy of misconceptions and sometimes distrust. But that does not affect Ireland's response to strangers, which is uniformly open, friendly, welcoming and curious.

What about flags? Everyone has seen, on television, flags being used in Ireland as potent and emotive symbols of political allegiance. It is unfortunately true that a small minority in Ireland – chiefly Northern Ireland – see the Union Flag and the Irish Tricolour as little else. If you have the slightest concern about this, simply don't fly a flag. Nobody will pass comment; maritime flag etiquette is less rigorously observed here. In the southern half of the island, flags are never an issue.

The coast of Northern Ireland and its harbours, like the rest of the province, are a bit of a chequerboard of religious and political allegiances. The orange and the green alternate; some places are predominantly Unionist, others Nationalist, many a mixture. A list would not be appropriate here: if there is a distinct preference one way or the other, it is usually plain to see. It adds colour (often literally), interest and almost always a spice of humour to a cruise in these waters. The story goes that an Irish yacht, correctly dressed with her tricolour ensign, and her courtesy red ensign at the spreader, made her way into the harbour at Carnlough, County Antrim. A spectator commented to his friend "Now there goes a very confused wee boat."

It is to be hoped that nobody else will try to sort it out once and for all.

Irish Tánaiste and Minister of Foreign Affairs Eamon Gilmore welcoming Elizabeth II to Dublin in 2011, the first visit to the city by a British monarch for a century. The visit was a tremendous success and set new standards of mutual respect and friendship between the two nations.

Below, top to bottom: Ensigns being correctly flown at Inishbofin (Co. Galway), Ballycotton and Bantry Bay (Co.Cork)

Bibliography

Brown, Alison and Crosbie, Jane, *Strangford's Shores*, Cottage Publications 1996-2007

Carroll, Michael J., *The Castles and Fortified Houses of West Cork*, Bantry Studios 2001

Clark, Wallace, *Sailing Round Ireland*, Batsford 1976

Clark, Wallace, *Rathlin: Its Island Story*, Impact 1988

Dwyer, Kevin, *Dwyer's Ireland*, The Collins Press 2010

Dwyer, Kevin, *Ireland – Our Island Home*, The Collins Press 1997

Enright, Damien, *A Place Near Heaven*, Gill & Macmillan 2004

Feehan, John M., *The Secret Places of the West Cork Coast,* Royal Carbery Books 1990

Flanagan, Deirdre and Flanagan, Laurence, *Irish Place Names*, Gill & Macmillan 2004

Forbes, R.F. (Editor), *The Oxford History of Ireland*, OUP 1989

Harvey, Ros and Clark, Wallace, *Donegal Islands,* Laurel Cottage

Hiscock, Eric, *South West Irish Harbours and Bays*, Imrays 1937

Hopkin, Alannah, *Eating Scenery*, Collins 2008

Ireland, John de Courcy, *Ireland and the Irish in Maritime History*, Glendale Press 1986

Kean, Norman, (Editor), *East and North Coasts of Ireland Sailing Directions*, 11th ed., ICC Publications 2008

Kean, Norman, (Editor), *South and West Coasts of Ireland Sailing Directions*, 12th ed., ICC Publications 2008

McCarron, Donal, *Landfall Ireland*, Colourpoint 2003

McCarthy, Pete, *McCarthy's Bar,* Hodder & Stoughton 2000

McIvor, Aidan, *A History of the Irish Naval Service*, Irish Academic Press 1994.

McMullen, Richard T (RT), *Down Channel*, Rupert Hart Davis 1951 (1869)

Nairn, Richard, *Ireland's Coastline,* Collins 2005

Phelan, Andrew, *Ireland from the Sea*, Wolfhound Press 1998

1,200-year-old drystone wall of the monastery on Inishmurray

Donegal Harbour

Phelan, Andrew, *Turning Tides – a Voyage round the Irish Sea*, Wolfhound Press 2003

Rainsbury, David, *Irish Sea Pilot*, Imrays 2009

Reed's Nautical Almanac

Rutherford, Iain, *At the Tiller*, Blackie, 1946

Severin, Tim, *The Brendan Voyage*, Hutchinson 1978

Siggins, Lorna, *Mayday! Mayday! Heroic Air-Sea Rescues in Irish Waters*, Gill & McMillan 2004

Somerville, Christopher, *Coast*, BBC Books 2005

Somerville-Large, Peter, *Ireland's Islands*, Gill & McMillan 1999

Somerville-Large, Peter, *The Coast of West Cork*, Appletree Press 1991

Swanson, Graham, *Cruising Cork and Kerry*, Imrays 2005

Taylor, Richard M., *The Lighthouses of Ireland*, Collins 2004

UK Hydrographic Office, *Irish Coast Pilot*, NP40, 2010

Villiers-Tuthill, Kathleen, *Alexander Nimmo and the Western District,* Connemara Girl Publications 2006

Watson, Philip, *Rathlin, Nature & Folklore*, Stone Country Press 2011

Wilcox, Robert, *Southern Ireland Cruising Companion*, Wiley Nautical 2009

Wilson, T.G., *The Irish Lighthouse Service*, Allen Figgis 1968

Walsh, David, *Oileáin*, Pesda Press 2005

Opposite: *Gola*

420s racing at Galway Bay Sailing Club

243

Acknowledgements

This book is the fruit of many people's labours.

We wish especially to thank the Officers and Committee of the Irish Cruising Club, in particular James Nixon and Club Commodore David Tucker, whose enthusiasm for the project was unbounded, and vital; ICC member Kevin Dwyer, whose eager assistance and stunning photographs have been invaluable; Edward Mason, Editor of the Clyde Cruising Club's *Sailing Directions* and co-author with Mike Balmforth of *Cruising Scotland*; the staff of the Commissioners of Irish Lights, in particular Desmond O'Brien, Deirdre O'Neill and Robert Sparkes; the staff of the UK Hydrographic Office, in particular Roger Millard; also Sally Barnes, John Clementson, Rory Conlon, Eddie Diver, Kieran Flatt, Peter and Susan Gray, Heather Greer, Emmett Johnston, Hugh Kennedy, Sam and Kay McDowell, Paud Murphy, William Nixon, Martin O'Malley, Libby Purves, Niall Quinn, Brian Sheridan, Karen Sleat, Chris Stillman, Ed Wheeler, David Whitehead and Padraig Whooley.

Photographs are by Geraldine Hennigan, except:

Kenneth Allen: 224 Ballymastocker

Ken Atkinson: 26 trawlers, 27 top, 37 both, 38 bottom right, 56 Mizen, 86 top (both), 158 Baily, 160 Rosslare, 166 Optimists, 195 sunset, 241 red ensign, 248 St Brendan, 251 Fenit

Mike Balmforth: 11 Bofin Harbour and Barloge, 24 left, 28 bottom left, 33 bottom, 48 Lough Hyne, 51 North Harbour, 58 Blaskets, 63 Lawrence Cove, 74 bottom, 75 bottom right, 76, 85 Inishvickillane, 87 Illauntannig, 96 Bikes for Hire, 97 all three, 98 top, 120 cliffs, 129 Stags, 131 Arranmore, 140 Inishmurray, 145 bottom, 147 Church Pool, 148 Chapel Bay & Ballagh Rocks, 151 lower right, 173 Lambay, Rockabill & Martello tower, 174 both, 175 sunrise, 179 Haulbowline, 181 Bar Pladdy, 184 St John's Point, 185 Annalong, 188 both, Angus Rock, 190 Audley's Roads & Killyleagh, 191, 192 Ringhaddy, 193 South Rock, 196, 199 Isle of Muck, 201 Glenarm, 207 Garvans, 208 Ballycastle, 209 top, 220 Inishowen Head, 227, 228 both, 230

Opposite: *Barloge, County Cork*

Replica Famine emigrant ship **Dunbrody** *at New Ross*

Horn Head, 238 Kinsale

Henry Barnwell: 241 Irish ensign

Ivy Barnwell: 56 top, 59 Dunboy

Adrian Bell: 71 Derreen, 83 Great Blasket (both), 116 Caher Island

Brian Black: 157 top, 172 bottom, 181 puffins, 186 St Patrick's Rock & sunrise, 189 *Courante*, 192 race crew, 222 deer, 223 seals

Bob Brown: 208 puffin

Sarah Brown: 19 dolphins, 42 dolphins, 51 shearwaters, 59 seal, 81 dolphin, 134 dolphins

Chris Bunting: 187 Strangford

John Campbell: 45 otters

Wallace Clark: 249

John Clementson: 159 Tuskar, 189 SeaGen, 254 Warrenpoint

Commissioners of Irish Lights: 139 Metal Man

Nigel Cox: 87 Gallarus

Eleanor Cudmore: 20 top, 250 Fastnet

Sam Davis: 185 Mountains of Mourne, 187 Ballydorn

Brian Deeney: 143 lower right.

John Delap: 60 centre left

Donald Demers: 90 *Galatea* & *Mayflower* (from his painting)

Ella Dover: 159 sunrise

Tommy Dover: 163, 164 *Granuaile*, 165 Wicklow Head

Hugo du Plessis: 84 Great Foze Rock

Kevin Dwyer: 2, 3, 21 bottom, 24 bottom, 29 aerial, 42 aerial, 43 aerial, 44 both, 60 Skellig, 67 Bantry House, 68 Dursey, 71 aerial, 73 Derrynane (both), 74 top, 75 top & bottom, 77 both, 78 Portmagee, 79 aerial, 99, 104 Roundstone, 109 aerial, 111 aerial, 113 aerial, 114 Inishturk, 117 aerial, 121 aerial, 154 Gweedore, 167 aerial, 169, 175 Drogheda, 178 aerial, 184 Warrenpoint, 206 Tory, 215 Barmouth, 216 both, 218 aerial, 219, 221 top, 225 top, 229, 231 both, 233, 234 Tory, 248 Ancient Monuments, 250 Great Skellig, 256 *Asgard II*

Espresso Addict: 86 centre left

Sarah Gallagher: 222 Macamish

The Guardian: 241 Eamon Gilmore and ER

Galway Harbour Company: 100 aerial

Marie Goggin: 66 Adrigole

Heather Greer: 19 oystercatchers, 23 bottom right, 95 Anchor Beach, 96 sunset, 109 flowers, 110, 112 sunset, 113 Ballynakill & Oliver's, 127 gale, 128 surf, 130 oystercatchers, 131 seal, 132 sea anemones, 158 Arklow Bank, 181 wave, 235, 256 Sunset walk on Sellerna beach

Cruising Ireland

The approaches to Clifden, Connemara; Fishing Point beacon in line with Clifden Castle, the Twelve Bens of Connemara beyond

Sculpture on Inishturk

Opposite: (top) Howth (bottom) Aran Sound, Co. Donegal

Bill Hogg: 106 Roundstone, 107 Slyne Head, 241 blue ensign

Emmett Johnston: 206 sharks, 213 shark breaching, 220 sharks

A/S David Jones & Irish Naval Service: 34 top

Edi Keating: 14 lower left, 50 Baltimore, 64 sheep, 65 Illnacullen, 88 beach

David & Hazel Lewis: 29 top, 31 Dungarvan, 32 top right, 33 centre left, 39 bottom, 48 Barloge, 49 Lot's Wife, 51 Sherkin, 52 Dún an Oir, 67 Glengarriff, 72 Sneem, 157 Poolbeg, 159 Ha'penny Bridge, 162 top, 168 Poolbeg, 170 Baily, 238 Arklow, 236, 237 Crosshaven, 247 Howth, 255 Courtmacsherry lifeboat

Donald MacDonald: 224 horse on Rathmullan beach

Tom McDonnell: 59 seal, 75 gannet, 204 eiders

Sam McDowell: 22 top, 209 bottom

Paul McSorley: 225 bottom

Freddie Moran: 28 top left, 181 sunset

Nigel Moyter: 122 shark

Rory Mullins: 62 Ardnakinna

W.M.Nixon: 12, 13 both, 14 *Ainmara*, 15 top, 23 bottom, 25 top right, 30 top and left, 33 bottom (both), 36 Cronins, 53 South Harbour, 56 centre right, 59 Derrynane, 64 Adrigole, 66 Glengarriff, 82 bottom, 88 Fenit, 95 Kinvara, 100 *MacDuach*, 109 Ardbear, 114 Derryinver & Killary, 156 both, 158 *Hallowe'en*, 167 bottom, 170 rainbow, 171,

187 *Ainmara,* 195 Carrickfergus, 202 Carnlough, 217, 218 yachts, 220 Greencastle, 168 *Cill Airne,* 172 Malahide, 181 Bangor, 182 top left, 222 drontheims, 238 Cahersiveen, 242, 248 Ballintoy

Joe Phelan: 52 Fastnet, 168 Grand Canal, 247 Derrynane

Angie Purcell: 94 cliffs, 190 Mount Stewart, 200 Antrim coast, 207 Causeway, 212 both

Niall Quinn: 1, 49 top, 103 Macdara's, 106 Inishlackan, 107 Joyce's Pass, 115 Inishturk

Stuart Ruttle: 30 bottom

Tim Severin: 9

Karen Sleat: 226 Macamish

Colin Speedie: 213 shark (upper)

Donal Walsh: 31 raft-up, 250 Dunmore East

Philip Watt: 202 lower left

Ed Wheeler: 26 top left, 78 Puffin Sound, 91 bottom, 93 cockpit, 98 bottom, 145 top, 205 Inishtrahull, 221 bottom, 252 Portmore

Harry Whelehan: 177 pigeon, 206 Rathlin, 210 lighthouse

David Whitehead: 230 West Town

Padraig Whooley: 28 whale, 47 whales off Galley Head, 89 dolphins, 126 dolphins, 224 whale

Wikimedia Commons: 41 *Lusitania,* 49 *Kowloon Bridge,* 84 Peig Sayers, 176 Newgrange, 194 Lipton, 208 Dulse & Yellow Man, 234 Rockall, 240

Bob Yates: 16

Index

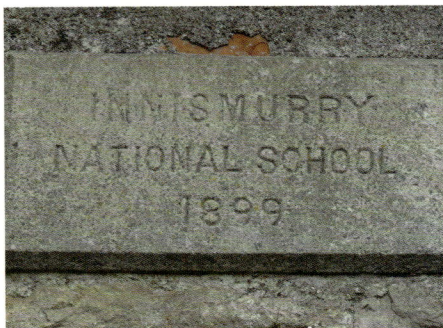

253

Opposite: *(top) Sunset over Clifden Bay*

(bottom) Courtmacsherry lifeboat comes alongside; Crew Member Kevin Young practises his rope trick under the watchful eye of Coxswain Sean O'Farrell

Donkeys on Dinish Island in Kilkieran Bay

Sunset walk on Sellerna beach, Connemara

The Irish sail training brigantine **Asgard II**, *built by Tyrrell's of Arklow in 1981.* **Asgard II** *sank in the Bay of Biscay in 2008, possibly as a result of striking a submerged object such as a container. There were no casualties.*